THE CAMPAIGN CONTINUES

THE CAMPAIGN CONTINUES

How Political Consultants and Campaign Tactics Affect Public Policy

Douglas A. Lathrop

Westport, Connecticut
London

Library of Congress Cataloging-in-Publication Data

Lathrop, Douglas A., 1971–
    The campaign continues : how political consultants and campaign tactics affect public policy / Douglas A. Lathrop.
        p.   cm.
    Includes bibliographical references and index.
    ISBN 0–275–97965–2 (alk. paper)
    1. Political planning—United States.   2. Political consultants—United States.   3. Politicians—United States.   4. Public opinion—United States.   I. Title.
    JK468.P64L38   2003
    320′.6′0973—dc21   2003046324

British Library Cataloguing in Publication Data is available.

Library of Congress Catalog Card Number: 2003046324
ISBN: 0–275–97965–2

First published in 2003

Praeger Publishers, 88 Post Road West, Westport, CT 06881
An imprint of Greenwood Publishing Group, Inc.
www.praeger.com

Printed in the United States of America

For my parents and Angie

Contents

Acknowledgments

I want to thank all of those who, after listening to my ideas and reading the book, offered their advice and constructive criticisms. I am especially indebted to Jerry Mileur and Jeff Sedgwick of the University of Massachusetts who encouraged me to transform my thesis into a published book. They were always available with kind words of encouragement and thoughtful insights long after I left graduate school. I would also like to single out the interview subjects for special praise. During the course of my research I was pleased to discover that the tension that is said to exist between political scientists and political practitioners is overstated. The people I interviewed were gracious, generous with their time, and honest with their answers. It is not an exaggeration to say that without their cooperation the project would not have come to fruition. Finally I would be remiss if I did not mention the unconditional support my parents and my wife have provided. In addition to reminding me of the importance of my research, they helped to keep me focused on the ultimate goal.

1

Political Consultants and Policy Making

During the fall of 1999 television viewers were introduced to "Flo," a spry, elderly woman with a message about Medicare. Flo wanted Americans, particularly senior citizens, to understand the inherent dangers of imposing a large-scale reform on Medicare. "We want the right Medicare reforms," she intoned, "that will let doctors decide what medicines are best, not government." She finishes her thirty-second monologue with a flourish, stating unequivocally, "I don't want big government in my medicine cabinet."[1] Although Flo's indignation seemed genuine, that was a testament to the actress who played the role. Flo and her message were really the brainchild of a media consulting firm working at the behest of the pharmaceutical industry.

Flo's television debut coincided with a heated congressional debate over the establishment of a prescription drug benefit for senior citizens. The implementation of a prescription drug program would be the greatest change to the American health care system since the introduction of Medicare in 1965. For senior citizens' interest groups such as the AARP the establishment of a prescription drug benefit is a top legislative priority and with good reason. Out-patient drugs are by far the most expensive item not covered by Medicare. According to the U.S. Census, 34 million senior citizens spent $42.8 billion on prescription drugs in 2000, an amount that some observers expect to triple by 2010.[2] An estimated 25 percent of Americans over sixty five pay at least $500 a year out of pocket for prescription medicines.[3] Needless to say, the financial stakes in a new government entitlement of that magnitude are enormous. Insurance companies, consumer groups, and drug makers all had a vested interest in a prescription drug benefit. The pharmaceutical industry in particular was concerned that the government, as a way to control costs, would mandate price caps on drugs and thus limit a growing source of revenue. Flo was created by Citizens for Better Medicare, a coalition of business groups and drug manufacturers, to deliver a pro industry message to the general public in the hope of influencing congressional action. Her presence on the airwaves drew scornful jeers from self-appointed government watchdog groups and consumer activists like Ralph Nader's Public Citizen. They claimed that she was a cynically contrived character spreading misleading industry propaganda under the guise of a public service announcement.

Although consumer advocates invest too much significance in Flo's powers of persuasion, they have a point. Certainly the advertisement's venue, a bowling alley, the central character, a benign, obviously middle-class elderly woman, and the language, ominous warnings about big government, were all crafted with care by political consultants to inspire trust and to relate to the broadest possible audience. It would be inappropriate, however, to join the chorus and cast value-laden aspersion on the motives of the people that created Flo. Indeed, the television ads starring Flo are less important for what they say than for what they represent. The ads are a manifestation of a new political ethic that celebrates the cleverness and skill needed to sell an abstract idea or political argument. It is an ethic that promotes the use of opinion polls to discern latent public sentiment and embraces focus group tested phraseology as a means to communicate with the public. Pundits and scholars have dubbed it the "permanent campaign." [4] Leading the nascent movement is a cadre of professional political operatives collectively referred to as "political consultants."

Informal campaign advisors have existed in American politics since the 1700s, but the twentieth century witnessed the professionalization of campaign advising under the rubric of political consulting. [5] Political consultants, loosely defined, are men and women with whom candidates contract for a fee to provide expertise on topics ranging from the aesthetic to the substantive; from physical appearance and demeanor to policy issues. They are readily distinguishable from other paid campaign workers, since they usually work for more than one client during an election and lack an intimate, personal connection to the candidate (a more rigorous definition will be provided later in the discussion). Independent consultants cooperate occasionally with political party leaders, but operate for the most part independently of the national party apparatus, though their party affiliation and especially their ideology often influences who their clients are. Consultants have no common pedigree, fixed training, or standard accreditation, and though many claim governmental and political experience, a significant number do not. Business marketing, academia, and journalism are among the diverse fields that have produced successful political consultants. This eclectic background may be attributed to the relative immaturity of the profession. As recently as the 1970s there were fewer than forty people who considered themselves full-time political consultants nationwide. [6] Despite their currency and a dearth of empirical evidence, politicians and party leaders place stock in consultants' abilities and believe that they have had a profound impact on campaigning and the electoral process in general.

As political consultants become more prominent in the American electoral process, they are simultaneously expanding their sphere of influence into the policy-making realm. No longer relegated to the limited scope of the campaign, many consultants remain principal advisors to the politician once in office. The flowering of a post-electoral relationship between public officials and consultants is due in large part to the advent of the permanent campaign. Major policy initiatives take on the trappings of a campaign as politicians court the public for support. Blurring the distinction between campaigning and governing places a premium on the specialized knowledge consultants possess in fields such as polling, mass marketing, and media relations. Beginning with the election of Jimmy Carter in 1976 and his elevation of campaign pollster Pat Caddell to full-time political advisor, consultants have held prominent, if often unofficial, positions in the executive branch. Successive occupants of the White House have embraced and expanded upon this practice. In the early 1990s this trend migrated to the legislative branch, where consultants employed their technical and communication skills to help clients wage policy battles in Congress.

Before speculating on the effects consultants may have on the policy-making process, a clear definition of what constitutes post-electoral consulting is needed. There are two essential components to post-electoral consulting, one dealing with the actors involved and the other with the techniques they use. A consultant involved with policymaking is somewhere between the official staff and an ad hoc counselor solicited by political leaders. They are paid for their services like official staff, but perform outside the conventional organizational loop.[7] To avoid confusion about who is considered a consultant, I have limited my analysis to those individuals who maintain an independent client base made up of several paying customers. Personal confidants or trusted civic figures who bend the ear of politicians, even if the advice is sought on a regular basis, are not consultants for two reasons: They do not earn a living as political advisors, and they are not in the regular employ of other political actors (this includes other politicians and interest groups).[8] The other aspect of post-electoral consulting is the incorporation of campaign methods into governing, as for example, the public relations blitz that paralleled the health care reform effort in 1993–1994, the hard sell of the Contract with America by Republican consultants, and the battle over a prescription drug benefit illustrate. Polling expertise, marketing skills, and the ability to sell a public policy to the general populace are as valuable after the election as they are during the campaign. In sum, post-electoral consulting is defined by the professionalization of the agents and the application of their trade to governing.

The growing presence of political consultants in the legislative process begs the question: What does it mean for American politics? Several important concerns are raised by post-electoral consulting. First, pursuing public, campaign-oriented strategies makes it more difficult for elected officials to negotiate in good faith. Given the institutional rivalry between the White House and Congress, exacerbated for years by persistent partisan division, creating legislation acceptable to both branches is a trying endeavor. The addition of consultants and their methods to the legislative process has altered the relationship between the executive and legislative branches by sharpening those divisions. Consultants are often accused of debasing the electoral process by encouraging candidates to recite market-tested phrases and creating a false sense of melodrama through overwrought appeals. They bring the same theatrics to governing, inflating rhetoric and making it harder for politicians to compromise. Second, political consultants, as private citizens crafting public policy, appear to escape accountability. The crux of a democratic society is the degree to which citizens control their elected representatives through frequent, regularly scheduled elections. Although a consultant's client is ultimately liable for policy decisions, consultants themselves are beyond the reach of electoral retribution. Third, despite their technical proficiency, many of the specialized skills consultants offer are overestimated and their role in helping shape legislation is dubious. Finally, there is concern that the use of high-priced consultants and pollsters to develop mass media lobbying campaigns further tilts the balance of power in favor of wealthy interest groups.

The unrelenting drive to sustain a positive public image and disseminate policy arguments to the general public has led the president and members of Congress to call upon political consultants. Yet their introduction into the legislative process has potentially harmful consequences for executive/legislative relations.[9] The nature of a campaign is fundamentally different from governing: Campaigns have endings resulting in a final victor; governing is an ongoing process without a clear-cut winner. Thus, successful campaign methods, such as negative advertising, are ill suited to governing, which requires a modicum of comity and reciprocity among the participants. Consultants are not responsible for feelings of hostility between the two parties, nor are consultants liable for personal traits such as stubbornness and arrogance that make cooperation difficult. However, as the 1994 health care reform and the Contract with America demonstrate, while consultants may not create animosity, their modus operandi can amplify it.

A serious concern for any political observer is the nebulous position consultants occupy in the policy process. Consultants, by advising politicians on the content and direction of public policy, are in essence quasi-public officials, beyond the scope of democratic accountability. Political consultants, for example, are not regulated by the financial disclosure provisions, income restrictions, and ethics rules that elected officials and their staffs must follow. The relationship between the professional consultant and a politician is more nuanced than a simplistic rendering of the politician as the puppet and the consultant as the puppet master and, despite the source of the idea, the elected official remains answerable to his constituents. But consultants, using their technical skill and political expertise, wield considerable influence over public policy and thrive outside the reach of public oversight. Concern about democratic accountability is also the focal point of criticism from interest group scholars who argue that political consultants further tip the balance of political power in favor of the wealthy.[10] In the latest policy battle over prescription drugs, for example, consultants hired by pharmaceutical manufacturers launched a multi million-dollar advertising and direct mail campaign to forestall legislation at the state and federal level that would have imposed price controls on drugs. Consumer advocates, as well as neutral observers, claim that this campaign was instrumental in slowing legislative progress despite continued popular support for some measure of government intervention.[11]

For political elites, a policy battle is often reduced to how the conflict is understood by the general public, with each side attempting to frame the debate to its own advantage. Consultants, by virtue of their command over communication media and mastery of polling techniques, are an integral participant in the effort to stimulate, mold, and channel public opinion. Political science is replete with arguments about the merits and deficiencies of the practical application of social science. I do not wish to add to them by engaging in an ad nauseam discussion regarding the intrinsic value and normative implications of polling and focus groups for American politics. My concern is not polling and focus groups per se, but their use by consultants to shape policy and coordinate public campaigns.

Many critics contend that polls are at best an uncertain snapshot of the public mood at a point in time and are often self-serving, misleading, and inaccurate. Moreover, even well-crafted polls can obscure public sentiment rather than illuminate it. The Clinton health care reform effort provides a telling example. Throughout the debate public ambivalence was the rule, with a vast majority expressing satisfaction with their own health care but simultaneously declaring a nationwide health care crisis.[12] Consultants can cloud the polling results by "spinning" and skewing data to reflect certain policy preferences. Although a consultant who presents a client with a rosy scenario may be accused of professional dishonesty, the consequences for the policy maker who utilizes a questionable poll are more severe. During the 1995 budget confrontation with President Clinton, members of the House Republican majority were bolstered by poll ratings indicating that the public supported their uncompromising position. But Republican consultants who conducted the polls were later accused of presenting a sanitized version of the results that produced an inaccurate portrait of the public mood.[13] Meanwhile, President Clinton, under the influence of consultant Dick Morris, was accused by members of his own party of abandoning traditional Democratic concerns in a cynical bid to capture Republican issues.

Despite its malleable nature, public opinion polling has a valid scientific foundation. The same cannot be said for focus groups, a popular complement to polling within the consulting profession. The focus group, a small non random sample of citizens, provides qualitative depth lacking in a poll and can reveal the primal emotions that animate public sentiment. Focus groups are a useful way to gain beneficial insight from ordinary people, but they are unscientific and can lead to dubious assumptions about public opinion. Consultants who generalize results to the greater population and base policy recommendations on focus groups are essentially reading tea leaves. The prevalence of focus groups is not inherently dangerous, provided the limitations of the methodology are acknowledged by the consumers. The danger is over reliance and misappropriation of the data.

Other techniques used to stimulate public support for an issue, such as direct mail and media advertising, can obscure and corrupt public sentiment as much as reveal it. One of the common invectives hurled at consultants is that they manipulate voter emotions and cater to the basest instincts of the electorate.[14] Some consultants, in their more candid moments, confess that they do not respect many of their political clients, nor do they hold the voters in high esteem. Their disdain for the public is motivated by the belief that voters tend to ignore rational arguments, responding instead to visceral emotional appeals. Rather than elevate debate on the merits of the issues, consultants encourage their clients to speak in the coarse language of demagoguery. As Paul Corcoran points out, contemporary political discussion requires "the virtual abandonment of sustained argument in favor of one sentence paragraphs, bold emotional assertions, and clichés."[15] Critics contend consultant methods foster ambiguity and the politics of symbolism through euphemism, metaphor, and puffery.[16] Through media advertising and direct mail, consultants can reach out and energize a significant number of citizens. Contrived grassroots activity (what is mockingly referred to as "astroturf campaigning") is an increasingly popular tactic engaged by interest groups seeking to influence legislation as it moves through Congress. These so-called outside strategies are rapidly becoming just as important as conventional Washington lobbying. But a partnership between political consultants and interest groups to mobilize an army of grassroots supporters presents a warped vision of constituent pressure and calls into question the authenticity of contact between the voter and the legislator.

Political scholar E. E. Schattschneider once described the chorus of interest groups as "singing with an upper class accent."[17] The interest group community is more diverse than it was when Schattschneider made that remark, but the influence and access enjoyed by well-funded interests continue to animate scholarly debate and inspire political reformers. The employment of political consultants by interest groups has added another facet to the discussion. Political scientists have raised legitimate questions about wealthy groups using political consultants to define the terms of policy debates and overwhelm other interest-group voices. In a system that depends on the mass media to communicate with citizens, there are concerns that political consultants, in the employ of interest groups, further advantage elite interests at the expense of the disorganized and impoverished.

ORGANIZATION OF THE BOOK

The concerns outlined previously should not be misinterpreted as a broad indictment of the consulting profession. In this book I will endeavor to avoid the mistakes of earlier authors, who readily blamed consultants for a variety of problems based on their proximity, and will seek to evaluate consultants without malice aforethought. There are plenty of bad things to say about consultants and many are well deserved, but consultants, it should be remembered, are servants of their political masters. Even in their most rarefied state they are not the architects of public policy. Their role in the legislative process, while it should be examined carefully, should not be treated casually as a corruption of the system without firm evidence. Political consultants need to be held accountable and should be examined critically. Some recent articles raise important questions about the nature of the profession and its role in a democratic society.[18] Unfortunately, too many writers begin with an a priori assumption that political consultants are bad. Although it may be gratifying to blame consultants for failures in our political system, it is not especially informative. Some authors compound their initial misconception by using caricatures to describe other political actors. In order to elevate consultants to "kingmaker" status, voters and politicians must be reduced in kind. It is fairly common to stumble upon descriptions of the politician writ large as a venal, self-serving cipher waiting to be told what to say by his consultant. Voters are characterized as an ignorant, passive mass that is easily duped by clever campaign tricks. My goal is to cast a critical but not jaundiced eye on a fairly new method of influencing the course of pending legislation.

In 1989 Mark Petracca offered several explanations why political science had overlooked political consulting. The silence, he argued, is attributable to a number of factors: "First, compared with voters, PAC's or interest groups, consultants are far more difficult to study. There are no readily available data sources to either identify consultants or document their activities. Second, the considerable variation in what it means to consult and in the activities of professional consultants makes it difficult to identify the essence of consulting."[19] The gap was a source of frustration to scholars, as Stephen Medvic noted: "missing from political science journals are both quantitative and qualitative analyses of political consulting (or, for that matter, any reference to consulting at all). Furthermore, even the few books that have been written on the subject lack a theoretical foundation with which to explain the role of political consultants in American campaigns."[20] Ten years later it appears this shortcoming is being rectified, albeit slowly. A growing number books and articles are using primary interviews and the rich data provided by mandatory FEC reports to explore political consulting. The new works are tackling important questions, such as the relationship of consultants with the political parties, their responsibility for escalating campaign costs, and their role in initiative drives and referendums. A larger bibliography will probably solve the other major problem with the literature: the prevalent bias against the political consulting profession. As more scholars analyze political consulting, a wider spectrum of opinion is likely to emerge, but one notable blind spot still remains. Most of the literature dealing with political consultants, whether impressionistic or empirical, limits the analysis to campaigns. It is a reasonable parameter, since the campaign has been the consultants' professional reason for being. Consultants, however, do not go into hibernation after the election; they do not sever ties with successful clients, as some earlier works suggest. In fact, a growing number of consultants remain closely involved with their clients in office, providing advice and plotting strategy. Elected officials are not the only figures in the policy process who are using consultants. Interest groups are discovering the advantages of grassroots lobbying to augment their usual Washington activities. Through consultants with experience in political campaigns and mass communications, interest groups are able to take their arguments directly to the voter in the hope that voters will in turn contact their legislators on behalf of the interest group. As the profession continues to expand, one area sorely in need of attention is the role consultants play with respect to the policy process *after* the election.

The focus of this book is on issues that are qualitative in nature and not easily reducible for statistical analysis. The study, therefore, does not purport to present a "theory" of post-electoral consulting, meaning a procedure to predict future consultant activity in governance based upon established, quantifiable criteria. Rather, it focuses on a descriptive account of consultants emerging from the campaign to play an important role in governing. In particular, it chronicles the consultant-led and inspired public relations campaigns that mirror large-scale public policy initiatives. Using several case studies in combination with elite interviews, the goal of the book is to demonstrate the changes wrought on the legislative process by political consultants.

The book is divided into seven chapters. Chapter 2 provides a brief history of political consulting. Although some of the services political consultants perform have deep historical roots in American politics, a class of professionals devoted to providing strategic campaign advice for a fee is a twentieth century phenomenon. Their rise to prominence has been abetted by a number of well-documented changes in our political culture, such as the declining significance of political parties, the concurrent rise in candidate-centered campaigns, and the emergence of television as the dominant communications medium. The second chapter also includes a detailed description of the direct mail, mass media advertising, and polling techniques and strategies practiced by political consultants. Although each technique is discussed separately, in practice they are usually part of a seamless, unified public relations campaign. Polling and focus groups are used to devise the message and uncover the most receptive audience; direct mail and media advertising are the mediums to deliver the message.

In order to evaluate the impact of political consultants on the legislative process, a baseline needs to be established. In Chapter 3 the Medicare case study provides an example of lawmaking before consultants became involved. It exemplifies the traditional understanding of the legislative process typified by behind-the-scenes negotiations between the White House and congressional leaders, relentless lobbying of legislators by vested interests, and the horse trading that occurs between legislators. The fight to pass Medicare pitted President Lyndon Johnson and his numerous allies on Capitol Hill against powerful organized interests and conservative legislators who were skeptical of Johnson's program. The American Medical Association, which had twenty years earlier defeated President Truman's health care initiative by presenting it as "socialized medicine," vociferously opposed Medicare. They were joined by a phalanx of drug and insurance companies who feared a large government presence in the health care industry.[21] The political battle between the two camps was fierce, but it was waged within the corridors of power and was not augmented by the consultant-led public relations campaign characteristic of later conflicts.

Chapter 4 presents the first case study with manifest consultant activity. It chronicles another ambitious attempt to reform the American health care system. Unlike Johnson's proposal, however, the Clinton health care reform resulted in a humiliating defeat for the president and the congressional Democrats.[22] Aside from the outcome, the Clinton proposal differed from Medicare by virtue of the massive media and grassroots war coordinated by political consultants. During the year-long effort, America witnessed one of the most intense public policy campaigns in history. Hundreds of millions of dollars were spent by supporters and opponents of the Clinton plan through political consultants in an effort to stimulate, massage, and shape public opinion.[23] Given the public ambivalence toward the state of American health care, President Clinton and his supporters were convinced that they had to "sell" the proposal to the American people. But the debate was defined by the opponents, who successfully played upon public fears of bureaucratic control and incompetence. Throughout 1994, anxious legislators watched public support for the Clinton initiative evaporate.

Chapter 5 illustrates the extent to which political consultants are currently involved in the governing process. In many respects, the Contract with America represents the culminating achievement of political consulting. Consultants were enmeshed with the Contract from its creation to its transformation into legislation. In terms of policy, the ten plank platform signed by 367 House Republican candidates is a summary of conservative boilerplate: tax cuts, welfare reform, tort reform, regulatory relief, and so on. What made the Contract unique was the formidable marketing and polling scheme buttressing the ideas. Although the objectives were familiar, the language and themes were a synthesis of focus group information and public opinion polling designed to provoke a positive public reaction.[24] The election did not halt the marketing juggernaut; in fact, it picked up speed. Many of the consultants who were instrumental in crafting the Contract remained active advisors to the new majority as they shepherded the agenda through Congress.

In several respects the Clinton health care reform and the Contract with America and provided a template for future campaigns. The lessons drawn from the successes and failures of the 1990s have been incorporated into contemporary battles to shape the terms of debate regarding a prescription drug benefit. Chapter 6 offers a glimpse at a more mature example of post-electoral consulting. The public campaigns swirling around prescription drug benefit legislation and the movement to establish private accounts within Social Security are, in large part, built from the mold set in the 1990s. Like in earlier examples, the issue-inspired dueling opinion polls as well as television and print ads are targeted to voters and elite decision makers alike. The prescription drug battle also saw the emergence of a powerful new public relations weapon: the interactive Web site. The Internet has become a valuable tool used to deliver information and motivate grassroots activity.

Chapter 7 will assess the influence political consultants have had on the legislative process by gauging the impressions of select individuals who are intimately familiar with the events described in the case studies. Interviewees will be asked to comment on the three questions presented at the outset of the study. First, what effect has the introduction of public, campaign-oriented strategies had on the prospects for cooperation among elected officials? Second, do political consultants violate the principles of democratic accountability? Finally, are their methods suitable for governing?

The eighth and final chapter offers concluding remarks and speculation for the future. Chapter 8 will also present a comparison of the various case studies. Over the past thirty-five years the legislative process has become more complicated. It would be inaccurate to claim this change is due simply to the introduction of political consultants. Yet, it would not be an exaggeration to claim that the multi-million dollar advertising campaigns, the direct-mail salvos, and the incessant polling conducted by political consultants have managed to alter the nature of the legislative process. Along with the conventional activities that mark the process, committee hearings, negotiations between the White House and Congress, and interest group lobbying, public relations campaigns are a regular feature.

NOTES

1. Nancy McVicar, "Drug Lobby Accused of Airing Misleading Ads," *Ft. Lauderdale Sun-Sentinel*, 29 June 2000, A1.

2. "Cost Overdose: Growth in Drug Spending for the Elderly 1992–2010," (Washington, D.C.: Families USA, 2000).

3. David Rosebaum, "The Pill Box: The Gathering Storm over Prescription Drugs," *New York Times*, 14 November 1999, sec. 4, p. 1.

4. The term "permanent campaign" was coined by journalist and political advisor Sidney Blumenthal. The concept has surfaced in other books dealing with elections, most notably Gary Jacobson, *The Politics of Congressional Elections*, 3rd ed. (Boston: Little Brown, 1992); Paul Herrnson, *Congressional Elections: Campaigning at Home and in Washington* (Washington, D.C.: CQ Press, 1995); and Anthony King, *Running Scared: Why America's Politicians Campaign Too Much and Govern Too Little* (New York: The Free Press, 1997). More recently, Thomas Mann and Norman Ornstein produced an edited volume addressing the public policy concerns raised by the permanent campaign. See Thomas Mann and Norman Ornstein, eds., *The Permanent Campaign and Its Future* (Washington, D.C.: The Brookings Institution, 2000).

5. Indeed, some political communications scholars argue that modern-day political consultants are the progeny of colonial and early American campaign operatives. In their estimation, the advisors who came up with pithy slogans of the nineteenth century, such as "Tippecanoe and Tyler Too" are analogous to the professional ad men who devised Ronald Reagan's "Morning in America" pitch.

6. The latest count of political consultants appearing in the trade publication *Campaigns & Elections* puts the number of professional firms at over 2,300 nationwide, with thirty-eight specialties ranging from direct mail to television post-production.

7. Not all consultants receive compensation directly from the client. In order to avoid legal restrictions and sticky questions from the press, some consultants are paid by political party organizations. Clinton White House consultants Paul Begala and James Carville often worked pro bono. They did, however, reap significant financial benefits from their close association with the president through other paying clients.

8. The incipient growth of an industry based on dispensing policy advice is chronicled in two noteworthy books, James Smith, *The Idea Brokers: Think Tanks and the Rise of the New Policy Elite* (New York: The Free Press, 1991) and Robert Wood, *Whatever*

Possessed the President? Academic Experts and Presidential Policy1960–1988 (Amherst: University of Massachusetts Press, 1993). Smith presents a thorough history of think tanks as powerful non governmental institutions. Wood analyzes the twentieth-century phenomenon of academics as policy makers.

9. For an elaboration on the dynamic between the president and Congress, particularly in light of the divided government phenomenon see: Louis Fisher, *The Politics of Shared Power: Congress and the Executive*, 4th ed. (College Station: Texas A & M University Press, 1998) and James Thurber, *Divided Democracy: Cooperation and Conflict Between the President and Congress* (Washington, D.C.: CQ Press, 1991). The normative implications of divided government are addressed in David Mayhew, *Divided We Between the President and Congress* (Washington, D.C.: CQ Press, 1991) and, Morris Fiorina, *Divided Government* (New York: MacMillan, 1992).

10. Darrell West and Burdett Loomis, *The Sound of Money: How Political Interests Get What They Want* (New York: WW. Norton, 1998).

11. "Rx Industry Goes for KO," *Public Citizen*, November 2000, 11; Juliet Eilperin and Thomas B. Edsall, "Ad Blitz Erodes Democrats' Edge on Prescription Drugs," *Washington Post*, 27 October 2000, A14

12. Lawrence Jacobs and Robert Y. Shapiro, "Questioning Conventional Wisdom on Public Opinion toward Health Reform, *PS: Political Science and Politics* 19 (1994): 208–211.

13. Elizabeth Drew, *Showdown: The Struggle between the Gingrich Congress and the Clinton White House* (New York: Simon and Schuster, 1996).

14. W. Lance Bennett, *The Governing Crisis: Media, Money, and Marketing in American Elections* (New York: St. Martin's Press, 1992).

15. Paul Corcoran, *Political Language and Rhetoric* (New York: Prentice-Hall, 1979), 159.

16. Larry Sabato, *The Rise of Political Consultants: New Ways of Winning Elections* (New York: Basic Books, 1981), chapter 1.

17. E. E. Schattschneider, *The Semi-Sovereign People: A Realist's View of Democracy in America* (New York: Holt, Reinhart & Winston, 1960), 8.

18. James Thurber, "Are Campaign Pros Destroying Democracy?" *Campaigns & Elections*, August 1998, 55–61; Mark Petracca, "Political Consultants and Democratic Governance," *PS: Political Science & Politics* 14 (1989): 11–29.

19. Petracca, "Political Consultants," 11.

20. Medvic, Stephen. "Is There a Spin Doctor in the House? The Impact of Political Consultants in Congressional Campaigns." Ph.D. diss., Purdue University, 1997, 4.

21. John A. Andrew III, *Lyndon Johnson and the Great Society* (Chicago: Ivan Dee, 1998), 99–101.

22. There are two noteworthy book length discussions of the Clinton health care reform: Theda Skocpol, *Boomerang: Clinton's Health Security Effort and the Turn against Government in US Politics* (New York: WW. Norton, 1996), Haynes Johnson and David Broder, *The System: The American Way of Politics at the Breaking Point* (Boston: Little Brown, 1996). Skocpol's book is well argued and insightful, but at times it reads like a DNC editorial, dismissing all reform opponents as obstructionists whose arguments lack merit. The book fairly hums with an undercurrent favoring state control over health care. Johnson and Broder provide a lengthy journalistic narrative of the entire campaign. They colorfully describe the political wrangling over the doomed proposal.

23. Scholars at the Annenberg Public Policy Center at the University of Pennsylvania estimated that opponents to the Clinton plan spent nearly $200 million dollars to defeat the proposal.

24. Elizabeth Kolbert, "The Vocabulary of Votes - Frank Luntz," *New York Times Magazine*, 26 March 1995, 47– 48.

2

Political Consultants: Historical Origins and Methods

Behind-the-scenes political advisors have been fixtures in American elections since the early days of the republic. In the nineteenth century, the national party system provided an opportunity for savvy, regional power brokers to influence elections from the shadowy confines of political clubs. During the halcyon days of the party system, political bargains were made in legendary "smoke-filled rooms" by party bosses. The party bosses were in effect the men who chose the candidates and supplied the organizational talent and political know-how to get them elected. Although bossism came to be embodied by the cigar-chomping characters of Tammany Hall, they were actually a diverse lot. Martin Van Buren, for instance, the skillful tactician who ensured the election of Andrew Jackson in 1828, was a party builder and a man with his own national ambitions.[1] Republican party activist Mark Hanna was a wealthy Ohio financier who masterminded William McKinley's campaign for the White House. Backroom advisors were so prominent in American politics that toward the end of the nineteenth century they became part of popular culture, exemplified by the satirist Thomas Nast's famous caricature of the party boss as an unscrupulous, corpulent, money-grubbing fixer. These early party advisors performed many tasks that are familiar to modern-day political consultants, such as fundraising and campaign strategy. However, it would be inaccurate and perhaps disingenuous to claim that Martin Van Buren and Mark Hanna are the forefathers of political consulting, since it ignores a critical difference between political consultants and nineteenth century party bosses. Their personal motives notwithstanding, neither Van Buren nor Hanna considered campaign advising to be a vocation. The campaign was always a means to an end, not the defining moment. Consultants, on the other hand, are transfixed by the campaign and, even though a growing number remain in close contact with clients after the election, their post-electoral activities are not interested in party building. Consultants may perform an age-old service, but they are in fact a new breed of political actor.

The powerful party stalwarts who dominated American elections in the nineteenth century have disappeared, and it seems political consultants have taken their place. Whether consultants are partly to blame for party decline or whether consultants are simply opportunists who took advantage of a decrepit system is a point of contention. There is no question that industry pioneers had little use for party organizations and despite a recent trend toward cooperation with party leaders, consultants still fiercely guard their independence. But the historical record suggests that consultants owe their preeminence to fortune as much as to their ambition. The meteoric rise of political consultants from obscurity to notability is due to the confluence of several unrelated political, social, and technological developments. Assorted political reforms intended to "clean up" politics and give citizens greater influence weakened political parties and ushered in the era of the candidate-centered campaign. New laws opened a window for entrepreneurial consultants as candidates replaced party regulars with freelance campaign advisors. Consultants also benefited from the greater social and geographic mobility enjoyed by average citizens. Fluid migration from state to state created large blocs of voters with enervated ties to the community. Meanwhile, a permeable social strata diminished traditional party loyalties among citizens. Lastly, technological advances in communications, most notably the arrival of the television age, altered the venue of political activity. Campaigns that are fought largely on the airwaves created a marked demand for advisors with experience in the new media technology.

According to Dan Nimmo, modern political consultants are the direct descendants of public relations specialists of the 1920s.[2] The business discipline of public relations was created out of a corporate necessity to rehabilitate a tarnished public image. Prior to the turn of the century, dominant industrialists and financiers had little to fear from public approbation, since the government was unwilling to interfere with the free market. But in the early 1900s public outrage, fed by a series of inflammatory exposes recounting predatory business practices, posed a threat to corporate power. With the emergence of the Progressives as a political force willing to use the state to limit the excesses of corporations, companies began to curry support from the general public as a means to protect them from government intervention.[3] Initially, public relations was intended as a defensive strategy to counter unflattering newspaper reports, but it shortly became a crucial offensive weapon as businesses sought to enlarge markets for their products. By the 1920s, public relations and mass marketing were an integral part of the corporate culture.

It was not long before the public relations specialists who transformed corporate images gained the attention of politicians. Edward Bernays, a pioneer in modern public relations, was an early advocate of public relations in government service and he offered his insights into public behavior, honed by selling Ivory soap and Lucky Strike cigarettes, to President Calvin Coolidge.[4] In his books *Crystallizing Public Opinion* (1923) and *The Engineering of Public Consent* (1955), Bernays outlined the practical necessity of governmental public relations in a democratic society. He even went so far as to suggest a cabinet-level position for a PR expert. Bernays's well-earned reputation as a master salesman gave his viewpoint credibility in some political circles. He was, after all, the man credited with obliterating the social taboo against female cigarette smokers. But his vision of a secretary of public communication never came to fruition. Even the modern presidential press secretary, the individual charged with "selling" the president's policies, bears scant resemblance to his cousin the marketing executive. Nevertheless, as the advertising profession matured into a full-fledged industry, politicians tapped ad agencies for talent during presidential campaigns. As recounted by Stanley Kelley Jr. in *Professional Public Relations and Political Power*, the Eisenhower campaign relied heavily on marketing expertise provided by the New York firm of Batten, Barton, Durstine, and Osborn (BBD&O) and subsequent campaigns by Kennedy and Nixon also used professional ad agencies.[5] In the 1950s and the 1960s commercial marketing firms often took on political clients, but vain attempts to package politicians like frozen dinners or dish detergent were viewed with skepticism by some political figures and with outright hostility by others. Senator Hubert Humphrey, for instance, was vocally derisive of efforts to market leaders as if they were commercial goods. By the early 1970s most Madison Avenue ad agencies abandoned overt political activity. Concerns about profitability and competition from specialists such as political consultants convinced marketing executives to quit campaigning.

By the time Madison Avenue left politics, several important lessons had been imparted to political operatives, lessons that would inform the actions of future political consultants. Political consultants, for example, embraced the maxims ascribing the brief attention span of a consumer. Marketing provided a new vocabulary for campaign discourse. Nationally, political slogans, which had existed since at least the Jacksonian era, were infused with a commercial tone. Moreover, common political speech and correspondence became more abbreviated. Although it would be an exaggeration to claim that marketing is responsible for the triumph of sound-bite politics, there are visible roots.

Nimmo's political consultant family tree identifies the public relations man as the patriarch, but in doing so he neglects another important branch: the academic ancestors. Political consulting owes as much to social science as it does to business marketing. Political consultants have profited directly from the development of scientifically valid public opinion polling and benefited generally from the vast literature concerning voter behavior and elections. Despite the overt hostility exhibited between some scholars and political consultants, their relationship is more symbiotic than antagonistic. Consultants provide topics and data to study and analyze, while academics supply consultants with the theoretical foundation that guide their analyses of voter behavior and public opinion.

The advent of reliable, scientifically sampled opinion polls in the 1930s was a landmark event in the history of political consulting. Although it would be several decades before commercial pollsters emerged as influential political figures in their own right, polls quickly became ubiquitous features in campaigns. The value of in-house pollsters was clearly illustrated in the 1960s, when John F. Kennedy hired Lou Harris to be his public opinion analyst for his presidential campaign. Harris wasted no time proving his worth. Conventional political wisdom held that Kennedy, based on his Catholicism and his gilded background, would do poorly in an impoverished, overwhelmingly Protestant state like West Virginia. But Harris convincingly shattered this presumption with polling data indicating Kennedy's message resonated with West Virginia voters.[6] Kennedy won West Virginia and Harris silenced the skeptics. In later presidencies, pollsters moved beyond providing strategic analysis and became intimate political advisors. Pat Caddell was a member of Jimmy Carter's inner circle and Richard Wirthlin performed a similar function for Ronald Reagan. In the 1990s nearly every influential politician retained the services of a pollster.

It should come as no surprise that the first full-fledged political consulting firm, Campaigns Inc., would emerge in California. In many respects, the trends that shaped California politics in the early twentieth century presaged national events. California was home to an anemic party system further debilitated by an atomized, highly mobile electorate. Moreover, the vast size of the state encouraged candidates to explore new ways of reaching the voters. By the 1930s radio ads and five-minute movie shorts, the precursors to television ads, were used in statewide campaigns. Campaigns Inc. was founded by Clem Whitaker and Leona Baxter in the mid 1930s. Whitaker, a former political reporter with the *Sacramento Union*, and Baxter, a corporate publicist, quickly became important figures in California politics. Their first major success was a 1933 campaign in support of a flood control and irrigation development project in northern California. The plan was opposed by utility companies who believed it posed a threat to private power. Outspent by a four to one ratio, Whitaker and Baxter nevertheless prevailed over the utility companies by using clever radio and newspaper advertising. In 1934 Whitaker and Baxter confirmed their reputation as extraordinary political strategists by assisting in the defeat of populist gubernatorial candidate, Upton Sinclair.[7] From the 1930s to the late 1950s, Campaigns Inc. worked on dozens of statewide campaigns and built an impressive winning record. Although Whitaker and Baxter were conservative and worked primarily for Republican candidates, the couple disdained the official party apparatus. They made it clear they served candidates out of ideological sympathy and financial interest, not out of a sense of partisan loyalty. According to Stephen Medvic, they "radically broke from convention by not only controlling every aspect of a campaign, but doing so without any reliance on parties whatsoever."[8] Whitaker and Baxter were also innovators in the technical aspects of campaigning. Their use of film and later television ushered in a new era of media-based campaigning. Whitaker and Baxter were not simply perfecting the way campaigns were run, they were revolutionizing the process.

In the decades following World War II the circumstances that propelled Campaigns Inc. to the heights of political power in California spread rapidly across the nation. The profound transformation of the American electoral process can be attributed to a variety of causes, but with regard to political consultants there are two fundamental factors that transcend all others. First, the invention and proliferation of television, coupled with the inevitable development of media-driven politics, created a demand for individuals with experience with the new medium. Television, among all other twentieth century communications innovations, has arguably had the greatest impact on American politics. It transformed the way elections were conducted, it changed the way politicians behaved, and, perhaps most important, it altered how voters viewed the political process.[9] Second, the weakening of the party system, brought about by an institutional shift away from party organizations and toward primary elections as the method for choosing party nominees, encouraged entrepreneurial candidacies, what Martin Wattenberg refers to as "the rise of candidate centered politics."[10] The entrance of novice candidates was a boon to political consultants whose advice-for-hire business filled the gap created by party absence.

For better or worse, television is inextricably tied to the political process. Although it is often lampooned for, among other things, fostering a false sense of melodrama and reducing politics to sound bites, television has succeeded in bringing an abundance of political information to the general public. Unfortunately for elected officials, the television age has complicated politics. Effective communication through television requires a cadre of experts who understand the artistic and commercial aspects of the medium. As television became the dominant means of communication between politicians and the general public, political consultants, some with experience in commercial advertising, thrived. Media-driven campaigns forced amateurs out in favor of professionals. As Paul Herrnson notes, "The overall effect of technological change was to transform most campaigns from labor intensive grass-roots undertakings at which local party committees excelled, to money-driven, merchandised activities requiring the services of skilled experts."[11] The breadth of television's influence on American politics cannot be overstated. Not only did it fundamentally alter the nature of political communication; it created a virtually insatiable need for campaign cash. Political consultants stepped into the void and became indispensable fundraisers as well as for-hire media experts.

Television is partly responsible for the professionalization of campaign advising, but the decline of the political parties is the reason why professionals are in such great demand. In the post-war era, parties lost their hold on voters. Throughout the latter half of the twentieth century the number of unaffiliated voters rose, while party registration dwindled. By the 1960s and 1970s, public perception of the parties had changed. Survey research indicated that many citizens did not believe there were important differences between the Democratic and Republican parties. The parties exacerbated the situation with self-inflicted wounds. The well intentioned but damaging efforts to reform party structure took power away from the leaders and essentially crippled them. As a result of the reforms, individuals could seek and gain the party nomination without any cooperation from party leaders. William Crotty and Gary Jacobson describe the new environment: "A prospective candidate with sufficient personal wealth or PAC resources can run for office wherever he decides. He need have no political experience, no ties to the party whose nomination he seeks and no particular roots in the community or bond to the people he seeks to represent."[12] With their gate-keeping function removed, party leaders became superfluous. Jacobson further adds, "primary elections have largely deprived parties of the most important source of influence over elected officials. Parties no longer control access to the ballot and, therefore, to political office."[13] But weakened parties did not decrease the demand for expert political advice. On the contrary, the unprecedented number of political novices who captured party nominations through primaries magnified the need for professional advisors. As the party bosses slowly receded into the background, maverick political operatives like Joe Napolitan and David Garth leaped into the fray and began cultivating reputations as a new breed of kingmakers.[14]

As a group, political consultants have proven to be innovators and risk-taking opportunists. Political consultants have been at the forefront of the transformation of American electoral politics, from the incorporation of business marketing techniques into campaigns to the establishment of polling as a irreplaceable campaign tool. Their value to candidates and their exalted position in politics is predicated on the mastery of a specific skill subset. Some of the skills, such as polling, require technical knowledge and an understanding of scientific methodology. Other skills are based on keen political intuition and a firm grasp of business marketing principles.

TECHNIQUES AND TACTICS

The greatest indication that political consulting has reached industrial maturity is the wide range of services offered by professional firms. Within *The Political Pages*, a listing of professional consulting firms compiled by the trade magazine *Campaigns & Elections*, there are thirty-eight subdivisions ranging from television post production to direct mail services. Technological innovations have made campaigns an exceedingly complicated enterprise. A contemporary campaign involves complex tasks such as conducting polls or focus groups, media advertising, and direct mail, that often require professional help. Political consultants provide a unique service just like lawyers who dispense advice on campaign regulations or accountants who manage the books. The degree of specialization in political consulting parallels their deep penetration of the electoral process. At the federal level, it is becoming increasingly rare for a candidate, particularly an incumbent, to forgo the services of a political consultant. Presidential candidates and, more recently, Senate candidates usually hire several consultants. In 1996, for example, the Republican presidential candidate, Bob Dole, employed over fifty professional consultants from around the country.[15] In his failed bid for a California Senate seat, Republican candidate Michael Huffington passed $21 million through political consultants.[16] Judging by the enormous sums of money that are funneled through political consultants, their services are in great demand.[17] However, the robust growth enjoyed by the industry cannot be solely attributed to candidates' willingness to hire them. Political consultants are also profiting from the explosion of grassroots lobbying.[18]

It is not unusual for a major policy initiative to be followed by an elaborate public relations campaign, complete with television ads, Web sites, focus groups and staged public events. As policy battles have come to resemble campaigns, the pressure to garner public support has driven politicians to seek help from the people best able to cultivate, shape, and stimulate public sentiment. The knowledge and skills of experienced campaign operatives are an indispensable part of the public relations strategy in a high-profile policy debate. Although capturing the debate and selling the issue have not supplanted the traditional means of policymaking, committee work, negotiations between political leaders, and face-to-face lobbying are still paramount, a public relations campaign is a crucial complementary strategy. Despite the elemental differences between a policy campaign and a candidate campaign (winning an elective office and winning a policy debate are not completely analogous), the techniques used by consultants are roughly the same. Direct mail, an important fundraising tool during a candidate campaign, is employed to create grassroots activity. Media advertising performs the same function for issues as it does for candidates by raising awareness and disseminating information. Finally, polling and focus groups are used to track public sentiment throughout the debate. It enables partisans to measure the effectiveness of the media effort and alter their strategy accordingly.

Direct Mail

At its core political direct mail is simplicity. If you peel away the high-tech veneer, direct mail is a reasonably old-fashioned way for politicians to communicate with their supporters. The mail does not require satellite uplinks, television cameras, or fancy computer graphics. In fact, a successful direct mail campaign consists of two basic parts: a clever, well-crafted message and a precisely targeted list of recipients. Its basic design, however, belies a complicated mission.

Political direct mail emerged as a fundraising gimmick at the turn of the century. As early as 1916, politicians were using the mail to reach supporters. A fundraising appeal, for example, sent out under President Woodrow Wilson's signature resulted in 300,000 donations to the Democratic National Committee. Direct mail appeals continued to be used sporadically during the 1930s as New Deal supporters were solicited by mail for donations to the Democratic party.[19] The presidential campaigns of Dwight Eisenhower, Barry Goldwater, and George Wallace all utilized direct mail as a supplementary fundraising vehicle and as a way of bypassing the usual money men. The early efforts, however, were hampered by primitive technology and disorganization. In the 1960s and 1970s the power of direct mail was fully harnessed by early pioneers in the field, such as Richard Viguerie, Morris Dees, and Roger Craver.[20] These men combined marketing savvy with keen political insight to create the modern direct mail operation. The ingenuity and entrepreneurial skill of early direct mail consultants was abetted by two unrelated historical events: rapid innovations in computer technology and campaign finance regulation. Computers and sophisticated printers allowed direct mail consultants to produce prodigious amounts of high-quality mail (the importance of the aesthetic will be explained later in greater detail). Computers also enabled direct mail consultants to produce increasingly precise lists based on demographic information. During the 1970s direct mail operatives received an unintended boost through campaign finance reform laws that limited the amount of direct contributions to candidates. The legislation limited individual contributions, but language controlling expenditures was struck down by the Supreme Court as unconstitutional. The failure to contain costs was a boon to direct mail consultants, who became indispensable fundraisers. As costs continued to escalate, the statutory caps on donations forced candidates to seek funds from a broader population. Direct mail became the standard fundraising tool used to tap the small donor market.[21]

Although direct mail emerged as a fundraising device, raising money is only one aspect of contemporary direct mail activity. Lobbyists and political parties employ direct mail as part of a grassroots strategy to win support for a particular policy issue.[22] Issue mailings are not intended to solicit funds, but to sway public opinion. The mailings are explicitly designed to create a groundswell of public sentiment around an issue that will in turn translate into pressure on elected officials. But an issue mailing is not an innocuous method of persuasion and has spawned controversy by employing inflammatory and, some say, deliberately misleading language. Direct mail whether it is a positive reinforcement, encouraging recipients to call or write in support of a policy or a negative call to arms, relies on visceral emotions to spur the reader to action. Direct mail consultants understand a truism of human behavior: Fear and anger are powerful motivating forces. Critics argue that the cynical, calculated manipulation of voters' emotions harms the political process by polarizing policy debates and coarsening public dialogue. Moreover, by inciting voters to sound off to their elected representatives, direct mail consultants "have made it hard to tell the difference between manufactured public opinion and genuine explosions of public sentiment."[23]

The critics may be unduly alarmed. Prompting a reader to action is only the first link in a causal chain that must remain unbroken for the letter to be considered a success. Direct mail consultants endorse the conventional wisdom, buttressed by numerous congressional scholars, that politicians care about their constituents' opinions and will tread cautiously when a substantial number express an unambiguous position on an issue.[24] Despite the well-documented validity of this proposition, channeling public pressure through a direct mail campaign is not easy, nor is it simple to trace. A mass-mailed fundraising appeal can be evaluated based on the amount of money that comes in as a result of the letter. Unfortunately, such facile calculus is not applicable to an issue-advocacy letter. Direct mail appeals compete for voters' attention with more immediate concerns, such as working, family, and leisure time. The mailing must overcome these natural barriers as well as voter apathy and provoke a sufficient number of recipients to contact their legislators. Furthermore, contact must rise above a subjective threshold or it may never capture the attention of the legislature. But raising an issue to prominence is no guarantee legislators will respond in accordance with the mailing. Indeed, some legislators are suspicious of contrived mailings and dismiss the flood of letters and phone calls urged by a mailing.[25] Despite the fragility of this arrangement, political consultants use direct mail because it plays on the instinctive fear most legislators have of public disapproval.[26]

A successful direct mail effort is an artful combination of statistical inference and impassioned prose. To create a viable mailing list, direct mail consultants use detailed demographic information and behavioral assumptions based on selected characteristics of the audience. Quasi-scientific generalizations enable mailers to eliminate segments of the population and concentrate on potentially receptive groups. A mailing opposing English-only instruction in public schools, for instance, would likely target voters with Hispanic and Asian surnames. If list production has a formula, then letter writing has a feel. Copywriting relies on intuition and an instinctive sense of what will provoke a visceral reaction. As Richard Armstrong puts it, "Writing a direct mail letter has less to do with sheer creativity and more to do with manipulating human emotions and playing upon basic human needs."[27] A direct mail appeal is laden with evocative symbolism and heated rhetoric expressly designed to trigger a powerful emotional response.

The first step in a direct mail campaign is generating a mailing list. Political parties and interest groups maintain in-house lists of contributors and dues-paying members. These lists are sufficient to communicate with known supporters, but if the issue requires a broader outreach the in-house list must be supplemented with lists obtained from brokers. Some of the larger direct mail operations take custody of lists after a campaign and subsequently rent them to smaller companies.[28] According to Dennis Johnson, "Commercial firms compile lists on nearly every conceivable demographic variable, one such firm, I Rent America, advertises some 220 million names on computer files. Clients can rent the names of 266,302 active donors to Handgun Control Inc., the 154,551 alumni of Outward Bound, or the 345,895 subscribers to the *Vegetarian Times* magazine."[29]

Just like a sculptors clay, the list needs to be manipulated before it can be unveiled. Sophisticated computer software programs enable direct mail consultants to filter and enhance the list. By using information provided by government agencies such as the U.S. Census Bureau and the FEC, direct mail consultants shape the unrefined list. Computers overlay a template that groups the population into subsets based on ethnicity, gender, income level, or party affiliation. The census, for example, places voters into neighborhoods or districts of 1,000 to 1,600 individuals who share similar social and demographic traits. Direct mail consultants benefit greatly from the sea of data produced by governments at all levels, most of which is part of the public domain and inexpensive to obtain.[30] Direct mail consultants can use this information to target specific geographic areas. Given the technology, it is relatively easy to produce a list of all the homeowing, registered Democrats in a particular county over age 65 with incomes less than $40,000. Computers have, in a sense, shattered the limitations on list production. Not only have they enabled political consultants to produce well-tailored lists; computers have allowed groups to gather an unprecedented amount of valuable data. The trafficking of personal information has raised concerns with right-to-privacy advocates, but despite their complaints the government has refrained from overt regulation, favoring disclosure requirements and opt-out clauses as the best way to restrain direct mail contact.

A viable list is the basis of a successful direct mail effort, but the list is worthless without an effective pitch. The content of the letter mixes crass commercial gimmickry with an overt emotional appeal. This is a volatile combination that leads some critics to argue direct mail is a dishonest and inflammatory campaign tactic. Practitioners make no apologies for the shrill tone that pervades issue appeals and they scoff at the suggestion that their goal could be accomplished with neutral, dispassionate language. According to Eva Pusateri, a conservative direct mail consultant, "All politics is emotional. Each [political] issue needs to be developed on the voters' level and brought home to them...Emotion, either positive or negative, needs to be communicated."[31]

Direct mail copywriting has two component parts: appearance and language. Commercial gimmickry is most evident in the design and aesthetic appeal of the mailing. Direct mail consultants understand that they face a difficult task in differentiating their mailing from all other "junk mail." Consultants pay careful attention to the smallest detail, no matter how seemingly insignificant. Every aspect of the letter is analyzed deliberately, from the typeface, to the color and texture of the paper, to the placement of stamps on the envelope . Direct mail consultants are also not above subterfuge. In order to entice the recipient to open and read their mailing, consultants have developed several clever disguises that mask the true character of direct mail. Stylistic imitation is common because there are no civil or criminal penalties for such deception unless the content of the letter can be proven to be fraudulent.[32]

The false official letter is among the most popular designs used by consultants. The official letter mimics an important government document and grabs the recipient's attention with a stern warning about "penalties for misuse" and a bold statement declaring "this document not to be forwarded" (bulk mail is never forwarded).[33] The personal letter is another familiar outreach method. Whereas the official letter jolts the reader with apprehension, the personal letter invites the reader with an intimate approach. Personal letters eschew the standard accouterments of mass mailings such as metered postage and window envelopes in favor of "live" stamps and heavier stock paper to simulate stationery. Advances in laser printing and computer technology enable consultants to produce mass mailed letters that appear to be handwritten notes.[34] The disguises are only limited by the imagination of the direct mail consultant, and they are constantly searching for a new eye-catching approach. In the early 1990s fake newspapers gained wide popularity. The paper contains slanted stories and editorials about an issue, but is otherwise difficult to distinguish from other small community papers.[35]

In terms of the language used in the letter there are no hard and fast rules, only general guidelines. According to practitioners, the most important ingredient is emotion. Their experience has taught them that appeals to reason are not as effective as appeals to the heart. A cold, aloof, dispassionate discourse on an issue will not arouse the reader, but an impassioned provocative letter will generate action. Yet direct mail consultants are careful not to overindulge in emotional rhetoric. Sanctimonious letters that browbeat the reader or letters filled with invective can alienate the audience rather than stimulate it. The language should be simple and direct and should not include complex abstractions or obscure vocabulary. A simple letter works best, not because the readers are dumb, but because the scan reader can grasp the main argument without reading the entire letter.[36]

Proponents of the Clinton health care reform would undoubtedly agree with Larry Sabato, who claims "Direct mail is often nothing more than mass produced, lovingly refined hate mail [and] is thus the conveyor of misinformation and the purveyor of oversimplification and superheated emotionalism, all of which are notoriously destructive to rational political decision-making."[37] Sabato's hyperbolic characterization overstates the case, but there is reasonable concern that direct mail may have a corrosive effect on communication between legislators and constituents. By encouraging people to flood their senators' and representatives' offices with postcards, letters, and phone calls, direct mail has clouded the distinction between contrived public outcries and unprovoked expressions of public opinion.

Mass Media Advertising

Of the three activities generally associated with political consulting, media advertising, direct mail, and public opinion polling, advertising has the deepest historical roots. Political advertising came about as a practical necessity in a geographically expansive nation with a far flung population. In the eighteenth century, newspapers and pamphlets were disseminated among the citizenry, extolling the virtues of some candidates and, in a precursor to modern negative advertising, trumpeting the foibles of other candidates. These were essential forms of political communication, particularly in campaigns for national office, where the candidates were often incapable of traveling to every corner of the territory. In the nineteenth century new technologies supplemented the rustic examples of the founding period. Lithography, and later photography, enabled campaigners to reproduce the same image with relative ease and advances in printing technology provided an expansive tableau. Before long, political slogans and portraits were ubiquitous. According to political communications scholar Kathleen Hall Jamieson, "Through most of the nineteenth century, American were able to eat on, sleep with, wipe their mouths on, or blow their noses in political advertising, for political aspirants imprinted their likenesses, their slogans, and their promises on bandannas and handkerchiefs, tablecloths and coverlets."[38]

The creative use of print mediums notwithstanding, political advertising did not come to full maturity until the twentieth century, when techniques invented by business marketers began to infiltrate politics. Although mass marketing candidates for public office has been loudly denounced by a succession of journalists, academics, and politicians as an affront to principled politics, corporate experience offers important insights into public behavior. Gary Mauser claims, "Marketing has developed a body of knowledge and expertise pertaining to methods of analyzing and persuading large groups of people with appropriate adaptation, these procedures may be extended to political campaigns."[39] If voters can be considered analogous to consumers and candidates to products, then marketing and advertising not only make sense, but also are necessary.

Twentieth century advances in communications technology also changed the nature of political advertising. The invention of the radio brought political advertising into people's homes and enabled candidates to speak to a vast audience in their own voices. But without question the greatest, most potent medium with respect to political advertising has been television. In modern campaigns, candidates and issue advocacy groups still use newspapers and radio for political advertising, but usually as a complementary feature of a strategy focused around television. As Nicholas O'shaughessy accurately points out, "Political marketing employs a constellation of mediums, but television remains the supreme gift to politicians."[40]

The proliferation of television coincided with the rise of the independent political consultant and, in a sense, they are an inseparable pair. It is impossible to discuss the impact of television on the political process thoroughly without mentioning the acknowledged masters of the medium: political consultants. Nor is it feasible to analyze political consultants without devoting significant attention to their advertising efforts on television. Television advertising is the political consultants' golden goose that provides a continuous supply of money. The enormous sums required to campaign on television facilitated the expansion of political consulting over the course of thirty years from an insignificant part-time occupation to a large-scale, multi faceted industry. It appears growth will continue well into the twenty-first century as issue advocacy campaigns become more common. Consultants stand to make substantial profits from public policy battles waged between corporations, trade associations, and public interest groups as they use advertising campaigns to sway public opinion. Non candidate related political advertising is now a staple at many large firms. According to principals at Sawyer-Miller, a leading consulting firm, "Where once companies tried to influence public issues mainly by back-door lobbying on Capitol Hill, they now increasingly campaign directly for mass public support, which they believe will move the legislators more effectively."[41]

It is not an exaggeration to say that contemporary campaigns, particularly campaigns for federal offices, are waged largely on television. Television has surpassed all other media forms to become the primary conduit of political information for the American people. A variety of academic disciplines, from sociology to political science, have provided a virtual mountain of statistics concerning public viewing habits and their implication for political decision making. Without digressing into a tedious recitation of numbers, there are several figures that illustrate television's pervasiveness. According to census statistics, 99 percent of American homes own at least one television and the average citizen watches it roughly four hours a day. As a source of political news, television is unmatched. According to surveys conducted by the Roper Organization, in national elections 75 percent of those surveyed indicated that they received the majority of their political news from television.[42] In terms of its impact on voter behavior, however, the results are mixed. Some scholars have concluded that the persuasive capacity of television is limited as it serves simply to reinforce preexisting attitudes. But other scholars counter that it has a deterministic effect in campaigns, particularly among less educated voters.[43] From a political consultant's perspective, the ongoing academic debate regarding television and politics is interesting, but ultimately irrelevant. Television is essentially the only game in town and if your client is not on it, then he is at a distinct disadvantage. In the words of political consultant Frank Luntz, "Candidates have come to accept paid television advertising as the primary mode of interaction with the electorate. The reason is both clear and simple: it reaches virtually every voter."[44] The same logic holds true for issue campaigns.

An effective media strategy is comprised of four components: thorough and accurate background research, creative story-boarding and visual presentation, a well planned air time strategy, and a concerted effort to amplify the theme via free media. Political consultants are involved in every stage, coordinating all the activity. Integrated political consulting firms can often provide a politician or an interest group with a broad range of campaign services, from thematic story-boarding to the actual production and editing of television and radio spots. Smaller firms often subcontract with specialists to produce the same level of service.[45]

Mass media consultants begin with the explicit understanding that television advertising is extremely costly. In most campaigns it is the single largest expenditure, taking up the lion's share of the campaign budget. With that in mind, consultants never undertake commercial production without adequate background research. Consultants are often criticized for selecting issues based on advertising viability. In other words, matters that concern the voters which are difficult to encapsulate in an ad campaign are ignored in favor of visceral, easy-to-grasp slogans. However, consultants' commitment to detailed research reflects a different dynamic. Research-driven commercials put the voter in charge of issue selection. According to Gary Nordlinger, an experienced Democratic consultant, the most important facet of political advertising is "the use of survey research and opposition research to develop an understanding of what concerns the public."[46]

Once the background research is complete, the artistic process begins in earnest. An obligation to issue research does not change the fact that television is a visual medium that works best with evocative imagery. As Robert Denton and Gary Woodward ruefully observe, "The form and content of an ad must be designed to create an emotional response in a viewer. We vote with our hearts, not our minds."[47]Although stylistic differences abound among media consultants, many advocate a storytelling approach when drafting a political commercial. Storytelling connects the candidate with viewers by drawing on familiar American values such as hard work, family, and patriotism. Often in this milieu candidates take on the trappings of popular culture figures. During his 1992 presidential campaign, for example, Bill Clinton was successfully cast as the archetypal Horatio Alger character in his "Man from Hope" television commercials. His hardscrabble life and his up-from-his-boot-straps personal history were tailor made for this type of appeal. This style works just as well in an issue format without a candidate centerpiece. During the 1994 health care reform effort Goddard-Claussen, a political consulting firm specializing in media relations, created the infamous Harry and Louise ad campaign. This middle-class couple narrated a devastating story of the potential hazards that could befall average Americans if the Clinton plan were enacted. The commercial was deemed so harmful to the reform effort that Dan Rostenkowski, chairman of the Ways and Means Committee, negotiated with the sponsors to have it taken off the air.[48] In the 106th Congress, the pharmaceutical industry was able generate public doubt about the wisdom of stronger government regulation over drug prices by using a battle-tested political advertising formula. The drug company message was channeled through a feisty, elderly woman named Flo, a character built from the Harry and Louise template.[49]

Creating a strong visual rendition of the campaign theme is the glamorous aspect of a media strategy. But the most rousing ad will be useless unless it reaches the proper audience. In order to ensure expensive commercials have the greatest impact, media consultants put together a precise time-buying strategy. Media consultants base their decisions on demographic research, focus groups, ratings studies, and pricing data that target a specific audience. A poorly targeted ad is essentially a waste of money and in some cases can prove detrimental to your campaign. Robert Nelson, a California-based political consultant, explains, "if you are a hostile, bombastic older male [candidate], you probably shouldn't spend a lot of time buying Murphy Brown television commercials. You'll be paying to advertise to a group of people who whenever they see you will remember how much they dislike you."[50] The emergence of cable television has, in some respects, made time buying easier for political consultants. Abundant channels have depressed the cost of advertising on television and provided several options for consultants. More important, the channels that cater to special interests present a narrow, demographically consistent audience. A commercial with an environmental theme, for example, can reach environmentally sensitive voters by airing on Outdoor Living, Home and Garden Television, and the Discovery Channel.

In order to stretch the advertising dollar, consultants also attempt to capitalize on the free media provided by television news programs. Amplifying a campaign theme via free media is difficult, since most journalists are unwilling to become echo chambers for candidates. Some consultants accomplish this by creating newsworthy commercials. These commercials are either so controversial in nature or innovative in design that they attract the attention of journalists. The Harry and Louise ads, for instance, gained a much broader audience after the Clinton administration and media elites began discussing them.[51] Commercials sponsored by Citizens for a Better Medicare so outraged liberal interest groups and their allies in Congress that they were mentioned by name in a series of counter ads, but their vociferous condemnation may have worked against them by simply raising the advertisements' profile (and indirectly the drug industry's position) with the voters.[52] Consultants also encourage their clients to parrot commercial themes when they are interviewed by reporters. Repetition of common words and phrases creates a synergy between paid advertising and free media. Republican consultant Ed Gillespie likens repetition to an amplifier. He claims, "It's important to have a lot of smaller megaphones going off at the same time. If they're going off at the same time with different messages it's just noise. If they're going off at the same time with the same message, it's an echo chamber."[53] Some consultants, in an attempt to take advantage of media credibility, try to blur the line between paid media and free media by creating commercials that mimic news footage.

I would be remiss if I did not mention the role newspapers and radio play in a public relations campaign. Although television is the primary advertising method, newspapers and radio can be an effective complement by reinforcing the message delivered on television. As a print medium newspapers can put forward a more detailed, complex argument than an average thirty-second television spot. Thus, themes presented on television can be explained in newspaper ads. Furthermore, newspaper space is cheap and always available. As for radio, it nearly matches television in sheer ubiquity. Radio ads played on popular stations during "drive time" (morning and evening rush hours) can reach a vast audience of voters. Moreover, the very nature of radio facilitates much more precise demographic targeting than television. Station formats such as easy listening or adult contemporary draw remarkably homogenous audiences. More important, radio draws on a listener's imagination. According to media consultants Don Sweitzer and David Heller, "Radio is the most intimate of all media, its impact is significant because the images it conveys exist in the listeners mind."[54]

Political advertising is subject to the same sort of criticism leveled at direct mail: It is overly melodramatic, it champions image over substance, and it is corrosively negative.[55] From an academic perspective, the onus is placed squarely on the shoulders of political consultants. In his book, *The Rise of Political Consultants*, Larry Sabato questions "their glorification of style over substance, their hero worship of imagery idols; and their trivialization of politics with an over indulgent, insatiable appetite for gimmicks, slogans, and star politics."[56] Lance Bennett has a more insidious view. He claims political consultants, through the magic of advertising, preserve an illegitimate status quo. Bennett states, "When signs of political illegitimacy begin to appear, image-laden techniques can create the illusion of legitimacy to dispel serious consideration of the underlying problem."[57] Other writers blame advertising for presenting a false set of simplistic solutions to difficult policy problems. These scholars grant marketing and advertising an unwarranted amount of power over the political process. In truth, advertising has a muffled, imprecise effect. In America, individuals possess considerable freedom to decide between candidates and between public policies. Advertising, far from having a decisive impact, is just one of several factors that influence public opinion.

The Internet and the World Wide Web

Political consultants, as a professional group, have eagerly embraced new technologies. Whitaker and Baxter's innovative use of billboards and radio advertising during the 1930s and Richard Viguerie's ground-breaking application of computers to organize his mail lists in the 1970s are two excellent examples. In the 1990s the rapid emergence of the World Wide Web presented political consultants with another venue in which to practice their skills. Political consultants are using Web sites to complement traditional direct mail outreach and as a supplemental advertising medium. In a short period of time, the Internet has proven to be a cost-effective way to deliver a message and generate grassroots activity.

According to the Pew Research Center, an estimated 104 million Americans had access to the Internet at the end of 2000, with over 58 million counted as daily users. More significant, a growing number of Americans are going on line to get news and political information.[58] Political scientists are currently evaluating what the burgeoning online community means to American politics. Suffice it to say that the jury is still out, but prescient political consultants, as usual, are not waiting for the endorsement of academics. They are using the Internet in a myriad of ways, ranging from advertising to fundraising. In the 2002 consultant directory provided by *Campaigns & Elections* magazine lists twenty eight firms that bill themselves as Internet specialists, not including the larger firms that employ the Internet as a piece of an overall business model. Seven years ago this category did not exist.

Political consultants have discovered that Web sites are flexible mediums that can mimic some of the strongest attributes of a direct mail appeal at a lower cost. They are visually compelling, they can provide an assortment of emotion-laden narrative examples, and they can deliver a wealth of startling statistics. Web sites also own a particular advantage over direct mail in the sense that they are interactive. A visitor to a web site can instantly register an opinion via e-mail, join an organization, or even donate money using a credit card. Direct mail, in contrast, relies on a recipients willingness to take time to write a check or fill out a form. The Web's utility was on display during the 106th Congress as President Clinton and his allies attempted to pass prescription drug benefit legislation. The coalition group Citizens for a Better Medicare used a Web site, callyourgrandma.com, to rally young people to call their elders and convince them to lobby Congress against President Clinton's plan. The site even offered free phone cards to people who logged on.[59] Not to be outdone, Seniors USA, a liberal organization sponsored by the labor unions, launched an Internet campaign in June 2001 to encourage seniors to e-mail legislators and the White House to protest the high cost of prescription drugs. Their announced goal was 1 million e-mail contacts over a five-day period. The effect of second-order grassroots outreach like callyourgrandma.com or coordinated e-mail campaigns like Seniors USA is unknown. Consultants are willing to gamble with Web sites because they are inexpensive, unlike television advertising or a mass mailing that require large capital investments.

Web sites are not without shortcomings. Direct mail, and even to a lesser extent television advertising, can be directed to a receptive audience. Political consultants can refine a mass mailing with little difficulty using a rich assortment of easily obtainable demographic information. In a similar fashion, consultants use viewer information to determine the most effective time to show a television ad. Web sites, however, must rely on random Internet traffic to reach citizens. The self-selection bias makes it uncertain whether the Web site is attracting new converts or whether it is speaking in a vacuum. There is no tried and true formula to attract citizens predisposed to the message as there is with a direct mail campaign. Internet boosters, however, claim that Web sites have a viral trait that compensates for its limitations. The existence of a Web site can be promoted by visitors through word of mouth, or more likely, e-mail. Thus, one visitor can easily relay information to several friends who may visit the Web site themselves and in turn tell more people.[60] It is premature to assess the impact of the Internet on American politics; it is too early to tell if it will have a similar transformational effect that television had in the mid twentieth century. Yet given the vast proliferation of Internet access and the growing volume of e-mail traffic, it is reasonable to assume that the Internet will become a prominent component of future consolidated public relations campaigns.

Public Opinion Polling

The role of public opinion in our political system is an historically contentious topic. Concerns over the nature and volatility of public sentiment animated critical debates during the Constitutional Convention and were important rhetorical fodder for the authors of *The Federalist Papers*. Two centuries have not cooled the passion surrounding the debate, nor has time solved some of the fundamental questions. Modern scholars, echoing voices from the founding generation, continue to debate issues, such as the wisdom of majority opinion and the use of political institutions as a buffer between public opinion and public policy.[61] In the twentieth century, the dilemma posed by public opinion was complicated further by the triumph of scientific polling. When politicians and thinkers of the eighteenth and nineteenth centuries engaged in debate about public opinion, it was amorphous and abstract. Only the brazen or the foolish claimed to know the public's wishes. But in our era public opinion has taken concrete form in the shape of poll numbers. Contemporary pundits discuss public opinion as if it is instrument, like a thermometer, to be periodically consulted. The ability to point to numerical renderings of public sentiment has influenced the course of public policy. Although it would be an overstatement to assert public policy is the cumulative result of opinion polls, there is ample evidence to suggest that opinion polls play a strategic role during policy formulation.

Even before scientific, randomly sampled polls became a fixture in American politics, politicians and journalists attempted to plumb the depths of public opinion. The earliest type of public opinion polls were straw polls conducted by newspapers and magazines during the nineteenth century. These polls usually consisted of random man-on-the-street interviews conducted by reporters or, in some cases, mailed questionnaires to subscribers. The results were unscientific and irregular, since the surveyed population was invariably too small and insufficiently heterogeneous to accurately reflect the general populace. Despite their penchant for inaccuracy, straw polls remained standard until the 1930s.[62] In 1936, in an event that eventually took on mythic status, George Gallup, a young Ph.D. from Iowa, changed the face of polling virtually overnight by predicting Franklin Roosevelt's reelection with a randomly sampled poll. Gallup's results challenged a much larger but less scientific poll taken by the respected national magazine *The Literary Digest*. Gallup's methodology revolutionized polling and laid the foundation for the polling industry.

Gallup was an effusive promoter of the benevolent power of public opinion polling. According to Irving Crespi, "Gallup claimed poll results can be considered a mandate from the people that should be followed by the nations leaders because those results represent what the people want, what legislation they favor, what they oppose, and what policy directions they want government to follow."[63] But many politicians remained skeptical and some, such as President Harry Truman, were openly hostile to public opinion polling. Truman considered polls to be an abdication of responsible leadership. In his estimation, only weak, vacillating politicians pandered to public opinion.[64] Evidently, Truman's aversion was not shared by his successors in the White House, as every president since Eisenhower has employed a pollster. It is important to note, however, that president's are quick to refute any suggestion that policy positions are the result of polls. In fact, most political leaders would argue that they use polls to shape their preexisting position; not to adopt whatever captures the majority support.[65]

Gallup and his contemporaries, Elmo Roper and Arthur Crossley, considered polling to be a non partisan endeavor and avoided close ties to either political party. In the 1960s and 1970s, however, a new generation of commercial pollsters emerged who readily sold their services to candidates. For-hire pollsters, such as Patrick Caddell, Richard Wirthlin, Peter Hart, Lou Harris, and Bob Teeter, emerged as prominent figures in political campaigns. Initially, pollsters were relegated to the periphery of the advisor circle, but some transcended their lowly status and became trusted political confidants. These men did more than simply report polling results. They interpreted the data, developed models and theories of voting behavior, and used their numbers to plot governing strategy.[66]

The evolution of the pollster from a lower-echelon campaign operative to a prominent political advisor has altered the kind of advice they proffer. Pollsters are frequently asked to assess the popularity of policy initiatives, a role that is qualitatively different from conducting candidate polls. Even a well-designed candidate poll is prone to error resulting from voter ignorance and ambiguous responses. These problems are magnified in a policy poll. Depending on the profile and complexity of an issue, there may be a high number of non respondents, people who refuse to be interviewed, or of respondents who give no opinion. With a small number of potential respondents qualified to give an informed opinion, issue polls often force the pollster to speculate based on a limited data set. In these instances a pollster is not so much a specialist providing reliable information as an oracle trying vainly to predict the future. Nevertheless, issue polls are commissioned regularly by elected officials to gauge public support for new legislation.

Commercial pollsters can provide clients with an assortment of polls that vary in cost and utility. The baseline poll (sometimes referred to as the benchmark poll) is taken at the outset of a campaign and is generally used to provide information that will guide subsequent decisions. The poll probes the public for positions that generate strong responses, either positive or negative, that can be incorporated into the media campaign. A poll on immigration policy, for instance, may indicate that people are extremely uncomfortable with the prospect of government identity cards as a means of curbing illegal immigration. Opponents to immigration reform can then use the identity card as the centerpiece of a media campaign against the legislation. The baseline poll is also used to determine the relative strength of the opposition. During the 1994 health care debate, for example, a number of polls indicated that public support for health care reform was strong, but pollsters working on behalf of a coalition opposed to the Clinton plan discovered that support for the actual plan was soft and that public apprehension over governmental control was high. Based on these results, the coalition launched a massive media campaign designed to exploit public concern.[67]

The baseline poll is crucial to establishing a strategic plan, but considering the fluid nature of a policy debate the initial results need to be augmented by tracking polls. Tracking polls provide campaigns with a means of measuring daily fluctuations in public opinion by continuous polling over a four to five-day period. The utility of a tracking poll can perhaps best be described in sports parlance, where the tracking poll is the scoreboard telling the players who is ahead and who is behind. Although it is expensive, tracking polls enable consultants to measure the impact of the other elements of the public relations campaign. In other words, a well-implemented tracking poll can ascertain whether commercials and direct mail appeals are having the desired effect.

The last type of survey cannot be accurately described as a poll. "Focus groups," according to Herbert Asher, "are not polls but in-depth interviews with a small number of people (usually 10 to 20) who often are selected to represent broad demographic groups."[68] Discussions are led by a moderator, who is charged with keeping the group on topic and facilitating comments from the members. Focus groups perform a reciprocal function by providing qualitative depth that is sometimes missing from a poll. In terms of a public relations campaign, focus groups can often supply the vocabulary used to sell a particular policy. Frank Luntz, the pollster behind the Contract with America, is a firm believer in the power of focus groups as a means to construct debate language. From his perspective, the political party that utilizes the terms and phrases that resonate with the voters has already won the argument.[69] Critics contend this is an exercise in semantics and reduces policy choices to euphemisms, but focus group supporters remain undaunted. Stan Greenberg, President Clinton's pollster, employed a high-tech version of the focus group method called "dial groups". In a dial group "Each viewer holds a little electronic box with a dial that's connected to a computer. The viewers are instructed to adjust the dial on a scale of 0 to 100 as they react negatively or positively to the politician's words. The responses are simultaneously fed into the computer, which instantly produces a continuous line superimposed on a separate television monitor that the pollster can watch as the politician speaks."[70]

According to Dennis Johnson, an academic and part-time political consultant, "Focus groups and their electronic cousins, dial meter groups, have become the hot even faddish new tool in the pollster's arsenal. Under the name qualitative research, these tools reveal much about attitudes, fears, and preferences, but very little about public opinion at large."[71] Focus groups are unscientific and even their defenders acknowledge that they cannot be used to generalize to a larger population, but they can provide insights into why people think the way they do.

People tend to grant pollsters, in the words of Larry Sabato, "the right to philosophize grandly and to pontificate in terms normally reserved for a nation's governing elite."[72] Pollsters have secured a coveted spot on the political advisor totem pole by claiming to offer subjective information as objective facts, but poll consumers would do well to view these "facts" with a wary eye. Polls are burdened with a host of weaknesses ranging from flawed methodology to interpretive bias.[73] Structural defects are compounded by the fleeting, ever-changing nature of public opinion. Even if a poll is methodologically sound and free of bias, it is only a snapshot of public opinion whose value depreciates precipitously over time.

The greatest fear among the critics of public opinion polls is that elected officials will use them as a substitute for reasoned discourse and that public policy will amount to a popularity contest rather than a principled search for sound answers. As the British statesman Edmund Burke colorfully put it centuries ago, you elect your representatives "to be a pillar of the state, not a weathercock on the top of the edifice."[74] But the reality is more complicated than they imagine and hardly as alarming. Polls are undoubtedly used by politicians throughout the life span of legislation to provide strategic guidance, and political leaders constantly refer to them as a justification for a course of action. Polls, however, have a supporting rather than a deterministic role in the legislative process. Instead of using polls to develop policy, politicians use polls to develop a marketing approach to sell the policy.

CONCLUSION

In an effort to provide a rudimentary explanation of the favored techniques used by political consultants it has been necessary to compartmentalize them. In practice, direct mail, Web sites, media advertising, and public opinion polling are part of an integrated public relations campaign. Insights derived from polls are used to help develop the advertising and direct mail efforts, which in turn are designed with the intention of moving public opinion. The transfer of these campaign skills to the legislative process has required surprisingly little adjustment on the part of political consultants. Despite the fact that consultants during a public policy campaign are working on behalf of an idea or abstract ideology rather than an individual candidate, the talents honed during candidate campaigns can be applied with virtual ease. According to political consultant Matt

Reese, selling a policy is analogous to electing a candidate. "The job," he declares, "is to decide what truths to tell to whom, through what channels of communication, and how many times. You win votes, or win activity by repetitive persuasive contact."[75] But the nature of a campaign is fundamentally different than governing: Campaigns result in an undisputed victor; governing is an ongoing process. Thus, successful campaign methods, no matter how well they work in the service of an issue, may be ill suited to a process that demands conciliation and compromise. In the next few chapters the case studies will illustrate the potential hazards of employing campaign techniques in the legislative process.

NOTES

1. James Ceaser, *Presidential Selection: Theory and Development* (Princeton: Princeton University Press, 1979) ch. 3.

2. Dan Nimmo, *The Political Persuaders: The Techniques of Modern Elections* (Englewood Cliffs: Prentice-Hall, 1970), 34.

3. The genesis of public relations and the reasons for its emergence are presented in Stuart Ewan, *PR! A Social History of Spin* (New York: Basic Books, 1996).

4. Coolidge supporters brought in Bernays to transform the president from a cold, aloof introvert into a homespun figure people would trust in the White House. In one memorable scene, Bernays invited several Vaudevillians down to the White House to eat breakfast with Coolidge. The press coverage showed a warm, engaging man enjoying the company of popular entertainers. According to his biographer, Larry Tye, "Bernays proved that the skills he used to craft public attitudes toward cigarettes and cigars could be employed to reshape the image of elected officials." Larry Tye, *The Father of Spin: Edward L. Bernays & the Birth of Public Relations* (New York: Random House, 1998), 79.

5. Stanley Kelley, Jr. *Professional Public Relations and Political Power* (Baltimore: Johns Hopkins University Press, 1956). The Kennedy and Nixon experiences are recounted in Melvyn Bloom, *Public Relations and Presidential Campaigns: A Crisis in Democracy* (New York: Thomas Crowell, 1973) and Joe McGinnis, *The Selling of the President: 1968* (New York: Trident Press, 1969).

6. Robert Friedenberg, *Communications Consultants in Political Campaigns* (Westport: Praeger Publishers, 1997), 49.

7. For a lengthy but highly readable chronicle of Upton Sinclair's failed gubernatorial bid, see Greg Mitchell, *Campaign of the Century: Upton Sinclair's Race for Governor of California and the Birth of Media Politics* (New York: Random House, 1992).

8. Stephen Medvic, "Is There a Spin Doctor in the House? The Impact of Political Consultants in Congressional Campaigns" (Ph.D. diss., Purdue University, 1997), 34.

9. Even a summarized list of the excellent books discussing television and its role in the political process would be too ambitious, but I would be remiss without mentioning several important works: Edwin Diamond and Stephen Bates, *The Spot* (Cambridge: MIT Press, 1984); Doris Graber, *Media Power and Politics* (Washington, D.C.: CQ Press, 1984); and Kathleen Hall Jamieson, *Packaging the Presidency* (New York: Oxford University Press, 1988).

10. Martin Wattenberg, *The Rise of Candidate Centered Politics: Presidential Elections of the 1980s* (Cambridge: Harvard University Press, 1991).

11. Paul Herrnson, *Congressional Elections: Campaigning at Home and in Washington* (Washington, D.C.: CQ Press, 1995), 14.

12. William Crotty and Gary Jacobson, *American Parties in Decline* (Boston: Little, Brown and Co., 1980).

13. Gary Jacobson, *The Politics of Congressional Elections* 3rd ed. (New York: HarperCollins Publishers, 1992), 20.

14. David Chagall, *The New Kingmakers* (New York: Harcourt, Brace and Jovanovich, 1981)

15. "Meet the Puppetmasters," *U.S. News and World Report*, 11 March 1996, 29.

16. Michael Wiesskopf, "The Professionals' Touch," *Washington Post*, 8 November 1994, A1.

17. According to *Campaigns & Elections,* the industry revenues amounted to over $1 billion from 1993 to 1996. According to FEC reports, nearly half of the money spent during congressional campaigns, a sum approaching $200 million, passes through the hands of professional political consultants. See Steven Medvic, "Spin Doctor" and Eliza Newlin Carney, "Cashing In," *National Journal*, 6 June 1996, 1295.

18. "Increasingly, corporations, unions, trade associations, and issue advocacy groups directly attempt to identify and activate rank-and-file voters to contact presidents, governors, mayors, and legislators on their behalf or on the behalf of an issue position that they wish to promote. This component of the process is called grassroots lobbying." Michael Clark, "Selling the Issues," *Campaigns & Elections*, April/May 1993, 27.

19. Frank Luntz, *Candidates, Consultants and Campaigns: The Style and Substance of American Electioneering* (Oxford: Basil Blackwell, 1988), 147.

20. Richard Viguerie, the godfather of conservative direct mail operations, began his career by copying down the names of donors to the Goldwater campaign. In 1965 Viguerie, with the help of a few assistants, went to the Clerk of the House of Representatives and transcribed by hand a list of individuals who donated more than $50 to the Goldwater campaign. His original list, which numbered only 12,500, grew to over 30 million names of conservative individuals by 1977. See Richard Armstrong, *The Next Hurrah: The Communications Revolution in American Politics* (New York: Beech Tree Books, 1988).

21. Larry Sabato, *The Rise of Political Consultants: New Ways of Winning Elections* (New York: Basic Books, 1981), 224.

22. Tracy Weber, "The Darth Vaders of Direct Mail," *Los Angeles Times*, 3 March 1996, A1.

23. Stephen Engleberg, "A New Breed of Hired Hands Cultivates Grass-Roots Anger," *New York Times*, 17 March 1993, A1.

24. David Mayhew, *Congress: The Electoral Connection* (New Haven: Yale University Press, 1975); Richard Fenno, *Home Style: House Members and Their Districts* (Boston: Little Brown, 1973).

25. Elizabeth Kolbert, "The Special Interests Special Weapon," *New York Times*, 26 March 1995, A1.

26. Scholars continue to argue over the extent to which citizens exercise control over their representatives. David Mayhew and Richard Fenno maintain legislators naturally adopt a position of risk avoidance. Anthony King recently suggested legislators' palpable fear of voter retribution herds them away from tough policy decisions. According to R. Douglas Arnold, voters do not even have to pay careful attention to issues to exert influence over legislators. The potential for a reaction is enough to impact their decision. Arnold claims, "what is certain is that legislators will do their best to anticipate citizens' preferences, to avoid the most dangerous mine fields, and to chart as safe a course as possible through the treacherous territory before them [and] it makes little difference

whether legislators are responding to citizens' existing policy preferences or to the preferences they believe would arise if they voted carelessly." R. Douglas Arnold, "Can Citizens Control Their Representatives?" in *Congress Reconsidered*, ed. Lawrence C. Dodd and Bruce I. Oppenheimer (Washington, D.C.: CQ Press, 1993), 411. See also Fenno *Home Style* and Anthony King *Running Scared: Why America's Politicians Campaign Too Much and Govern Too Little* (New York: The Free Press, 1997).

27. Armstrong, *The Next Hurrah*, 88.

28. Viguerie and Associates actually includes a clause in their contracts specifying sole ownership of lists produced during a campaign.

29. Dennis W. Johnson, *No Place for Amateurs: How Political Consultants Are Reshaping American Democracy* (New York: Routledge, 2001), 152.

30. Friedenberg, *Communication Consultants*, 97.

31. Eva Pusateri, "Shock Mailers That Jolt Your Audience," *Campaigns & Elections*, May 1995, 42.

32. Gregg Easterbrook, "Junk Mail Politics," *The New Republic*, 25 April 1988, 18.

33. The National Taxpayers Union, a non profit association concerned with government spending, sent out letters resembling IRS mailings declaring: "IMPORTANT: CONTAINS YOUR 1984 STATEMENT." The actual letter describes how much money the average American taxpayer sends to Washington and closes with a pitch to join the NTU in opposing increased government spending. These tactics are not confined to conservative groups. The ACLU sends out ersatz indictments of conservative politicians and government officials, complete with a case number and the double red stripe border found on a real indictment. Armstrong, *The Next Hurrah*, 92.

34. Candidates have made extensive use of the personal letter. Some of the best examples include heartfelt letters written by candidates' wives discussing family life and imploring the voter to elect their husbands. One intrepid candidate even sent out a simulated children's letter written on yellow lined paper in large block letters.

35. The fake newspaper is a popular tactic because it is cheap to produce and fools many voters. In his 1992 congressional campaign, Rep. Carlos Moorhead's team put together a publication called the *California Statesman*. According to the *Los Angeles Times* "the lead article of the *California Statesman* declares that Moorhead will be overwhelmingly reelected Nov. 3 by broad-based support from both Republicans and Democrats, according to public opinion polls conducted by the *California Statesman*." Paul Feldman and Richard Simon, "Zeroing In," *Los Angeles Times*, 31 October 1992, A21.

36. Richard Schlackman and Jamie Douglas, "Attack Mail: The Silent Killer," *Campaigns & Elections*, July 1995, 25–27.

37. Sabato, *Consultants*, 329.

38. Kathleen Hall Jamieson, "The Evolution of Political Advertising in America," in *New Perspectives on Political Advertising*, ed. Lynda Kaid, Dan Nimmo, and Keith Sanders (Carbondale: Southern Illinois University Press, 1986), 11.

39. Gary Mauser, *Political Marketing: An Approach to Campaign Strategy* (New York: Praeger, 1983), 2.

40. Nicholas O'shaughnessy, *The Phenomenon of Political Marketing* (New York: St. Martin's Press, 1990), 46.

41. Barry Siegal, "Spin Doctors to the World," *Los Angeles Times Magazine*, 24 November 1991, 22.

42. Luntz, *Candidates*, 157.

43. In a landmark study of television and campaigns, Thomas Patterson and Robert McClure concluded the vast majority of Americans are immune to political advertising

because other factors such as party affiliation, ideology, and racial or ethnic biases predispose them toward a candidate. See Thomas Patterson and Robert McClure, *The Unseeing Eye: The Myth of Television Power in National Politics* (New York: G.P. Putnam, 1976). Several scholars, while not disputing the general accuracy of Patterson and McClure's findings, argue television does have a significant impact among marginal voters. See Donald Cundy, "Political Commercials and Candidate Images: the Effect Can Be Substantial" in Kaid, Nimmo, and Sanders *New Perspectives on Political Advertising*, 210–235.

44. Luntz, *Candidates*, 73.

45. Sabato, *Consultants*, 120.

46. Friedenberg, *Communications Consultants*, 165.

47. Robert Denton and Gary Woodward, *Political Communication in America* 2nd ed. (New York: Praeger, 1990), 59.

48. Michael Wiesskopf, "Harry and Louise to Vacation During Hearings," *Washington Post*, 24 May 1994, A1.

49. Dan Morgan, "On Air and Rising," *Washington Post*, 2 May 2000, A1.

50. Amy Wallace, "Buying Time for Candidates, *Los Angeles Times*, 25 April 1994, A1.

51. Kathleen Hall Jamieson, "When Harry Met Louise," *Washington Post*, 15 August 1994, A19.

52. Shawn Zeller, "Say It Ain't So, Flo," *National Journal*, 9 October 1999, p. 2910.

53. Kevin Merida, "The GOP's Town Criers," *Washington Post*, 10 July 1997, A1.

54. Don Sweitzer and David Heller, "Radio Tips: 10 Ways to Give Your Campaign Ads More Punch," *Campaigns & Elections*, May 1996, 40.

55. It is beyond the pale of my study to discuss the flaws in political advertising. Needless to say, this subject has been exhaustively examined by a number of scholars including Kathleen Hall Jamieson, Larry Sabato, Nicholas O'shaughnessy, Lance Bennett, and Dan Nimmo. There is even a popular sub genre devoted to negative advertising.

56. Sabato, *Consultants*, 204.

57. W. Lance Bennett, *The Governing Crisis: Media, Money and Marketing in American Elections* (New York: St. Martin's Press, 1992), 105.

58. Susannah Fox, "Time Online," Pew Internet and American Life Project, 16 July 2001.

59. Mark Hosenball, "Flo's Big Dollar Backers," *Newsweek*, 25 September 2000, 26.

60. Roger Stone, "Using the Internet to Build Citizen Armies," *Campaigns & Elections*, April 2001, 46.

61. There is a rich body of literature discussing the normative implications of public opinion in a democratic society. Many authors take the position that unadulterated public opinion poses a direct threat to democratic institutions and should be treated delicately. They would probably agree with Oscar Wilde's famous quip: "public opinion is simply an invention which takes community ignorance and elevates it to the level of political force." See Benjamin Ginsberg and Martin Shefter, *Politics By Other Means* (New York: Basic Books, 1990); John Geer, *From Tea Leaves to Opinion Polls* (New York: Columbia University Press, 1996); and James Fishkin, *The Voice of the People: Public Opinion and Democracy* (New Haven: Yale University Press, 1995).

62. The history of the straw poll era is covered in Susan Herbst, *Numbered Voices: How Opinion Polling Has Shaped American Politics* (Chicago: University of Chicago Press, 1993), 69–89.

63. Irving Crespi, *Public Opinion Polls and Democracy* (Boulder: Westview Press, 1989), 3.

64. Some of Truman's antagonism may be traced to his 1948 campaign. In a widely published poll, George Gallup had predicted Thomas Dewey would defeat Truman, but due to an interpretive error, Gallup's poll numbers were skewed and ultimately incorrect. Personal experience may have given Truman a reason to question the value of public opinion polling.

65. Crespi, *Public Opinion Polls and Democracy*, 25.

66. David Moore, *The Superpollsters: How They Measure and Manipulate Public Opinion in America* (New York: Four Walls Eight Windows, 1992).

67. Darrell West, Diane Heith, and Chris Goodwin, "Harry and Louise Go to Washington: Political Advertising and Health Reform," *Journal of Health Politics, Policy and Law* 21, (1996): 35–66.

68. Herbert Asher, *Polling and the Public: What Every Citizen Should Know* (Washington, D.C.: CQ Press, 1992), 100.

69. Peter Stone, "Man with a Message," *National Journal*, 19 April 1997, 751.

70. James Barnes, "Polls Apart," *National Journal*, 10 July 1993, 1753.

71. Johnson, *No Place for Amateurs*, 102.

72. Sabato, *Consultants*, 74.

73. The literature on survey research methodology is voluminous and impossible to cite completely. Two noteworthy works by Crespi and Asher, however, cogently summarize the inherent weaknesses in scientific polling and put public opinion in perspective, see Crespi, *Public Opinion Polls*; and Asher, *Polling and the Public*.

74. Lawrence Grossman,

75. Michael Clark, "Selling the Issues," *Campaigns & Elections*, April/May 1993, 28.

3

Medicare: Policy Making before the Permanent Campaign

The Contract with America offers an interesting glimpse of the legislative process. Like most real-world examples, the events of the 104th Congress broaden some of the colorless descriptions found in textbooks and reveal a dynamic, often unpredictable system enriched by personality and charged with ideology: New Gingrich, with his fiery brand of conservatism, locked in a high-stakes battle with President Clinton and his congressional allies. It has all the elements of compelling political theater. It is no surprise that the Republican revolution spawned a number of best-selling journalistic exposes. The Contract also illustrates lawmakers' powerful fascination with public opinion. The legislative process, when viewed through the lens provided by the Contract, shows legislators determination to harness the power of public opinion and use it as a weapon to bludgeon their adversaries.

The Founders were wary of the power of public opinion, and their apprehension about the "tyranny of the majority" led them to create a system to check the momentary impulses of the general public. Since the 1700s, public opinion has undergone a radical metamorphosis. Where it used to be ephemeral and slightly mysterious, social science has quantified it and made it seem concrete. Scientific polling has given public opinion the substance it lacked during Madison's day. This, in turn, has altered the link between the legislature and public opinion. The ability to "see" public opinion has inspired politicians to manipulate it.[1]

Legislators and other political actors expend vast amounts of money, time, and effort in order to secure and sustain public support for their agendas. This behavior has had a profound effect on the legislative process. By courting public sentiment aggressively, politicians have unwittingly blurred the line distinguishing governing from campaigning until a division is no longer recognizable. In the 1990s it became exceedingly rare for a major legislative initiative not to be accompanied by an expertly designed and professionally administered public relations campaign. The conflation of campaigning and governing presents obvious opportunities for political consultants who possess indispensable campaign experience and technical expertise. Their expanded role is clearly evident in the Contract with America. However, despite incontrovertible evidence of post-electoral consulting, it is impossible to speculate on the impact that political consultants may have on policy making without putting the actions described in the later chapters into a broader context. In short, without an historical account of the legislative process absent the presence of political consultants, any conclusions drawn from the cases described later in the book could be fundamentally flawed. The passage of Medicare in 1965 is an appropriate baseline with which to assess later examples of consultant activity. In 1965 professional political consultants were a rarity and were confined to campaign work

Before proceeding with a discussion of Medicare, a fuller definition and description of the permanent campaign must be provided.[2] It is the phenomenon that distinguishes the Contract with America and the Clinton health care reform from Medicare and it undergirds the analysis of post-electoral consulting. The permanent campaign, the idea that a boundary between campaigning and governing existed that eroded during the 1980s, has been examined at length by several political scientists and journalists. For some political practitioners, a separation between governing and campaigning is an academic conceit, a contrivance that does not exist in reality.[3] In a democracy, electoral consequences are invariably part of the decision makers' calculus.[4] The permanent campaign theory does not imply that an impermeable barrier has always divided campaigning and governing, but that modern behavior is so different in degree from the past that it has become different in kind.[5] The hallmarks of the permanent campaign, campaign specialists masquerading as policy advisors, multi million dollar advertising schemes, and ceaseless polling, are not analogous to earlier examples of public outreach.

THE LEGISLATIVE HISTORY OF MEDICARE

In 1965 the political consultant, at least as we know him today, did not exist. It would be several years before formation of the American Association of Political Consultants and thus signify the birth of a profession. The absence of political consultants from the Medicare debate differentiates it from the Contract with America and the other case studies. As we shall see in the next few chapters, the legislative strategies exhibit tell-tale signs of consultant influence. Although President Lyndon Johnson cultivated public support and entreated citizens to contact their representatives and senators on behalf of Medicare, he did so without the extravagant public relations spectacle that followed President Clinton's health care reform. The cornerstone of the White House approach was a high-level, behind-the-scenes effort to influence legislators such as House Ways and Means Chairman Wilbur Mills and Senate Finance Chairman Russell Long. Interest groups, with the notable exception of the American Medical Association (AMA), also eschewed grassroots efforts and largely confined their activities within the corridors of power.

Medicare's enactment in 1965 was the culmination of a legislative battle that spanned nearly three decades. It pitted New Deal liberals, attempting to fulfill plans outlined by the original authors of the Social Security Act, against a phalanx of conservative politicians and interest groups led by the American Medical Association. For anyone interested in exploring the legislative process through the case-study method, Medicare presents a well-defined example. Through its many preludes and false starts, Medicare featured all the elements scholars traditionally associate with the legislative process: ideological conflicts between conservatives and liberals, institutional clashes between the president and Congress, and the manifest manuervings of interest groups. It also underscored the unbounded personal autonomy enjoyed by House committee chairmen before the legislative reforms of the 1970s.

The idea of government-sponsored health insurance germinated during the New Deal. Several members of President Franklin D. Roosevelt's brain trust encouraged him to include health care as part of his sweeping Social Security program, but Roosevelt demurred. A cursory survey of the political landscape led Roosevelt to conclude that incorporating health care could jeopardize his entire proposal. Physicians and insurance companies had repeatedly vowed to fight any legislation that instituted excessive governmental control over the health care industry. The AMA, the leading professional association representing American doctors, was on record expressing adamant disapproval of government health care. As early as 1920 the AMA released a statement declaring their "opposition to the institution of any plan embodying the system of compulsory contributory insurance provided, controlled, or regulated by any state or federal government."[6] The group equated government health care with government interference and claimed any federal attempt to manage health care would lead down a slippery slope to socialism. In congressional hearings and in paid advertisements spokesmen for the AMA presented a dark view of the future in which patient services were rationed by the government and citizens could no longer choose their own doctors.[7] The fear of heavy-handed government control in the form of "socialized medicine" was articulated in the 1940s and became the cornerstone of the AMA's argument against Medicare.

Alarmist prognostications notwithstanding, throughout the 1940s and 1950s the AMA had little cause for concern. Despite the fact that Democrats controlled both chambers of Congress and the White House continuously from 1939 to 1946, they did not, according to Ted Marmor, enjoy a "programmatic majority" for government-sponsored health care. The House and Senate were dominated by a conservative coalition made up of Republicans and Southern Democrats who opposed activist government intervention and the expansion of social programs.[8] The coalition was sympathetic to the AMA's position and used their influence to stymie health care legislation in committees. The strength of the conservative coalition was evident in 1948 when President Harry Truman made national health insurance a domestic priority for his administration. Truman campaigned hard for the Wagner-Murray-Dingell bill, a bill intended to provide universal health insurance, but he was unable to sway conservative lawmakers.

His attempt to marshal public support for the proposal also met with defeat at the hands of a massive public relations campaign sponsored by the AMA. In a move that eerily presaged the Health Insurers Association of America (HIAA) campaign against the Clinton health care plan, the AMA hired Whitaker and Baxter, the prestigious political consulting firm from California, to develop a national ad campaign demonizing Truman's proposal. Using a clever mix of newspaper advertising and ghost-written editorials, Whitaker and Baxter's $2-million ad campaign succeeded in portraying the Truman plan as "socialized medicine."[9] After the ad blitz began, public support for health care reform plummeted.

During the Eisenhower years national health insurance remained off the public agenda. Every year, liberal members of Congress would introduce legislation that would subsequently disappear in committee. After a series of fruitless congressional sessions, experts working at the Department of Health, Education and Welfare (HEW) and the Social Security Administration, in conjunction with their congressional allies, changed tactics. They recognized earlier examples of health legislation were too ambitious and attracted opposition from a variety of perspectives. The core group of universal health care opponents believed that compulsory, government-sponsored health insurance violated American principles of independence and self-reliance. These members were philosophically opposed to statist welfare programs in all forms. They did not, however, represent an absolute majority. Their position was strengthened by an alliance of convenience with other lawmakers who were more concerned about the enormous financial burden the federal government would incur in an attempt to insure every American citizen. They were unwilling to commit the government to a program of this magnitude. In order to deflect criticism and simultaneously shrink the scope of the plan, Medicare supporters decided to limit the proposal to the elderly.[10] There were strong moral and economic arguments to expand the Social Security system to include health care for the aged. Many older Americans were retired and could no longer afford private insurance. Even though they tended to suffer from worse health, an overwhelming number did not have means to protect themselves. Medicare advocates believed that the government had a moral imperative to help its older citizens. Intervention was defended on economic grounds as well, since a government plan covering the elderly would help lower premiums for other age brackets.[11] By 1957, supporters in Congress and in HEW created the legislative template for Medicare.

As the 1950s drew to a close, health care once again emerged as a viable national issue. John F. Kennedy, on advice from his pollster Lou Harris, incorporated health care into his presidential campaign. In the Senate, Kennedy had introduced a version of the House bill and announced that enactment of Medicare would be one of his chief legislative goals if he were elected president. Although the Republican candidate Richard Nixon was reticent to discuss health care, Kennedy succeeded in reviving public interest in health care reform.

The Kennedy administration began with great promise and vision, but he was saddled with a number of debilitating handicaps that ultimately precluded serious consideration of Medicare. First, he possessed a weak electoral mandate. His victory over Richard Nixon was the narrowest margin since 1880, and thus he could not claim his election was an unqualified public endorsement of his agenda.[12] Second, he faced formidable conservative opposition in Congress. Southern Democrats were particularly wary of a northern, urban Democrat like Kennedy. Aside from these immutable factors, Kennedy made the situation more complicated by unveiling a long list of priorities. His domestic agenda was cluttered with major pieces of legislation, including a complete overhaul of the tax code, a massive increase in federal aid for education, and an ambitious space-exploration program. These issues depleted his limited political capital and forced Kennedy to pare back his efforts on behalf of Medicare. He could ill afford to squander his influence with Congress and perhaps incur the enmity of men like Wilbur Mills by badgering them to support a Medicare bill.[13]

Without Mills's cooperation, Kennedy, under the counsel of Wilbur Cohen and his domestic policy advisors, decided to bypass the House and work through the Senate. Although the Constitution stipulates all tax bills must originate in the House, Democrats and liberal Republicans sidestepped this provision by attaching Medicare as an amendment to a welfare bill that had already passed the House. The amendment passed and Kennedy achieved a major but fleeting victory.[14] During the conference committee obstinate House conferees refused to discuss Medicare and the bill died in conference.

It may be reasonably asserted that the catalyst for Medicare's passage was the 1964 election. Without the 1964 election, which brought an influx of liberal congressmen to add to Lyndon Johnson's popular mandate, Medicare would likely have remained an idealistic but unreachable goal. The addition of 37 new, mostly liberal Democratic congressmen swelled the House Democratic majority to 295 members. In the Senate, Democrats increased their total to 68. But the raw numbers are not as significant as the ideological outlook of the 89th Congress.[15] The new members were able to surmount the obstructionist tactics practiced by the conservative coalition that had thwarted social legislation in the two previous Congresses. President Johnson, whose unprecedented margin of victory over Senator Barry Goldwater was interpreted as an endorsement of his ambitious agenda, matched the activist fervor on Capitol Hill. According to Johnson biographer Doris Kearns Goodwin, the 1964 election presented a rare opportunity and "produced a blend of interests, needs, convictions, and alliances powerful enough to go beyond the normal pattern of slow incremental change."[16]

In the House of Representatives, the liberal cohort had an immediate impact on the institutional structure. First, they forced the House to adopt new rules restricting the power of the Rules Committee. Under the direction of conservative Democrat Howard Smith, the Rules Committee had bottled up a number of progressive bills by refusing to report a rule for floor consideration. The new rules permitted the chairmen of legislative committees, if recognized by the Speaker, to call up bills that had languished in the Rules Committee for over twenty-one days. Second, the addition of new members on committees altered the balance of power between conservative and liberal forces. On the Ways and Means Committee, for example, Democrats increased their number by two, creating a seventeen to eight ratio with liberal supporters outnumbering conservatives fourteen to eleven. For the first time a "programmatic majority" for Medicare existed in the House of Representatives.

President Johnson's determination to pass Medicare provoked a combative response from the AMA. Throughout the Kennedy administration the AMA had lobbied legislators and conducted sporadic advertising campaigns highlighting the deficiencies of Medicare. In 1965 the AMA raised its level of operations and unveiled a $1- million lobbying campaign that included TV, radio, and newspaper ads. The AMA campaign was unprecedented in terms of cost. According to *Congressional Quarterly* in 1965, "There have been only two occasions when lobbying spending by any organization for any full year reached or exceeded $900,000."[17] The AMA surpassed that mark in three months. Yet the AMA's massive public relations campaign should be interpreted as an act of desperation rather than as part of a formidable long-range strategy. The campaign was largely unnoticed by lawmakers, and the public seemed unaffected by revived cries of socialism. By 1965 the hysteria that could be generated by any mention of socialism (a euphemism for communism) had abated. The AMA was hampered by another crucial weakness. Despite the vast sum spent in 1965, the campaign had a primitive design. Modern public relations campaigns, like the one developed for the Contract with America, use poll data and demographic information to target specific audiences where the ads will have the greatest impact. The AMA spent millions of dollars, but the outreach was haphazard and lacked focus.

Although President Johnson was the most visible force behind Medicare, Representative Wilbur Mills may have played a more pivotal role. His decision to support Medicare after opposing it for nearly a decade was considered by many participants as the "missing link" needed for passage.[18] Mills's change of heart is a fine example of political pragmatism. He recognized his autonomy as Ways and Means Chairman was threatened by the liberal make up of the 89th Congress and he was not willing to sacrifice his reputation by fighting a futile battle against Medicare. His choice was made easier by the Johnson administration's willingness to offer a major concession. Mills had expressed reservations toward earlier versions of Medicare concerning the financing scheme and was especially critical of sublimating Medicare into the Social Security trust fund. The Johnson administration bill kept Medicare financing separate from Social Security.

Once Mills decided to support Medicare, he exerted tremendous influence over the substance of the bill. In fact, it is accurate to say that he is responsible for the existing scope of Medicare. Aside from the administration's bill, there were two other bills purporting to be superior versions of Medicare. The Republicans introduced an alternative with a broader range of benefits that was financed through general revenue taxes instead of a payroll deduction. A third plan, endorsed by the AMA, was even more generous, calling for an expansion of the Kerr-Mills Act which permitted the federal and state governments to purchase health insurance on behalf of impoverished elderly. The AMA's plan, however, was voluntary.[19] The AMA's abrupt reversal of their opposition to government-sponsored health care was a cynical exercise in political symbolism. They believed they could embarrass the administration by supporting a bill with more generous benefits. The ploy, however, turned out to be an enormous tactical blunder. Instead of engaging in a time-consuming battle over various proposals, Mills decided to combine elements of all three plans into a new bill. His brilliant legislative maneuver expanded coverage and simultaneously preempted the opponents' arguments. The Mills version easily passed the House by a 313 to 115 roll-call vote.

Medicare had even less trouble in the Senate. The Senate had already demonstrated its receptiveness to Medicare, passing previous incarnations of the bill twice, only to have them falter in conference committee with the House. There were, however, some delicate moments. The Senate Finance Committee, the committee with jurisdiction over Medicare, was led by the mercurial senator from Louisiana, Russell Long. Senator Long was not opposed to Medicare in principle, but he was unwilling to let it pass through his committee without leaving his mark. Driven by what critics said was overweening pride and personal ambition, Long began tinkering with the Mills version. Supporters were concerned that Long's efforts to improve the bill would dismantle it and result in a lengthy conference committee.[20] Personal entreaties to Senator Long by President Johnson along with the cooperation of several Democratic committee members succeeded in keeping the Senate-sponsored changes minimal. On 9 July 1965, Medicare passed the Senate by a vote of 68 to 21.[21]

On 30 July 1965, barely seven months after Medicare had been introduced in Congress, President Johnson signed it into law. But the actions of the 89th Congress should be viewed as part of a larger thirty-year struggle to put together a viable piece of legislation. Fittingly and symbolically, President Johnson conducted a signing ceremony in Independence, Missouri, Harry Truman's hometown, as homage to the former president. It was an historic and bittersweet moment that reminded all the witnesses how long they had been fighting for it and how many failures they had endured.

WHY DID IT PASS? EXPLANATIONS FOR MEDICARE

The chronology of the Medicare debate is a reflection of a complex legislative system buffeted by many external and internal forces. The historical account highlights several important incidents, such as Wilbur Mills's reversal on Medicare, the election of Lyndon Johnson, the change in the ideological makeup of the Congress, and the diminished influence of reactionary interest groups. All contributed to Medicare's enactment. But discussing Medicare without the language of political science makes it seem as if Medicare were a serendipitous event; worse still it makes the legislative process seem incoherent and inexplicable. Description alone does not explain *why* it took thirty years for the program to became a reality or why in 1965 passage was virtually assured.

Policy making is an activity that involves a myriad of choices for legislators and presidents. For political scientists, discovering and analyzing the motives behind the choices is an unending quest. A great deal of thought and research has been conducted in an effort to distill the factors that comprise the decision-making calculus. It is a trying endeavor that involves assumptions about human behavior and usually forces scholars to flatten the legislative process so that it can fit into a research design. The very nature of the division and separation of variables is a contrivance that distinguishes academic study from political reality. Congressmen, for instance, often scoff at the notion that their decisions are the product of applied arithmetic.[22] The analytical challenge is summarized by Roger Davidson and Walter Oleszek who state, "To unravel the chain of causality involved in congressional decision making would require a comprehensive model embracing demographic, sociological, psychological, and political motivations. Simplified models, without a doubt, pinpoint important components of legislative decisions. As with all complex human behavior, however, such decisions elude wholly satisfactory description."[23] Congressional votes taken on a single issue should be examined, interpreted, and labeled with caution. Nevertheless, a number of excellent works provide insight into the motives behind major policy proposals. With regard to Medicare, it appears constituency, presidential pressure, and ideology all played a significant part in its passage.

One of the more intriguing aspects of Medicare is the long string of failures and false starts that preceded its passage in 1965. The significance of these failures has been duly noted in several historic accounts of Medicare, but each work is colored by optimism inspired by the Great Society and seems to treat Medicare as an inevitable outgrowth of New Deal policies. John Kingdon offers a sophisticated and satisfying explanation for Medicare's emergence as a national priority. Kingdon posits major policy initiatives as the result of three streams, problem recognition, policy solutions, and politics, converging to open a narrow window of legislative opportunity. The streams, according to Kingdon, "are largely independent of one another, and each develops according to its own dynamics and rules. But at some critical junctures the three streams are joined, and the policy changes grow out of that coupling of problems, policy proposals, and politics."[24] Medicare fits well into his conceptual framework. By the 1960s a growing number of academics and policy experts in government had concluded that the lack of affordable health care for the elderly was an urgent problem. The overall number of senior citizens was increasing and they were living longer, but without the benefit of health insurance. Knowledgeable observers feared their numbers would eventually overwhelm the private health care system unless the government intervened. By the time Lyndon Johnson was inaugurated in 1965, a policy solution had taken shape, molded and revised by years of discussion on Capitol Hill and within the health care bureaucracy. The final piece of the puzzle was the landslide election in 1964. It created a friendly environment for Medicare and enabled partisans to push the measure through Congress. Kingdon's argument is implicit in James Sundquist's description of Medicare politics, "The final measure was the product of 15 years of refinement and liberalization since the first Federal Security Agency, and 8 years of continuous public debate since

Aime Forand presented his original proposal. Many of the changes were made to meet Republican objectives and embodied ideas that the Republicans could claim as their own."[25]

Kingdon's work suggests that Medicare was the culmination of unique events. For years, health policy experts knew that there was a problem; and they and their allies in Congress spent considerable time attempting to construct a legislative response. The decision in the late 1950s to limit coverage to the elderly in order to avoid the trouble that plagued the Truman bill was a crucial step toward enactment. But until the 1964 election, which returned an activist president to the White House along with a cadre of liberal representatives, Medicare remained an unlikely possibility. The window of opportunity did not stay open for long. The 1966 mid term elections were a disaster for Democrats as they lost forty-seven seats in the House, far more than the thirty-seven they gained in 1964. Given the circumstances, it appears doubtful that Johnson could have shepherded Medicare through the 90th Congress. Civil unrest at home and the tragedy unfolding in Vietnam ate away at Johnson's prestige and public support. As health policy scholar Lawrence Brown notes, "Medicare was an incidental consequence of political convergences and coalitions so rare that they dominate U.S. politics for perhaps ten years in a century."[26]

Congressional scholars Richard Fenno and David Mayhew present compelling arguments for why it proved so difficult to pass Medicare prior to the 89th Congress. For both authors, constituency is the locus of their analysis of congressional behavior. Their work argues that legislators' desire to be reelected and to serve the constituencies that put them in office are the driving force behind many policy decisions. In *Home Style*, Fenno develops a complex description of constituency that goes far beyond the geographic representation. Fenno maintains there are four concentric circles of constituency with varying degrees of influence over a legislator's behavior. Aside from the geographic constituency, which is made up of all the citizens residing in the prescribed district or state, a legislator pays special attention to the needs of his reelection constituency, his primary constituency, and his personal constituency. The reelection constituency are people that the legislator expects will support him, such as party stalwarts and long-time supporters. The primary constituency are those especially active in the primary campaign. The personal constituency is comprised of intimate associates who the legislator may seek out for advice.[27] Fenno's contribution puts the early success of the AMA into clearer perspective. During the 1950s and early 1960s, the AMA's extraordinary influence over the process eclipsed its relatively small membership. The organization was able to achieve this in part because so many of its members were trusted friends of congressmen or were community leaders in their own right. They constituted a specialized constituency whose opinion, particularly in medical matters, was taken seriously by members of Congress.

David Mayhew bolsters Fenno's analysis in his seminal work, *Congress: The Electoral Connection*. Mayhew posits that reelection is the primary goal of all legislators, whom he characterizes as "single-minded seekers of reelection." This consuming ambition has predictable effects on public policy. According to this logic, broad policy proposals that provide diffuse benefits to the disorganized are marginalized in favor of particularized programs that can translate into electoral support. "Congress," Mayhew claims, "will favor the passage of transfer programs when they are championed by powerful interest groups against unorganized opposition [but] will be reluctant to legislate new programs benefiting the unorganized over the opposition of the organized."[28] This analysis accounts for the tepid response Medicare received in Congress prior to 1964. Doctors' loud protestations against Medicare were not matched by any coherent public outcry in support of the program. The AMA's voice reverberated through Congress because the public remained silent.

The frameworks created by Fenno and Mayhew are strongest when explaining why Medicare failed to pass Congress, but their rationale falters slightly when examining the events of 1965. Explaining why narrow interests triumph over diffuse ones is relatively easy, and so is explaining efforts to obtain benefits or prevent costs for attentive constituencies. In *The Logic of Congressional Action*, R. Douglas Arnold amplifies Fenno and Mayhew's explanations by offering a more advanced theory of the electoral concerns that motivate legislators. Mayhew and Fenno limit their analysis to active participants in politics and give short shrift to the mass of indifferent voters. Arnold, on the other hand, imbues this bloc of voters with a great deal of power. He claims that inattentive publics can affect legislators' decisions because "latent or unfocused opinions can be quickly transformed into very real opinions with enormous political repercussions."[29] Capable legislators endeavor to anticipate public response to bills and rarely confuse unformed public opinion with no opinion at all. The landslide election of 1964 was taken as a strong indication of the public's position regarding Medicare. Johnson had made it his number-one legislative priority so his election could be interpreted as an endorsement of his social policies. Although the public was not clamoring for Medicare, Johnson's crushing victory induced some otherwise skeptical legislators to support the president's agenda.

Congress, of course, does not consider issues in a political vacuum. Congressional decision making cannot be readily uncoupled from the larger constitutional framework, and, as Louis Fisher notes, "To study one branch of government in isolation from the others is an exercise in make-believe. Very few operations of Congress and the presidency are genuinely independent or autonomous."[30] The president's shadow looms over the entire process and his position, particularly on major policy initiatives, and is often the impetus for congressional action. It is true that Congress functions independent of the executive branch, but it is impossible to imagine a legislative proposal on the order of Medicare emerging from Congress without forceful, committed leadership from the president.

Lyndon Johnson's decision to make Medicare his primary domestic priority was crucial to congressional action. As every grade school civics text makes clear, it is beyond the president's power to order Congress to take action. Yet the president is obviously more than just an interested bystander watching the legislative process from afar. His agenda, even in times of divided government, focuses congressional attention and provides the context for future debate. During the post-war era, when presidential power was seen to have grown with respect to Congress, it became popular to speak of "presidential dominance."[31] The aphorism, "the president proposes and the Congress disposes," was commonly used to describe the relationship between the legislative and executive branches. This is a distortion of the true relationship, as Congress is quite capable of pursing its own public policy course.

Paul Light, who portrays the president as a legislative facilitator, offers a more accurate description. According to Light, the president's most important skill is his "ability to link abstract public support to specific legislative measures" and highlight important issues for the Congress.[32] Johnson's indefatigable enthusiasm for Medicare and his relentless pursuit of its passage kept congressional attention centered on the issue. Johnson's muscular lobbying was intended, in part, to keep Congress from becoming distracted. His experience in the Senate taught him a valuable lesson about the tendency for legislation to drift aimlessly unless a powerful force guided its path. President Johnson explained his philosophy in his autobiography, stating that "there is only one way for a President to deal with Congress and that is continuously, incessantly, and without interruption."[33]

Johnson's vigorous effort, however, would have been for naught if he had not possessed a vast reservoir of political capital. The president's real power, the power to persuade according to Richard Neustadt, is predicated on his prestige and public popularity.[34] His prestige is the standing he has with other important political figures. Johnson, as a former Senate Majority Leader, was intimate with many power brokers on Capitol Hill. His personal rapport with committee chairmen and the elected leadership of the House and Senate was vital to his standing in Congress. Although many stories about Lyndon Johnson are apocryphal, there is little doubt that he was a man who was consumed by politics and thoroughly enjoyed the rough and tumble nature of lawmaking. Historians and biographers have produced a veritable hagiography depicting Johnson's highly personal style of politics. The other half of the president's power, from Neustadt's perspective, emanates from his public popularity. At the outset of the 89th Congress, President Johnson enjoyed tremendous public support. His public approval rating remained over 60 percent until the summer of 1966. Thus, in 1965 President Johnson, drawing upon a deep well of public support and his own prodigious political skill, was a formidable force in the legislative process, and given the circumstances, it seems unlikely that Congress would blatantly disregard his wishes concerning Medicare.

Johnson cannot take sole credit for his impressive string of legislative accomplishments. The 1964 elections radically altered the ideological makeup of Congress. The conservative coalition was weakened by the influx of new urban and suburban northeastern Democrats. In both the House and the Senate, conservative forces saw the number of legislative victories decrease by 60 percent during the 89th Congress.[35] In committee and on the House and Senate floors, the tacit alliance that had blocked progressive legislation during the early 1960s fell apart in the face an overwhelming liberal majority. The new members had an activist bent and did not need prompting from the White House to support a progressive measure like Medicare. According to a study of presidential success conducted by Joseph Cooper and Gary Bombardier, "Johnson could win victories denied to Kennedy because he was drawing on a larger population of fellow partisans, a population in which the northern Democrats alone could come very close to furnishing all the votes needed for a majority."[36] In the 89th Congress, progressive measures like Medicare enjoyed a programmatic majority for the first time since the New Deal.

At the outset of this section I stated that no single perspective offered a completely satisfactory explanation for the events that culminated in Medicare. This is a facile, bordering on axiomatic, conjecture. Of course no single theory could account for the passage of a complex and ambitious policy like Medicare, but the strength or utility of a theory is not predicated on its ability to clarify everything. Moreover, if competing explanations for public policy were invalidated by one all-encompassing theory, studying politics would be a pointless exercise, since every vantage point would yield the same view. Reality may not be as precise or formulaic as theories portend it to be, but the application of rigorous political science theory demystifies the legislative process and enables observers to comprehend the underlying factors that propel legislation through Congress.

Medicare became law only thirty-eight years ago, but in many ways its experience seems akin to legislative action from the distant past. The insular Washington, D.C., community that fought and negotiated Medicare's final form still exists. The president, Congress, and interest groups all engage in practices that would be familiar to Lyndon Johnson and his contemporaries. Yet the emergence of the permanent campaign and the blossoming of a post-electoral relationship between political consultants and polcy makers has altered the nature of conflict and compromise. Political consultants and the widespread application of campaign techniques and tactics has had a discernible impact on the policy-making process.

NOTES

1. Susan Herbst, *Numbered Voices: How Opinion Polling Has Shaped American Politics* (Chicago: University of Chicago Press, 1993).

2. A recent book dealing with the permanent campaign: Hugh Heclo offers this definition, "The permanent campaign is a non-stop process seeking to manipulate sources of public approval to engage in the act of governing itself." Hugh Heclo, "Campaigning and Governing: A Conspectus," in *The Permanent Campaign and Its Future*, ed. Thomas Mann and Norman Ornstein (Washington, D.C.: The Brookings Instiution, 2000).

3. Bill McInturff, interview by author, Alexandria, VA, 28 April 2000.

4. Some authors suggest that our attitude toward elections and our elected officials' obsession with retaining office is a uniquely American characteristic. Anthony King opines, "In most democratic countries other than the United States, the holding of elections and the consequent need to electioneer are seem as occasional intrusions into an ongoing governmental process rather than as an integral and continuous part of that process." Some of this undoubtedly stems from weak party identification among the electorate and the concurrent predominance of entrepreneurial candidates. Several classic studies of

congressional behavior demonstrate how independence from party leads to enhanced emphasis on constituent service. As Gary Jacobson observes, "Incumbents pursue reelection throughout their term in office so their campaign strategies are visible in all their dealings with constituents." Anthony King, *Running Scared: Why America's Politicians Campaign Too Much and Govern Too Little* (New York: The Free Press, 1997); Gary Jacobson, *The Politics of Congressional Elections* (New York: HarperCollins, 1992). See also Richard Fenno, *Home Style: House Members in Their Districts* (Boston: Little Brown, 1973).

5. Evidence of the permanent campaign is presented by several scholars from various perspectives. According to congressional scholar Timothy Cook, the ways in which congressional actors negotiate with other political actors has been forever changed. He states, "It is no longer easy to shape events on the Hill or move a bill along simply by contacting a few strategically placed people. Instead, persuading constituents to lobby their representatives or write Congress *en massé* has become the accepted way of getting things done." With regard to the presidency, scholars such as Samuel Kernell and Stephen Skowronek have analyzed the growing tendency of the president to use the rhetoric of the campaign to marshal public support for his proposals. Timothy Cook, *Making Laws and Making News: Media Strategies in the U.S. House of Representatives* (Washington, D.C.: The Brookings Institution, 1989); Samuel Kernell, *Going Public: New Strategies of Presidential Leadership,* 2nd ed. (Washington, D.C.: CQ Press, 1993); Stephen Skowronek, *Politics Presidents Make: Leadership from John Adams to Bill Clinton* (Cambridge: Harvard University Press, 1997).

6. Eugene Feingold, *Medicare Policy and Politics* (San Francisco: Chandler, 1966), 89.

7. The history of the Medicare care debate is drawn mainly from four books and supplemented with journalistic accounts taken from the *New York Times* and *Congressional Quarterly*. See Theodore Marmor, *The Politics of Medicare* (Chicago: Aldine, 1970); Sheri David, *With Dignity: The Search for Medicare and Medicaid* (Westport: Greenwood Press, 1985); Feingold, *Medicare Policy and Politics*; (Lawrence Jacobs, *The Health of Nations: Public Opinion and the Making of British and American Health Policy* (Ithaca: Cornell University Press, 1993).

8. The informal voting alliance between conservative Southern Democrats and Republicans emerged in the early 1930s in response to FDR's activist agenda and remained a fixture in Congress until the 1980s when large numbers of conservative Southerners abandoned the Democratic party and became Republicans. See Mack Shelley II, *The Permanent Majority: The Conservative Coalition in the United States Congress* (Tuscaloosa: University of Alabama Press, 1983).

9. Marmor, *The Politics of Medicare*, 13. The AMA's proto-grassroots campaign is covered in greater detail in Stanley Kelley's seminal work on political consulting. See Stanley Kelley Jr., *Professional Public Relations and Political Power* (Baltimore: Johns Hopkins University Press, 1956).

10. Although dozens of academic experts and bureaucrats were involved in developing Medicare, the decision to limit eligibility to the elderly can be traced to a few influential figures: Wilbur Cohen, a secretary of HEW under Truman and former academic; Bob Ball, a Social Security commissioner; and Anthony Celebrezze.

11. David, *With Dignity*, 27.

12. The importance of public prestige and the perception of the President's popularity among other Washington elites is explained in Richard Nuestadt's *Presidential Power and the Modern Presidents* 3rd ed. (New York: The Free Press, 1990).

13. Events beyond Kennedy's control also interfered with Kennedy's legislative program. During his abbreviated presidency Kennedy was forced to content with a series of international crises precipitated by Cold War tensions. On the domestic front, racial tensions were erupting into confrontations between civil rights supporters and the Southern political establishment. See Arthur Schlesinger, *A Thousand Days: John F. Kennedy in the White House.*

14. "Medicare Chronology," *CQ Weekly Report*, 30 July 1965, 1494.

15. John D. Morris, "Congress Begins, Johnson Reports State of the Nation," *New York Times*, 5 January 1965, A1.

16. Doris Kearns Goodwin, *Lyndon Johnson and the American Dream* 2nd ed. (New York: St. Martin's Press, 1991), 212.

17. "AMA Lobbying Spending," *CQ Weekly Report*, 25 June 1965, 1241.

18. Tom Wicker, "Medicare's Progress," *New York Times*, 25 March 1965, A1.

19. James L. Sundquist, *Politics and Policy: The Eisenhower, Kennedy, and Johnson Years* (Washington, D.C.: The Brookings Institution, 1968), 318.

20. David, *With Dignity*, 145.

21. John D. Morris, "Senate Passes Medicare Bill," *New York Times*, 10 July 1965, A1.

22. John Kingdon, *Congressmens' Voting Decisions* 3rd. (Ann Arbor: University of Michigan Press, 1989).

23. Roger Davidson and Walter Oleszek, *Congress and Its Members* 4th ed. (Washington, D.C.: CQ Press, 1994), 374.

24. John Kingdon, *Agendas, Alternatives, and Public Policies* (New York: HarperCollins Publishers, 1984), 19.

25. Sundquist, *Politics and Policy*, 320.

26. Lawrence Brown, "The Politics of Medicare and Health Reform, Then and Now," *Health Care Financing Review* 18 (1996): 163.

27. Fenno, *Home Style*, 11–23.

28. David Mayhew, *Congress: The Electoral Connection* (New Haven: Yale University Press), 137.

29. R. Douglas Arnold, *The Logic of Congressional Action* (New Haven: Yale University Press, 1990), 5.

30. Louis Fisher, *The Politics of Shared Power: Congress and the Executive* 3rd ed. (Washington, D.C.: CQ Press, 1993), ix.

31. Arthur Schlesinger, *The Imperial Presidency* (Boston: Houghton Mifflin, 1989).

32. Paul Light, "The Focusing Skill and Presidential Influence in Congress," in *Congressional Politics*, ed. Christopher Deering (Pacific Grove: Brooks/Cove, 1989), 240.

33. Lyndon Johnson, *The Vantage Point* (New York: Popular Library, 1971), 448.

34. Richard Neustadt, *Presidential Power*, 1–25.

35. Shelley, *The Permanent Majority*, 45.

36. Joseph Cooper and Gary Bombardier, "Presidential Leadership and Party Success," *Journal of Politics* 30 (1968), 1014–15.

4

The Clinton Health Care Reform Effort: Harry and Louise Steal the Show

The passage of Medicare in 1965 did not resolve the nation's medical access problems. The calculated political decision to limit Medicare coverage to seniors blunted opposition to the program, but it also ensured that future policy makers would likely revisit the issue. Ironically, the success and popularity of the program served to highlight systemic inadequacies in the American health care system. In the decades since the Great Society, health care costs outpaced economic growth to a significant degree and the number of uninsured Americans continued to multiply. Although public interest in health care issues waxed and waned during the 1970s and 1980s, health policy experts raised fears among some lawmakers by arguing that the nation was headed for a crisis that could only be avoided through government intervention.[1] Health experts' concern, though not their recommendations, was shared by American business leaders who witnessed a growing share of pre-tax corporate profits eaten away by health care costs for employees. By the late 1980s and early 1990s, health policy experts representing a wide spectrum of interests ranging from free-market proponents like Stanford University's Alain Enthoven to statist reformers like Senator Ted Kennedy, began sketching the outlines of various health care reform plans.[2] Despite ideological differences, knowledgeable observers from the left and the right agreed that the enormous contingent of uninsured Americans (close to 32 million by 1991) posed a threat to American economic stability. Elite attention coincided with renewed public concern over access to affordable health insurance.

The issue gained broader notice from national politicians during a 1991 special election to fill a vacant Pennsylvania senate seat. In that race, the Democratic candidate, Bryn Mawr College President Harris Wofford, trailed the Republican, former Bush Administration Attorney General Dick Thornburgh, by a significant margin. It appeared that Wofford's defeat was a foregone conclusion until his campaign seized upon health care as its defining issue. Wofford successfully capitalized on public apprehension over health insurance and medical costs and quickly erased Thornburgh's lead in the polls. The message he reiterated in his speeches and public appearances focused on his desire to reform the system and guarantee coverage for all Americans. His political consultants, which included future Clinton advisors James Carville and Paul Begala, came up with a powerful advertisement that featured Wofford's signature statement: "If criminals have a right to a lawyer, then I think average Americans have a right to a doctor." According to many political strategists, Thornburgh's inability or unwillingness to articulate a Republican response to health care was a crucial factor in his defeat.

In the 1992 presidential campaign, several of the Democratic contenders, including Nebraska Senator Bob Kerrey, Paul Tsongas, and the eventual nominee, Arkansas Governor Bill Clinton, took a lesson from Wofford and made health care reform a core issue in their campaigns. During the general election, Clinton highlighted his call for health care reform as a way to distinguish himself from the other two candidates, Ross Perot and incumbent President George Bush. Although he never released a detailed plan and only provided vague information to the press, his political pedigree as a centrist Democrat and his belief in market-based reform won praise among elite pundits and the voting populace as well.[3] Clinton's conviction that the American health care system was in desperate need of reform carried through the election; and shortly after he was inaugurated he announced the formation of a task force headed by his wife and Rhode Island business consultant Ira Magaziner. President Clinton's intended goal was to pass his health care bill by the end of summer 1993.

President Clinton's determination to enact health care reform early in his first term hearkens back to Lyndon Johnson's promise to make Medicare his number-one domestic priority. Unfortunately for President Clinton, the similarity ends there. President Clinton's experience is fundamentally different from Johnson's, both in terms of process and outcome. Scores of scholars and journalists have autopsied the Clinton health care reform and their combined efforts have produced a myriad of retrospective explanations for its failure. Some observers claim that Clinton misinterpreted his election, which he won with a plurality of votes, as a mandate for a wholesale restructuring of the American health care system.[4] This is a favorite of conservative commentators, who assert that Clinton's hubris led him to overestimate his public support and grossly underestimate public antipathy toward government intervention.[5] Their characterization is simplistic, but there is no doubt that public desire for an improved health care system was matched by apprehension over a new, massive government plan. Other observers, citing an institutional reason, point to the political dynamics on Capitol Hill. The Clinton health care reform, they argue, was the victim of the rise of entrepreneurial politics and the corresponding decline in party loyalty that appeared in Congress during the 1970s. Democratic party leaders, hampered by the emergence of candidate-centered politics, had difficulty sustaining party support for large-scale policy initiatives.[6] Moreover, many key legislators were members with long tenures who had cultivated personal relationships with interest groups, health care advocates, and lobbyists. Insurance companies, doctors, drug manufacturers, and hospitals were determined to use their ties with legislators to advance their singular interests. Beyond the intraparty concerns, the White House had to worry about a resurgent Republican minority in the House. The new generation of congressional Republicans, exemplified by their brash de facto leader Newt Gingrich, was philosophically opposed to plans to reshape health care through government intervention and their resolve further complicated the prospects of reform. Clinton's political foes were further bolstered by a series of scandals that broke during the first year of his administration.

Rather than engage in an ad nauseum analysis of the factors that led to the demise of the Clinton health care reform, I will use the events of 1993 and 1994 as a lens through which to examine the connection of professional political consultants to the legislative process. Consultants were heavily involved with the health care debate on both sides of the issue. Their actions appear to have shaped the course of events and were thought to have influenced the outcome to a significant degree. Some participants have even blamed them for the failure of the reform effort. Hillary Clinton, for instance, told the *New York Times* that she believed the health care debate "was lost on paid media and paid direct mail."[7] The First Lady's comment is certainly an exaggeration that ignores crucial institutional and political factors, but her frustrations with the process have merit. The manifest presence of political consultants at the core of a policy debate raises some interesting questions. First, does the blending of campaign tactics like direct mail and mass media advertising with governing threaten the prospects for compromise among elected officials by polarizing the public debate? In other words, do the pointed rhetoric and public appeals crafted by consultants corrupt the normal give and take of the legislative process. Second, using campaign tactics and tools to sell public policies to the American public often involves deception and a misrepresentation of the facts. Alarmist ads, focus groups, and biased polls may not be suitable means to communicate complex issues to the general public. Finally, consultants are specially trained political operatives who charge large fees for their services. This condition has created an organic elite bias among their clientele. During the health care reform debate, for example, insurance companies, hospitals, and drug manufacturers all employed political consultants. However, people with a great stake in the outcome, namely the poor and uninsured, were not able to afford the services of consultants. Are the disorganized and impoverished threatened by the hegemony of political consultants in an era of mass media politics?

THE LEGISLATIVE HISTORY OF THE
CLINTON HEALTH CARE REFORM EFFORT

In late January 1993 President Clinton announced that he was forming a task force comprised of health policy experts from business, academia, and government to study and eventually formulate a health care reform plan. From the outset, political pundits and media commentators questioned the wisdom of creating an unwieldy ad hoc coalition to draft such a major piece of legislation. In terms of design and procedure, the task force became a magnet for criticism. A strictly enforced media blackout only enhanced the sense of frustration among the groups left out of the task force meetings. Members of Congress, for example, grumbled that they were not regularly apprised of the task force's progress and that their input was discounted. In addition, many civil servants who had spent their entire careers studying, modifying, and working within the government health care system were suddenly swept aside in favor of a cadre of outside experts. But the greatest outcry came from health care lobbyists, who believed that their vested economic interests were under siege by Ira Magaziner and his inscrutable task force. Conservative groups were so furious at being frozen out of the process that they filed suit in federal court to open the task force proceedings for public comment.[8] Magaziner, however, was unperturbed by the negative reaction and defended the task force charter vigorously. He distrusted the insular Washington policy environment and believed that true reform could only come from a fresh perspective. According to Haynes Johnson and David Broder, Magaziner "wanted the specialized expertise, but did not want special interests to write the policy. Instead he wanted outside experts to challenge the conventional views of the health care bureaucrats and force them to document their assumptions."[9] The 500-person task force was comprised of health policy experts outside the Washington community, interest groups who were receptive to government reform, and select government officials. It met continuously from February to May 1993 and, after an exhaustive period of drafting sessions, produced a thoughtful, comprehensive document. Unfortunately, it was freighted with business-school jargon and technical terminology like "consumer purchasing alliances" and "regional health insurance cooperatives." The impenetrable vocabulary would have negative consequences later in the debate when the White House attempted to explain the details of the plan to the general public.[10]

Ironically, the first major obstacle to health care reform was the presidency. Scholars who study the presidency, like Paul Light, have noted that the president's ability to manage and direct his agenda is constrained by circumstance. Scarcity of time and unexpected crises interfere with the most rigorous scheduling and often force the president to scale back his initial plans.[11] Moreover, staff and cabinet officials fight among themselves for attention from the president. Early in Clinton's first term, health care advocates lost a decisive battle for the primary spot on the president's agenda to budget deficit hawks. Treasury Secretary Lloyd Bentsen and Budget Director Alice Rivlin argued successfully that it was more important for the country and for the Clinton presidency to address the budget deficit before embarking on any large-scale domestic programs.[12] The delay proved to be extremely costly, since it enabled interest groups to organize grassroots opposition and disseminate a contrary message through direct mail and mass media advertising. Bill Gradison, president of the Health Insurers' Association of America explained, "We had lots of time to get geared up. It [the delay] gave us more time to refine our message, raise our money, do internal staffing changes and have training sessions with members of our association as to what they could do with their home towns."[13] Clinton's inability to use the bully pulpit to present a cogent vision of reform early in the debate compromised his natural communications advantage over his opponents. Even after the formal introduction of the plan in the fall, President Clinton was forced to attend to a series of foreign policy crises. Events in Somalia and Haiti led the White House to abandon plans for a presidential health care awareness campaign. To make matters worse, following the suicide of White House lawyer and Clinton friend Vince Foster, burgeoning interest in the Whitewater affair drew press coverage away from health care. Opponents to the Clinton plan filled the communications void quickly and ably.

When President Clinton finally made his trek to Capitol Hill in late September 1993 to unveil his health care plan to Congress and the American public, its passage was already in jeopardy. The massive 1,300-page tome was one of the most ambitious domestic policy proposals ever produced by an American president, and for it to be realized as law would require solid Democratic support. Yet despite Democratic majorities in both chambers, President Clinton did not possess overwhelming support. In fact, by the fall of 1993 the president had dissipated much of the goodwill he had enjoyed in January. Two events can be singled out as reasons for his tepid support among congressional Democrats. First, Clinton's unwavering commitment to the North American Free Trade Agreement (NAFTA) put him at odds with a substantial number of Democrats, particularly laborites who believed that the treaty would lead to depressed wages and a loss of manufacturing jobs to Mexico. The ugly internecine conflict between pro labor and free market Democrats left a lasting bitterness among union supporters.[14] Second, the memory of the budget betrayal was still fresh in the minds of many House Democrats. Earlier that summer, President Clinton had implored House Democrats to vote for a controversial stimulus package that included a national fuel tax increase. It was a politically dangerous move for many legislators, especially those from swing districts. When Clinton jettisoned the fuel tax in a secret agreement with Midwestern senators, he infuriated House Democrats and left many of them wondering if they could trust the president.

Clinton's uncertain relationship with congressional Democrats would have consequences, but since most of them were ideologically disposed toward some sort of reform, they were not considered a serious threat to the process. Many White House aides and political strategists were more concerned with wooing the general public than with placating irate legislators. Since the general campaign, the president's pollsters had warned of a bifurcation in popular opinion concerning health care. The assessment was echoed by non partisan health opinion analysts, including Lawrence Jacobs of Harvard University, who noted, "The public is deeply ambivalent about how to change substantially government's involvement in health care: it supports reform but is uneasy about expanding government's role. This uneasiness is part of Americans' well known fear of big government and excessive regulation infringing on economic efficiency and individual freedom."[15] In light of the conflicted nature of public opinion, the Clinton administration faced a daunting task. In order to convince the public to support the plan they had to assure them that it would not cause a major disruption in their lives, while simultaneously countering the inflammatory claims of "big government" made by its opponents. This challenge proved to be too much for the Clinton administration, and they ultimately lost the message battle. Evidence of their failure can be found in opinion polls that indicate support for the goals espoused in the president's plan remained constant throughout the debate, while support for the actual plan plummeted.[16]

The legislative battle to pass comprehensive health care reform began in the fall of 1993 when the text of the president's plan was sent to Capitol Hill. According to House rules, the Speaker can refer a bill to multiple committees for concurrent markup. The procedure was initially designed to curb the power of recalcitrant committee chairmen, but it is also occasionally used to speed up the legislative process. Thus, when the Clinton bill was delivered to Congress in October, Speaker Foley sent it to three committees: Education and Labor, Ways and Means, and Energy and Commerce. The Education and Labor Committee is a bastion of Great Society liberals and urban Democrats. Although it had the weakest jurisdictional claim on the bill, it could be trusted to produce a favorable report. However, most knowledgeable observers expected the real work would be done by either the Ways and Means Committee or the Energy and Commerce Committee. Both were led by strong chairman who had decades of experience in health-related issues.[17] Furthermore, each committee had an indisputable proprietary interest in health legislation. Yet, in spite of their parliamentary skill and personal power, neither Ways and Means Chairman Dan Rostenkowski nor Energy and Commerce Chairman John Dingell could report a satisfactory bill. Members of both committees faced intense grassroots pressure stirred up by direct mail and mass media advertising. Lobbyists representing small businesses and insurance companies were relentless and made certain that undecided members knew what the potential electoral consequences would be if they voted for the Clinton plan.

The bill faltered first in the Commerce Committee. John Dingell, whose father had introduced the first universal health care legislation during the Truman administration, was trapped by two intractable forces on his committee.[18] On one side were liberal members who favored a Canadian-style, single-payer approach in which the federal government essentially manages the national health care system. On the other side were insurgent conservative Democrats led by Representative Jim Cooper. These members supported a free-market solution to health care access. The ideological divisions on the committee constrained Dingell's attempts to reach a compromise since any overture to one faction would cost him votes with the other faction. In June 1994, after several frustrating weeks of negotiation, Dingell informed Speaker Foley that it would be impossible to report a bill.

The Ways and Means Committee was not as polarized as the Commerce Committee, and Clinton administration officials believed Rostenkowski could cobble together a majority without abandoning the principles behind the legislation. Unfortunately, Rostenkowski never got an opportunity because he was indicted under federal corruption charges in late May 1994. Although Rostenkowski remained a member of the committee, House rules forced him to resign the chairmanship. His replacement, Representative Sam Gibbons, stubbornly refused to fulfill pledges made by Rostenkowski to certain members at the behest of constituent interests. Gibbon's fiery temper and unfamiliarity with the quid pro quo arrangements that had made Rostenkowski popular among Ways and Means members limited his influence over the committee. In Rostenkowski's absence, the committee was able to report a bill, but without his leadership the legislation lost focus.

The bill faced considerable difficulty in the Senate as well. Part of the problem stemmed from institutional characteristics unique to the Senate. The individual prerogatives afforded to members of the Senate, such as the filibuster and the hold, can slow and in some cases halt the legislative process. The Senate's penchant for indulging individual concerns was evident in the Senate Finance Committee, the committee with primary jurisdiction over health care reform. Finance Committee members, including its chairman, Senator Daniel Patrick Moynihan, were skeptical of the employer mandates and weak cost controls lodged within the administration's bill. The concern reflected the doubts of the Senate at large, and in late spring 1994 Moynihan told the White House that the bill in its current form could not survive on the Senate floor.

The continued string of mishaps and misfortunes on Capitol Hill did not dissuade the White House from pursuing health care reform. In fact, they stepped up the public relations campaign.[19] During the summer, the Clinton administration took the advice of its political consultants and brought the debate to the general public in the form of a national bus tour. The caravan (dubbed the "phony express" by Republicans) was matched by a national ad campaign produced by the Democratic National Committee.[20] But the White House underestimated the organizational capabilities and consultant-led public outreach conducted by their opponents. For months, groups using direct mail, television commercials, and phone banks had impressed upon the general public all the negative things associated with the Clinton plan. They had succeeded in defining the debate, and by the time the Clinton administration engaged in the bus tour, the communications war was already lost.[21] By late summer, public support for the plan was weakening, with a large number expressing outright opposition.

After July, the health care reform effort slouched toward its inevitable conclusion. House and Senate leaders told the White House that they intended to pull the Clinton bill from consideration and introduce a scaled-back version. In the House, the compromise bill introduced by Majority Leader Dick Gephardt drew opposition from the left as well as the right. Liberal Democrats were unwilling to support a bill that lacked universal coverage, while conservative Democrats were disillusioned by the leadership's willingness to pander to the left. In late August the Gephardt bill was withdrawn without a vote. In the Senate, George Mitchell browbeat, shamed, and pleaded with his fellow senators to support the measure without success. Mitchell pulled the bill from Senate consideration when it became apparent that a viable compromise could not be reached. On 26 September

1994, a year and four days after President Clinton made his impassioned speech before Congress, legislative leaders announced to the American public that health care reform would not be enacted during the 103rd Congress.[22]

The preceding abridged legislative history of the Clinton health care reform effort touches briefly upon the public nature of the fight, particularly the emphasis placed on grassroots lobbying and mass media advertising. The remainder of the discussion will focus on the role played by political consultants and the actions they took during the debate. Health care presents a compelling example of how political consultants and their campaign-oriented techniques have insinuated themselves into the legislative process. Their work has not gone unnoticed. According to David Broder, the public relations spectacle that followed health care "resembled in cost and complexity a presidential campaign without the candidates," and may be the harbinger of a new way of influencing public policy.[23] Scholars such as Kathleen Hall Jamieson marveled at the power political advertising had over the opinions of political leaders despite a lack of evidence that it influenced the general public.[24] Health care reform may have been a legislative failure for the Clinton administration, but turned out to be a triumph for political consulting.

CAMPAIGN TECHNIQUES AND POLICY MAKING

Since the emergence of the mass media oriented campaign, a great number of political observers (including academics, journalists, and citizens advocates) have raised concerns over the proliferation and content of political advertising (for the purposes of this discussion, I am speaking of television, radio, and print advertising, as well as direct mail outreach). Media commentators and good government groups such as Common Cause and Ralph Nader's Public Interest Research Group claim that negativity is the defining characteristic of the modern campaign and that scurrilous attack ads and personal mudslinging are its hallmarks. These critics generally blame consultants for the rise in negative advertising and hold them responsible, although without much empirical evidence, for a corresponding increase in voter cynicism. Political advertising also draws critical attention from academics who continue to debate the normative implications of mass marketing in the political system.[25] These concerns are not confined to candidate campaigns as observers who follow advocacy advertising continue to study the impact of ads on public policy debates.[26]

One of the main criticisms of political advertising is that advertisements on television and in the mail tend to polarize the political debate rather than enlighten citizens. Critics understand that a political advertisement will have, by definition, more in common with propaganda than with a public service announcement, but they contend that the inherent tendency toward boosterism is not an excuse to be deliberately misleading. Political advertising, like commercial advertising, should be held to some standard of truthfulness. Concrete evidence of critics' concerns appeared several times during the health care debate. A number of advertisements misled the general public through a selective appropriation of the facts and, in some rare instances, promoted an outright distortion of the truth.

The American Council for Health Care Reform, an umbrella conservative organization, sponsored one of the more egregious examples of inflammatory advertising. In a direct-mail campaign targeting elderly Americans, the group alleged that under the Clinton plan consumers would "face jail time if they bought extra health care."[27] The claim was based on a provision within the Clinton bill that stated anyone who offered or promised something of value to influence a "health care official" could be indicted for bribery. While the alarming prediction made in the ad is a technical possibility, the consultants who envisioned the scenario were not concerned with presenting a likely event. On the contrary, their express goal was to grab the recipient's attention with a shocking example. An ad produced on behalf of the Seniors Coalition is another case in point. In the commercial they assert that President Clinton's plan would eliminate Medicare, a statement sure to raise the ire of senior citizens. Again, this claim is lodged within the truth. If the Clinton plan were enacted, then the need for a separate government-funded insurance program for the elderly would be eliminated. Not surprising, this detail was left out of the ad. In both instances, consultants identified a viable demographic, senior citizens, and touched upon their fear of losing health care as a way to activate resistance to the Clinton plan.

In the push to exaggerate the danger posed by health care reform, some consultants melded fact with fiction. In a radio spot produced by Americans for Tax Reform, a conservative grassroots advocacy group, the truth became a casualty of the message. The ad depicts a plaintive mother who is seeking help for her sick child. The woman calls a government bureaucrat for permission to take the child to the hospital but she is put on hold. An ominous voice over warns that this is what awaits Americans if the Clinton plan is passed.[28] It is a visceral, powerful image, but it is completely untrue. None of the reform bills introduced during the 103rd Congress would have required citizens to call for government approval before visiting a doctor. Given the level of demagoguery found in some political ads, it is easy to understand the frustration of health care advocates. However, some liberal organizations that decried the inflammatory tactics used during the health care debate learned a valuable lesson from their political adversaries and, when political fortunes changed in 1994, they used similar ads to attack the conservative agenda. Consultants on both sides of the political spectrum defend their actions, at least according to preliminary survey data, and even maintain that they are performing a needed service.[29]

Perhaps the most visible advertisements in 1993 and 1994 were those featuring Harry and Louise, sponsored by the Health Insurance Association of America. The commercials were the brainchild of Goddard/Claussen, a California-based firm that specializes in referendums and issue-specific initiative campaigns. The ads, a well-balanced synthesis of demographic inference and political rhetoric, targeted the broad swath of middle-class voters with a financial stake in health care reform. In the ads, Harry and Louise, a white, middle-aged, obviously middle-class couple, discuss the risks associated with the Clinton plan, such as rationing, loss of consumer choice, and that great American bugbear: "big government." It was a clever pitch that avoided the hyperbolic claims made by other groups and instead focused on dampening public enthusiasm for reform.

Each Harry and Louise ad (there were several variations drafted to appeal to different demographic audiences) included a toll-free number that viewers could call to get more information or to register comments. According to the HIAA, nearly half a million people contacted the organization as a result of the ads. Among the 500,000, HIAA enlisted 45,000 to write letters to legislators, pen editorials for local papers, and make phone calls to other citizens. This dedicated corps of activists broadened the limited reach of HIAA and put pressure on legislators through relentless, repetitive communication. The HIAA, along with other like-minded organizations, was able to create the impression of a massive groundswell against the Clinton plan. Legislators, for instance, would return to their districts and be confronted with a well-organized, articulate group arguing against employer mandates. Meanwhile, legislative staff tallied hundreds of letters and postcards expressing opposition to elements of the reform legislation.[30]

Legislators and officials in the White House gave credit to the Harry and Louise campaign for turning public opinion against health care reform. However, despite the spate of news reports about the ad campaign, there is conflicting evidence that suggests that the ads may not have had a broad based impact on the general public's assessment of the Clinton plan.[31] Of course, they were never intended to move the entire nation. They were only aired in Washington, D.C., and New York media markets and in districts with particularly vulnerable congressmen. Nevertheless, the commercials were effective in influencing political elites, who were convinced the ads were responsible for the shift in public opinion. House Ways and Means Chairman Dan Rostenkowski claimed that the Harry and Louise ads were "the Willie Horton of the health care debate, they're increasing the heat without adding any light."[32] Rostenkowski's concern over the ads was so great that he took the unprecedented step of negotiating with the HIAA to have them taken off the air. The White House was also aggravated and unwittingly aided the ad campaign by publicly criticizing it, thus raising the ads' profile. The Clinton administration's communications team paid Goddard/Claussen a backhanded compliment by commissioning spoof commercials of Harry and Louise starring stage actor Jerry Stiller. These exaggerated reactions by the White House and congressional Democrats reveal the pervasive and systemic nature of the permanent campaign mentality. The close attention they paid to a medium-size insurance lobby ad campaign that only aired in New York and Washington is indicative of the warped perception many politicians have of power of political advertising. Kathleen Hall Jamieson explained the reaction: "Those candidates who believe that they were elected because of their consultants not their convictions are susceptible to ad phobia, an irrational but deeply held fear of the killer ad."[33]

If one accepts the argument made by Thomas Patterson and Robert McClure that most Americans are inured to political advertising, then the concern over deceptive tactics employed by political consultants is misplaced.[34] Who cares if they tell outright falsehoods if the people do not bother to listen? Many scholars agree with Patterson and McClure that political advertising is rarely a decisive factor in a citizen's decision-making calculus, but they stop short of claiming it has no measurable effect. Rather, the consensus among political communication scholars is that advertising seems to reinforce preexisting biases.[35] This assessment accurately describes the course of events during the health care debate. Opponents to the Clinton plan saturated the airwaves and mailboxes with a message attuned to Americans' nascent distrust of centralized, bureaucratic authority. By the time the White House formulated a response, the plan was already synonymous with "big government" and all the negative images that phrase connotes. Indeed, Clinton administration officials later admitted they were unprepared for the scale of the paid advertising campaign. In essence, the political consultants played upon an established, prevailing bias in the American body politic and successfully persuaded policy makers that the public was opposed to reform.

The negativity and hyperbole found in television ads and direct-mail appeals seems to have made it more difficult for elected officials and interest groups to negotiate in good faith. From the outset of the reform effort, political consultants attached to the White House were eager to cast a set of villains in the health care debate. They believed that connecting failures in the system with publicly recognizable groups such as pharmaceutical manufacturers and HMO's would strengthen the administration's case for legislative action.[36] The First Lady and members of the task force took the advice seriously and wove a narrative that laid blame for America's health care woes on a select group of companies. Throughout her public appearances, for example, Mrs. Clinton made a point to condemn drug companies for "profiteering" on the backs of the elderly and infirm. The persistent rhetorical attacks from the White House compelled the Pharmaceutical Research and Manufacturers Association (PhRMA) to respond in kind.[37] The Clinton administration's aggressive campaign-style tactics hardened the resolve of the interest groups aligned against the reform plan and erased the possibility of a negotiated compromise. Spokespeople for various interest groups expressed puzzlement that the White House would pursue such an aggressive attack when the groups claimed to support a majority of the president's goals. Although PhRMA maintained it developed ads to defend its reputation, several other groups sponsored ads and direct-mail campaigns without provocation. Conservative activists such as Americans for Tax Reform (ATR) and Citizens for a Sound Economy (CSE) sent out literature and aired political attack ads before the Clinton plan was introduced to Congress.

The national attention and outcry spawned by political ads like Harry and Louise may have caught some health care experts off guard, but their success probably did not surprise the political consultants who created them. The ads and direct-mail salvos were all buttressed by sophisticated polling data and focus group research that gave consultants a clear picture of the general public's fears and apprehensions. Harry and Louise could not have existed without exhaustive survey research. Aside from their involvement with the ad campaign, pollsters occasionally plotted strategy and helped shape the rhetoric used by participants.

Contemporary critics of American government often claim political actions are "poll driven" in the sense that politicians measure the public's temperature before they commit to a course of action, but the truth is more complicated than these statements would lead us to believe. Instead of using polls to select their positions, politicians mainly use polls to learn how to sell their ideas. In other words, "to educate and direct public opinion itself."[38] Polls were also used by health care debate participants to develop strategies. Pollsters in the White House, for instance, used poll data to convince President Clinton to abandon a value-added tax as a possible funding mechanism for the plan.

Technological advances and the infusion of social science has given pollsters greater confidence in their abilities and, as a result, a more prominent position within the advisory hierarchy. Successful pollsters exhibit an uncanny blend of speed and precision, as their clients often demand results within a narrow time period. Stan Greenberg, President Clinton's pollster cum policy advisor, was the first presidential pollster to engage in interactive "real time" polling by employing a device known as the dial-a-meter. Using a small group of citizens who were carefully selected for their demographic characteristics, Greenberg asked them to watch President Clinton's health care speech and to register their reactions with a dial.[39] The aggregate results were then plotted on a graph and enabled Greenberg to discover with some degree of confidence what words inspired a positive response as well as what words drew a negative reaction. The sample was non random and unscientific, but it nevertheless provided a useful glimpse of unfiltered citizen reaction. Greenberg's Republican counterparts used similar means to discern words and phrases that engendered public doubts. GOP pollsters used focus groups and in-depth interviews to glean valuable snapshots of the public mood.

Reporters who covered health care in 1993 and 1994 routinely criticized leaders for the artificial, buzzword jargon they used when they discussed legislative options.[40] It sounded inauthentic and it seemed, in David Broder's estimation, to be scripted and spoken without reflection.[41] The reason for the disappointing quality of the rhetoric may have been polls and focus groups. Many of the words and phrases used in the debate were specifically selected in response to survey research. As Robin Toner of the *New York Times* pointed out, "politicians used polls to figure out how to talk about the issue, how to connect with voters anxiety, and how to allay their nightmares."[42] Politicians telling people what they want to hear is hardly a novel occurrence in American history. However, the development of tools and a methodology to divine a popular vocabulary is an evolutionary leap beyond the traditional interchange between politicians and the general public. Unfortunately, couching proposals in poll-tested phrases deprives the public of valuable information they can use to evaluate the merits of a public policy. Politicians who resort to euphemisms, clichés, and metaphors to describe policies are in essence evading their responsibilities to their constituents. Yet the real fault, if casting blame is appropriate, lies with consultants who peddle symbols as a substitute for information. By mining the public for evocative words, consultants can sheathe unpleasant elements in sugarcoated terminology, or conversely they can tar a reasonable proposition with slurs and innuendo. Evidence suggests that this does have an effect on the public. Independent pollsters who evaluated the Clinton plan found that while people knew very little about the proposed legislation, either in specific or general terms, they were able to describe their impressions of the plan using the same phrases found in political ads.[43]

In terms of the actual content of the plan, pollsters exerted little influence. However, there are a few notable exceptions. In the White House, for example, during the planning stages of the health plan, Stan Greenberg told the task force leaders that a payroll tax or anything resembling a tax would compromise the popularity of the reform goals. His advice was instrumental in shaping the financing arrangement, a design that eventually settled on employer mandates rather than a tax increase.[44] GOP pollsters also provided useful strategic information. In early 1994 they quietly urged their clients to oppose any health bill, no matter how benign. They based their advice on poll data that indicated the Democratic party would benefit in the fall elections if it could point to legislative achievement in health care. In the aftermath of the reform collapse, several health policy scholars vented their disgust at what they perceived to be a cynical, wholly political spectacle. "Policy makers," noted Lawrence Jacobs of Harvard University, "concentrated not on what works best but on what mattered and what would be acceptable in terms of public preferences and understandings."[45] His dismay was echoed by Dianne Heith of Brown University, who rejected the public pandering and mass marketing as a debasement of thoughtful policy making.[46]

Interest groups were not above manipulating poll results to bolster an established position. The National Federation of Independent Businesses (NFIB), an association representing small businesses, polled its 500,000 members on a weekly basis and transmitted the results to all 535 members of Congress.[47] The poll questions, however, were not neutral and were intended to provoke negative assessments of the Clinton plan. NFIB is considered a small to medium-size lobbying organization, but its influence transcends its size. Small-business owners, to paraphrase Richard Fenno, are a specialized constituency who tend to be community leaders in their own right.[48] Legislators who ignore the voices of small businessmen do so at their own peril. Therefore, small-business owners' opinion, especially if it is coordinated on a national scale, will gain the attention of members of Congress.

For some scholars who witnessed the tidal wave of advertising and direct mail in 1993 and 1994, the activities of political consultants inspired familiar concerns over elite bias and the normative implications of mass media politics.[49] As with the Contract with America, the groups that most heavily utilized the services of political consultants were organizations with a substantial financial stake in the outcome. Through the television, the radio, and the nation's mailboxes, pharmaceutical companies, hospitals, doctors, and, most important, insurance companies were able to disseminate their points of view while groups with smaller budgets, namely consumer advocates and organizations representing the poor, were shut out. It was, as many health care advocates claimed afterward, not a fair fight. According to one estimate, groups opposed to the Clinton health plan outspent those that favored it by more than a two-to-one margin in political advertising. The HIAA alone spent nearly $16 million on the Harry and Louise campaign.[50]

The FEC does not keep statistics on advocacy advertising. In 1994 advocacy advertising, like independent expenditures made by interest groups during the regular election cycle, is not regulated by the federal government; therefore, estimates of the expenditures are subject to dispute. Nevertheless, several scholars and reputable public interest groups have compiled data that show that overall advocacy advertising (television and print ads as well as direct-mail outreach) totaled over $250 million. A cursory survey of the organizations with the heaviest involvement reveals an unsurprising pro business, anti government bias. The HIAA and PhRMA spent nearly $34 million combined, a figure that dwarfs the combined total of the four largest health care advocate groups. The AFL-CIO, the Democratic National Committee, the Health Care Reform Project (a consumer group), and the American Conference of Health Care Workers spent a total of $11.3 million on advertising supporting health care reform. The disparity was most evident during the crucial months immediately following the introduction of the Clinton plan in Congress. From October 1993 to December 1993 the DNC spent only $150,000 on print ads, whereas PhRMA and the HIAA spent $17.5 million.[51] Each group funneled the money through well-known consultants such as Bill McInturff and Bill Hamilton.

This is a valid and serious concern, but politicians and scholars should keep in mind that advertising is just one of a myriad of informational outlets accessed by citizens. A combination of factors balance out the paid advertising advantage owned by well-funded interest groups. The Clinton administration, for example, benefited from overwhelmingly positive press coverage after the president's initial presentation before the Congress.[52] His inability to capitalize on the goodwill had nothing to do with political consultants or opposition ads. Health care advocates also used free media. The Robert Wood Johnson Foundation, a philanthropic organization devoted to public health issues, bought two hours of prime-time air from NBC to present a detailed explanation of the American health care system and what was required to reform it.[53] The foundation paid nearly $2.5 million for the air time and an additional $1 million to advertise the special. Although the foundation was not a declared supporter of the Clinton plan, representatives had participated in the health care task force and were on record supporting the goals outlined in the plan.

The lamentations and self-pitying protestations that emanated from the White House shortly after Senate Majority Leader Mitchell pulled health care from the Senate calendar sounded like sour grapes to many of President Clinton's adversaries. Republicans claimed, with some glee, that the president had made an enormous blunder by trying to foist a burdensome policy scheme on a skeptical general public. It is true that over the last several years a large portion of the electorate has come to distrust the government and in turn has become wary of new policy programs, especially when those initiatives are complex and the future consequences are unknown.[54] However, public opposition to the Clinton plan did not emerge sui generis. The latent antipathy needed to be activated and manipulated. In this sense, political consultants were invaluable contractors for the forces aligned against the White House.

After health care had been removed from the legislative agenda, a reporter asked political consultant Ben Goddard for his opinion about the result. In comments that eerily echoed those made by some of his predecessors in David Rosenbloom's book, *The Election Men*, Goddard claimed, "We dodged a very dangerous, overwhelming proposal that obviously most Americans did not support."[55] Goddard went on to credit the work done by his firm and fellow consultants in protecting Americans from the Clinton plan. His candid, if self-promoting remarks raise an interesting question about the place of the consultant in our political system. In Larry Sabato's landmark work, *The Rise of Political Consultants*, he chastises them for serving as candidate preselectors. Although Sabato's alarm seems to be out of proportion to the actual problem, there is reason to question the position of political consultants as unaccountable gatekeepers and interlocutors. The fact that Ben Goddard believes he did a public service by creating skewed, inflammatory advertising campaign should give scholars pause, particularly when there are survey data that suggest his opinion is not isolated among his profession. According to a study by James Thurber of American University, a large number of consultants believe that they are in a better position to decide policy matters than the average citizen.[56] Their paternalistic outlook is coupled with an unfortunate disdain for the political system, giving fuel to accusations that consultants harbor anti democratic tendencies.

CONCLUSION

The movement to pass comprehensive health care reform was an important event in the Clinton presidency and for the Democratic party in general. Its failure demonstrated a powerful undercurrent of public distrust for large-scale, government-sponsored policy initiatives, and it challenged the Clinton administration's assumptions about what the American people want from the federal government. It also brought to the surface the deep, pervasive divisions within the Democratic party and, conversely, helped to unify and galvanize the fledgling conservative movement in American politics. Although it would be an exaggeration to claim that health care begot the Contract with America, it is hard to imagine the triumph of the Republican party without the Democrats' disastrous pursuit of health care reform. But perhaps its most lasting significance in American political history will be as the archetypal example of mass media oriented, public policy campaigning. Veteran political reporters David Broder and Haynes Johnson remarked that the health care debate "represented the first time political figures had brought the entire complement of campaign tools to bear during a policy battle."[57] This is an observation that is confirmed by the enormous sum spent on political ads and direct mail, not to mention the incessant polling conducted by the White House, legislators, and interest groups.

It is tempting to draw conclusions concerning the ubiquitous presence of high-priced political consultants and their campaign-oriented tactics. Hillary Clinton condemned the negative ads and misrepresentations spread in direct mail for "poisoning the debate." In a fit of pique, she placed blame for the defeat of the legislation squarely on the shoulders of interest groups and political consultants (it seems ironic that an administration known for calculating political angles would criticize opponents for adopting the same strategy). HIAA President Bill Gradison, conversely, was effusive in his praise for the work done by political consultants on behalf of groups opposed to the plan. He claims, for example, that Harry and Louise were instrumental in turning public opinion against the statist approach favored by the Clinton administration. Both comments imbue political consultants with great power and influence over the legislative process, but it is impossible to validate either statement. As Theda Sckopol argues impressively in her book, *Boomerang*, the reform effort was hampered early on by a myriad of factors unrelated to public relations. Institutional tension between the White House and Congress, coupled with jurisdictional disputes within Congress, delayed consideration of the legislation. The sixteen-month sojourn through Congress opened dozens of opportunities to block the legislation.

It is an overstatement to claim political consultants are somehow culpable for the failure of health care reform, and it would be inaccurate to accuse them of corrupting the debate by serving private interests and public officials simultaneously. There is no evidence that Bill McInturff, Mandy Grunwald, or Bill Hamilton misled or influenced their public-sector clients at the behest of private interests. This is not to suggest that political consultants are excused from all responsibility for the ugly tenor of the health care debate. The public arguments that followed health care legislation were fraught with emotional rhetoric, market-tested symbolism, and demagoguery. The critical but highly dubious claims made by the contrived couple, Harry and Louise, about the Clinton plan represent just one example among dozens where the facts were obscured by clever advertising. At least the creators of Harry and Louise stuck to a defensible version of the facts, the same could not be said for some other attack ads. The consultants who worked on behalf of the Clinton plan were no better, as they eagerly identified groups that could fill the role of villain for public relations purposes. Aside from the heated and occasionally misleading rhetoric, consultants are also accountable for inflating the influence disparity between well-heeled interest groups and lesser-endowed counterparts. Political consultants are expensive, and the advice they provide costs money. Supporters of the Clinton plan claimed afterward that the positive message was drowned out in the wash of paid media. Preliminary data suggest that they may be right. Consumer organizations and service-sector unions, two groups claiming to represent the uninsured and the under insured, were outspent by a 4 to 1 margin by insurance companies and drug manufacturers opposed to the reform plan.

The nature of modern American politics virtually assures the continued presence of political consultants in policy debates. In the era of the permanent campaign, grassroots stimulation, public opinion polling, and political advertising are an indispensable addition to the legislative process. Political consultants, by virtue of their training and expertise, are the obvious choice to lead the campaigns. What this means for the American political system will be addressed in greater depth later in the book.

HEALTH CARE REFORM TIMELINE

Date	Significance
January 25, 1993	President Clinton announces the formation of the task force and appoints the First Lady and Ira Magaziner to lead it.
Feb - May, 1993	The Health Task Force meets behind closed doors. Over 500 health experts from business, academia, and government partake in a series of seminars and drafting sessions to design a viable plan.
September 5, 1993	The infamous Harry and Louise ads debut. The commercials would air throughout the debate and became symbols of the new style of consultant-inspired, policy campaigning.
September 22, 1993	President Clinton unveils his health care plan to the public and Congress in a nationally televised address. Polls show a broad majority support the President's goals, but are unsure about how to achieve them.
October 27, 1993	The actual text of the bill is delivered to Congress. In the House the bill is referred to the Ways and Means Committee, the Energy and Commerce Committee, and the Education and Labor Committee. In the Senate, the Finance Committee asserts jurisdiction.
November, 1993	Opponents to the Clinton plan, such as NFIB, HIAA, and the Christian Coalition begin developing a massive, coordinated public relations campaign to defeat the bill.
Nov - Dec, 1993	The House and Senate close the 1st Session of the 103rd Congress after taking some preliminary action concerning health care.
Feb - May, 1994	Committees in both chambers meet continuously to craft a bill that fulfills the President's intentions and can muster a majority on the floor.
May 31, 1994	House Ways and Means Chairman Rostenkowski is indicted and resigns the chairmanship. Gibbons takes over and fails to hold a coalition together.
May - July, 1994	Polls show public support for the Clinton plan is slipping. Direct mail and media advertising have successfully portrayed the plan as a risky "big government" venture.
June 9, 1994	Senator Moynihan advises the White House that a health plan with employer mandates would

	have difficulty passing the Senate Finance Committee.
June 28, 1994	House Energy and Commerce Chairman John Dingell admits defeat and fails to report a health care bill from his committee.
June 30, 1994	The Ways and Means Committee reports a modified version of the Clinton bill to the House. It lacks a guarantee of universal coverage and possesses a diluted employer mandate.
July 15, 1994	A Gallup poll reveals 55% of those polled "disapprove" of the Clinton plan. This is a sharp contrast to a similar poll conducted in September 1993 in which 59% of the respondents supported the plan.
July 21, 1994	House and Senate leaders remove the Clinton plan from floor consideration and pledge to introduce a new bill that is "less bureaucratic and provides for a longer phase in period."
July - Aug, 1994	The White House organizes a last ditch public campaign for health reform. A national bus tour sparks controversy and fails to ignite public support.
August 3, 1994	House Majority Leader Dick Gephardt and Senate Majority Leader George Mitchell introduce their new health care bill.
August 25, 1994	The House Democratic leadership decides not to risk a humiliating defeat and pulls the Gephardt bill from the floor.
September 26, 1994	Senate Majority Leader George Mitchell takes health care off the Senate calendar and states Congress will not pass a bill this year.

NOTES

1. More recent research suggests that the attention to overall costs is misleading. In a study conducted by the Brookings Institution, Jack Triplett argued that while gross costs have dramatically increased, the costs of individual procedures has fallen allowing a larger number people to enjoy the benefits of health care innovations. For example, cataract surgery used to be a dangerous, expensive operation involving several days in the hospital. Technological advances in laser surgery have made it a simple, affordable outpatient procedure. See Charles Morris, "Health Care Economy Nothing to Fear," *Atlantic Monthly*, December 1999, 86–96.

2. There are two book-length treatments that ably outline the history of the Clinton health care reform. *The System* by David Broder and Haynes Johnson is a journalistic account filled with illuminating anecdotes and insightful comments made by many of the inside players who were at the core of the debate. It is at times a wistful recollection of what could have been, but on the whole a solid example of political journalism. The other book is *Boomerang*, written by Harvard University sociologist Theda Skocpol. Her work is well researched and brings a much needed academic perspective, but her bias is re-

flected in her manifest disappointment with the outcome of the health care debate. In her estimation the people who fought against the Clinton plan were reactionary obstructionists whose opinions and arguments lacked merit. On occasion her emotion bursts through and the result is more an elegy to New Deal politics than a sober account of the issue. Nevertheless, taken together the books provide a detailed portrait of the debate and my own historical summary draws heavily from these two works. David Broder and Haynes Johnson, *The System: The American Way of Politics at the Breaking Point* (Boston: Little, Brown & Co., 1996); Theda Skocpol, *Boomerang: Clinton's Health Security Effort and the Turn Against Government in U.S. Politics* (New York: WW Norton, 1996).

3. Broder and Johnson, *The* System, 96.

4. Lawrence Jacobs, "Health Reform Impasse: The Politics of American Ambivalence toward Government," *Journal of Health Politics, Policy and Law* 18 (1993): 634.

5. James Fallows, "A Triumph of Misinformation," *Atlantic Monthly*, January 1995, 26.

6. Over the course of the health care debate House Democrats were split among three separate bills, including the administration's plan. Nearly ninety members were committed to a Canadian-style, single-payer plan. Their plan would nationalize the health insurance industry by instituting universal coverage under which the government would collect premiums. Revenues would be used to pay private-sector providers. On the other side of the spectrum, a large contingent of conservative and pro-business Democrats supported a bill introduced by Jim Cooper (D-TN) that embodied the principles of managed competition. It did not require that employers pay for most their employees insurance premiums, nor did it attempt to control insurance costs. Not only did these two bills compete with Clinton's own plan, they were sufficiently incompatible that a compromise between Cooper's bill and the single-payer version was out of the question. See Alissa Rubin, "Two Ideological Poles Frame Debate over Reform," *CQ Weekly Report*, 8 January 1994, 2–26.

7. Adam Clymer, "Clinton Says Administration Was Misunderstood on Health Care," *New York Times*, 3 October 1994, A12.

8. Dana Priest, "Anonymity is the Buzzword for Health Worker Bees," *Washington Post*, 17 February 1993, A13.

9. Broder and Johnson, *The System*, 113.

10. Skocpol, *Boomerang*, 53–57.

11. See Paul Light, "Presidential Policy Making," in *Researching the Presidency*, ed. George Edwards, John Kessel, and Bert Rockman (Pittsburgh: University of Pittsburgh Press, 1993); Jeffrey Tulis "The Interpretable Presidency," in *The Presidency and the Political System* 3rd ed., ed. Marshall Nelson (Washington, D.C.: CQ Press, 1990).

12. In Bob Woodward's book *The Agenda* he describes the arguments between health care supporters led by Hillary Clinton and the by-the-numbers deficit hawks in colorful detail. Woodward goes on to suggest that, despite the acknowledgment of a policy problem, many of Clinton's cabinet were skeptical of the health care reform task force and were alarmed at the course taken by Mrs. Clinton and Ira Magaziner. Bob Woodward, *The Agenda: Inside the Clinton White House* (New York: Simon and Schuster, 1994)

13. Darrell West, Diane Heith, and Chris Goodwin, "Harry and Louise Go to Washington: Political Advertising and Health Care Reform," *Journal of Health Politics, Policy and Law* 21 (1996), 40.

14. The AFL-CIO was so incensed with the Clinton administration that it withheld over $5 million to the Democratic National Committee for several months. NAFTA

alienated a core constituency at a critical moment in the nascent health care debate. According to an administration official AFL-CIO President Lane Kirkland told the White House "we have $ 7 million to spend. We can either spend it supporting health care or fighting NAFTA." In short, the unions exhausted themselves fighting a futile battle *against* the president that left little for health care. Broder and Johnson, *The System.*

15. Lawrence Jacobs, Robert Shapiro, and Eli Schulman "The Polls and Poll Trends: Medical Care in the United States," *Public Opinion Quarterly* 57, (1993), 394–427.

16. Rick Wartzman, "Small Companies Misunderstand Clinton Health Plan," *Wall Street Journal*, 24 September 1993, B2.

17. Broder and Johnson, *The System*, ch. 5 and 6.

18. Trudy Lieberman, "The Selling of Clinton-Lite," *Columbia Journalism Review*, March/April 1994, 20–24.

19. Paula Span, "Ad Ventures in Health Care," *Washington Post*, 18 March 1994, A14.

20. David Broder, "White House Takes On Harry and Louise," *Washington Post*, 8 July 1994, A1.

21. James Risen, "Health Reform Sprouts Intense Grassroots Lobbying Outside the Beltway," *Los Angeles Times*, 1 August 1994, A5.

22. Scokpol, *Boomerang*, ch. 6.

23. Dan Balz and David Broder, "Players in Health Care Debate Mobilize Consultants and Lobbyists," *Washington Post*, 10 October 1993, A4.

24. Kathleen Hall Jamieson, "When Harry Met Louise," *Washington Post*, 15 August 1994, A19.

25. Stephen Ansolabehere and Shanto Iyengar, *Going Negative: How Political Advertisements Shrink and Polarize the Electorate* (New York: The Free Press, 1995). Ansolabehere and Iyengar maintain that the rise in negative advertising is directly correlated with diminished voter turnout. Their conclusions have been challenged, however, by several scholars who question the impact of political advertising on voters' decisions. See Martin Wattenberg and Craig Leonard Watkins, "Negative Campaign Advertising: Demobilizer or Mobilizer?" *American Political Science Review* 93 (1999), 891–899.

26. Darrell West and Richard Francis, "Electronic Advocacy: Interest Groups and Public Policy Making," *PS: Political Science & Politics*, 29 (1996), 25–29.

27. Robert Pear, "Liars Attacking Health Plan to Scare Elderly, Groups Say," *New York Times*, 27 May 1994, A1.

28. Rick Wartzman, "Truth Lands in Intensive Care as New Ads Seek to Demonize Clinton's Health Reform Plan," *Wall Street Journal*, 29 April 1994, A16.

29. "Are Political Consultants Hurting or Helping Democracy?" *Center for Congressional and Presidential Studies* available at (http://auvm.american.edu/~ccps).

30. Skocpol, *Boomerang*, 138.

31. West, et. al. "Harry and Louise Go to Washington," 60.

32. Span, "Ad Ventures in Health Care," A14.

33. Jamieson, "When Harry Met Louise."

34. Thomas Patterson and Robert McClure, *The Unseeing Eye: The Myth of Television Power over National Politics* (New York: Putnam, 1976).

35. Lynda Kaid, Dan Nimmo, and Keith Sanders, eds. *New Perspectives on Political Advertising* (Carbondale: Southern Illinois University Press, 1986).

36. Broder and Johnson, *The System*, 90.

37. Howard Kurtz, "For Health Care Companies, a Major Ad Operation," *Washington Post*, 13 April 1993, A1.

38. Michael Zis, Lawrence Jacobs, and Robert Shapiro, "The Elusive Common Ground: The Politics of Public Opinion and Health Care Reform," *Generations*, Summer 1996, 7–13.

39. James Barnes, Polls Apart, *National Journal*, 12 November 1993, 1750.

40. Joe Klein, "Bloviational Fiesta," *Newsweek*, 22 August 1994, 21.

41. Broder and Johnson, The System, 275.

42. Robin Toner, "Following the Crowd on Health Care, and Getting Lost," *New York Times*, 20 March 1994, sec. 4, 1.

43. Lydia Saad, "Public Has Cold Feet on Health Care Reform," *The Gallup Poll Monthly*, August 1994, 2–6.

44. Richard L. Berke, "Clinton Aide Says Polls Had Role in Health Plan," *New York Times*, 9 December 1993, A20.

45. Jacobs, "Health Reform Impasse," 649.

46. Diane Heith,

47. Susan Headden, "The Little Lobby That Could," *U.S. News and World Report*, 12 September 1994, 45.

48. Richard Fenno, *Home Style: House Members in Their Districts* (Boston: Little, Brown, 1978), 26.

49. West and Francis, "Electronic Advocacy," 25–26.

50. Darell West and Burdett Loomis, *The Sound of Money: How Political Interests Get What They Want* (New York: WW Norton, 1998), 68.

51. West, et. al. "Harry and Louise Go To Washington," 46.

52. Skocpol, *Boomerang*, 107–113.

53. Bill Carter, "Buying the Air Time, Foundation Fosters NBC Program on Health," *New York Times*, 4 May 1994, A1.

54. Michael Cobb and James Kuklinski, "Changing Minds: Political Arguments and Political Persuasion," *American Journal of Political Science*, (1997), 91.

55. Robin Toner, "Harry and Louise and a Guy Named Ben," *New York Times*, 30 September 1994, A22.

56. Thurber, "Are Political Consultants Hurting or Helping Democracy?"

57. Broder and Johnson, *The System*, 125.

5

The Contract with America: Marketing the Revolution

During the first heady days of the 104th Congress, Speaker Newt Gingrich occasionally allowed his excitement at the prospects of a Republican legislative revolution to get the better of him. In these moments, he was given to making grandiose historical comparisons and hyperbolic comments about the significance of the 1994 election.[1] He likened himself, for example, to British prime ministers of the nineteenth century, perhaps forgetting for a moment that we live in a federal system of separated powers. In interviews and press conferences, he tirelessly compared the Republican takeover of Congress to other landmark events in American history.

When Gingrich's statements are viewed in retrospect, they seem either poignant or outrageous, depending on your political persuasion. Given the fact that most of the Contract with America, the legislative agenda the Republicans rode to victory in the House of Representatives, was not signed into law and that, by 1999, Newt Gingrich was no longer even a member of the House, it seems unlikely that historians will place the 104th Congress in the category reserved for epochs like Reconstruction or the New Deal. Yet the Republican victory in 1994 and the party's initial legislative successes are important from a political science perspective. The Contract with America is an unprecedented example of a nationalized congressional party platform that ran counter to much of the academic discussion of congressional electoral behavior.[2] Moreover, the Contract demonstrated a concerted effort on the part of the congressional majority to wrest control of the political agenda from the president. Since FDR, the theme running through scholarly analyses of executive-legislative relations has focused on presidential dominance. According to political scientist Richard Fleisher, "The 104th Congress has shown us that the conventional wisdom that Congress is dependent on leadership from the president is overstated."[3]

Another characteristic that made the Contract with America unique and truly significant is the role political consultants played throughout its transformation from a series of campaign promises and bromides into legislation. Political consultants were intimately involved in the public relations campaigns that paralleled the Contract's progress through the House of Representatives. During the first months of 1995, pollsters conducted focus groups and polls to discover the most effective language to sell the Republican ideas to the American people. Their efforts were joined by media specialists and direct-mail consultants who waged a guerrilla campaign for public support. Democrats, once they overcame the initial shock that followed the election, followed suit. The White House and congressional Democrats also employed the services of consultants to counter the marketing juggernaut put together by congressional Republicans.[4] Once engaged, the public relations battle between the Democrats, the Republicans and their interest-group allies was frenzied.

It would, however, be an exaggeration to say that salesmanship overshadowed the substance of the Republican agenda. Detractors claimed that the Contract was hollow and cynically derived, but it was not merely a compilation of poll-tested ideas. It was, underneath the rhetorical facade and slick packaging, a sober articulation of conservative priorities. The real lasting significance of the Contract is as an illustration of how politicians at the end of the twentieth century, with the help of political consultants, attempted to cultivate and harness public support for their policies after the election. It also shows how preoccupied our elected leaders are with the vagaries of public opinion. In this sense, the 104th Congress was an acknowledgment of the modern political condition in which selling a policy is just as crucial as developing it.

The Contract with America represents a peak in consultant involvement in the legislative process, and thus is a useful test case through which to explore the three questions outlined in Chapter 1. First, are campaign methods suitable for governing? Does the pursuit of public, campaign-oriented strategies obscure issues with platitudes and encourage style over substance? Campaign-style governing may also exacerbate partisan and institutional tensions, dividing the political community into polarized factions. Second, are political consultants involved in the legislative process a threat to democratic accountability? Political consultants have great influence with their clients, and therefore over the content of public policy, but they are not subject to the same restrictions and regulations that govern the behavior of permanent staff. Political consultants with private-sector clients may possess an inherent conflict of interest on matters of public policy. Third, several events that occurred during the 104th Congress call into question the reliability and efficacy of the techniques used by political consultants.

FOUNDATIONS OF THE CONTRACT WITH AMERICA

A common misconception about the Contract with America is that it was the brainchild of Republican political consultants and pollsters. In fact, the roots of the Contract are found in the House Republican Conference and in the fledgling conservative think tanks that emerged during the presidency of Ronald Reagan.

In the early 1980s a cadre of junior Republican congressmen formed the Conservative Opportunity Society (COS) as an aggressive advocate for Republican legislative proposals. The COS, whose charter members included future Speaker of the House Newt Gingrich, Majority Leader Dick Armey, and several other members of the 104th leadership team, was a breeding ground for conservative ideas. These legislators were disdainful of moderate leaders like Bob Michel, who worked with Democrats in order to influence public policy on the margins.

Instead of working within the boundaries prescribed by the majority party, the COS offered conservative alternatives to Democratic legislation.[5] Throughout the 1980s and the early 1990s the COS helped articulate Republican policies and transform ideas into viable legislation. Some of the items in the Contract are the progeny of COS proposals. The legislative brainstorming encouraged by the COS was supplemented off the Hill by several new think tanks devoted to conservative causes. Organizations such as the Heritage Foundation and the Competitive Enterprise Institute eschewed the traditional, detached role played by venerable think tanks like the Brookings Institution in favor of policy analysis conducted expressly to support a conservative agenda. According to James Smith, a think tank historian, the conservative think tanks functioned as a "secondhand dealer of ideas" with an admitted bias toward advocacy rather than objective research.[6]

George Bush's defeat in 1992 crystallized the need for new ideas and spurred Republicans to a critical reevaluation of their electoral strategy. Several internal polls conducted by the Republican National Committee indicated that rank-and-file members were disillusioned with the GOP and believed that it lacked a vision for the country. Party stalwarts seemed to be suggesting that it was not enough for the Republican party simply to stand against the Democratic agenda; they wanted their own platform. Newt Gingrich and his allies in the House of Representatives drew an important lesson from this and in 1993 and 1994 began planning what would eventually become the Contract with America. The goal was to develop a defensible set of alternatives to Democratic proposals on the basis of which all Republican candidates could campaign. After polling Republican incumbents and House challengers for ideas, the Republican conference staff drew up a list of the ten most popular items.[7]

The proposals that form the Contract with America can be divided roughly into two categories: standard Republican issues such as tax cuts and strengthening national defense, on the one hand, and populist measures like term limits and the line-item veto on the other. Issues championed by social conservatives such as abortion and school prayer were left off the Contract to cultivate support with independent voters. The Contract was publicly unveiled on September 27, 1994, in an elaborate ceremony on the steps of the U.S. Capitol. In a made-for-television event coordinated by the RNC and several Republican media consultants, 367 Republican House members and challengers signed a document pledging an open vote for the ten items on the Contract within the first 100 days of the 104th Congress. It was immediately assailed by Democratic critics, who described it as reactionary, obtuse, and misguided. One wag dubbed it the Contract *on* America. Nevertheless, the House Republican leaders could draw satisfaction from their remarkable success at unifying their candidates under a coherent party platform (see Table 5.1).[8]

Table 5.1
The Contract with America

Bill Title	Bill Number	Description
Congressional Accountability Act	HR 1	Ends congressional exemption from eleven laws governing safety and other workplace issues.
Line Item Veto/BBA	HR 2 HJ.Res 1	Grants the president the authority to veto portions of appropriations bills; a constitutional amendment requiring a balanced federal budget.
Taking Back Our Streets Act	HR 3	Increases state grants for prison con struction; gives localities flexibility to use federal anticrime funds.
Personal Responsibility Act	HR 4	Converts welfare programs into block grants to states; ends auto matic eligibility for welfare; caps welfare spending and imposes a time limit on welfare benefits.
Unfunded Mandate Reform Act	HR 5	Eliminates imposition of federal regulations without compensation to the states for enforcement.
American Dream Restoration Act	HR 6	A $500-per-child tax credit; eases the marriage penalty for joint filers; cuts capital gains taxes; expands IRA's
National Security Restoration Act	HR 7	Prohibits the use of US troops in UN missions under foreign co- mand; prohibits cuts in defense to finance social programs; provides funding for a missle defense system.
Senior Citizens Equity Act	HR 8	Repeals 1993 increase in Social Security benefits subject to income tax; permits beneficiaries to earn up to $30,000 without losing benefits.
Job Creation and Wage Enhancement Act	HR 9	Requires federal reimbursement for reductions in property value due to regulations; increases first year tax deductions for small businesses.
Common Sense Legal Reform Act	HR 10	Establishes national product liabil- ity law limits on punative damages.

Although consultants were not responsible for the content of the Contract, they were heavily involved in the marketing strategy behind it. Republican consultant Frank Luntz conducted dozens of focus groups and polls in order to find the best way to present the Contract. Luntz, building upon work he had done for the Republican party during the 1994 crime bill debate, tapped into populist resentment and anger at the federal government. He claimed that Americans were alienated from their government and that they had lost faith in our political system. People were no longer confident that their lives would be significantly better than those of their parents, and they blamed a bureaucratic, distant, and feckless government created by the hubris of both political parties and their office-holders.[9] His research supplied the vocabulary used in the Contract. His surveys, for example, indicated that people responded favorably to the idea of a contract and the legal implications it represented. He also found strong support for the Republican commitment to balance the federal budget, an idea the average citizen can readily understand. Once the language was crafted, Republican media consultants developed an innovative advertising strategy that included a national advertisement in *TV Guide*. *TV Guide* had never been used in a national political campaign, but the consultants ingeniously speculated that if the Contract were in *TV Guide* it would be seen by every member of the household several times over the course of a week.[10]

POLITICAL CONSULTANTS AND THE TRANSFORMATION OF THE CONTRACT

The activities of political consultants on behalf of the Contract during the election were not unusual. What was unusual was the continued effort they put forth after the election. Consultants were called upon regularly during the 104th Congress to help manage the public relations campaign for two reasons. First, consultants were brought in to combat the perceived negative coverage many Republicans leaders thought they were receiving in the mainstream press. Media bias is a common refrain among conservative politicians. Once they took power, the Republican leadership was convinced the press would not report their agenda fairly. Their concerns were bolstered by analysis of the network news coverage about the Contract. According to Republican estimates, nearly two-thirds of the network news stories concerning the Contract during the first 100 days were negative.[11] As a way of countering bad press, the Republicans employed media specialists and direct mail to penetrate, and in some cases bypass, the traditional media. Second, consultants were employed to maintain control of the public agenda and keep President Clinton and the congressional Democrats in a defensive posture. Numerous presidential scholars have addressed the inherent communications advantage the president possesses relative to the Congress.[12] The president, as a unitary political figure surrounded by a sophisticated communications apparatus, is able to command the attention of the media and the general public in a way that dwarfs the most visible, newsworthy senator or representative. GOP leaders and their interest group allies believed they could diminish the president's media superiority with a professionally orchestrated public relations campaign.

According to Republican pollsters, each item in the Contract with America drew majority support from the general public.[13] But public popularity is no guarantee of passage. Some issues faced serious obstacles in the form of vested interests and Democratic opposition in Congress. The Common Sense Legal Reform Act, for instance, was an expansive bill intended to establish national product liability law limits on punitive damages awarded in civil lawsuits. The bill was a high priority with an array of pro business organizations; namely, the National Federation of Independent Businesses, Citizens for a Sound Economy, the Chamber of Commerce, and the National Association of Wholesalers. In the lobbying battle over the legislation, pro business forces were opposed by a formidable interest group, the Association of Trial Lawyers of America (ATLA).[14] ATLA is a classic example of a lobby with influence disproportionate to its size. Interest-group theorists from David Truman and James Q. Wilson to Jonathan Rauch have described similar groups whose small numbers belie a tightly organized, well-financed, and respected presence on Capitol Hill. In addition, many representatives and senators are former trial lawyers themselves, giving the organization an unmatched personal connection with lawmakers. According to the the 1998 edition of the *Almanac of American Politics*, there were sixteen members of the trial bar serving in Congress.[15] Previous attempts to pass product liability reform legislation were thwarted by vigorous ATLA lobbying. ATLA bolstered its support on the Hill by remaining a conduit for campaign funds. According to FEC estimates, the trial bar provided over $60 million in campaign contributions to opponents of tort reform between 1988 and 1996.[16] In 1995 ATLA retained strong support in the Democratic caucus and had the sympathetic ear of President Clinton. Thus, even in a Republican Congress friendly to business interests, passage of the Common Sense Legal Reform Act was not assured.

To complement their traditional lobbying efforts in Congress, the pro business coalition engaged in an integrated public relations campaign directed by a group of political consultants. The public relations effort included all of the elements of an electoral campaign, direct-mail outreach, mass media advertising, and public opinion polling, in order to put public pressure on legislators to support product liability reform. The campaign was intended to create public outcry on behalf of the business group's position and exploit congressional sensitivity to constituent opinion. By casting the trial lawyers as the villains in a political drama, the business lobby hoped to make opposition to product liability reform politically dangerous. The public relations campaign sponsored by business interests was expensive (some estimates put the cost at over $17 million) but it was not, to use a crude metaphor, akin to using a sledgehammer to kill a fly.[17] The campaign was targeted precisely and followed a cyclical pattern. Public opinion polls were used to select districts where legislators appeared to be most vulnerable to a media campaign, and advertisements appeared in districts during congressional recesses when legislators would be home to hear from constituents. Media events were coordinated to occur in proximity to floor votes and, once the bill moved on to the White House, ads were targeted in states where support for President Clinton was suspect.

In early April 1995 the pro business coalition hired the media consulting firm Goddard/Claussen to create an ad campaign promoting product liability reform, a task that firm partner Ben Goddard thought they were well equipped to handle. According to Goddard, the strength of their firm is "boiling down complex issues to a message so visceral that it inspires viewers to gripe to their elected officials out of fear or anger. We can create from whole cloth a grassroots lobbying effort."[18] Goddard/Claussen was joined by the Murphy, Pintak, Gautier Agency, a well-regarded campaign firm specializing in attack ads. The campaign-style ads produced by both firms are an example of emotionally manipulative tactics designed to provoke an angry response rather than provide useful information. One particular advertisement, for example, depicted a field of Little League ball players who slowly disappeared while a narrator explained "frivolous" lawsuits had made Little League too expensive to insure. Another more ominous ad featured small-town firemen who were reluctant to perform CPR because of the threat of lawsuits. Neither ad attempted to present the legitimate merits of product liability reform. Instead, the ads tried to energize the viewers with raw emotion.[19] By some accounts, the ads had the desired effect. A spokesman for Citizens for a Sound Economy claimed that several representatives contacted the group and requested the ads be taken off the air. The group complied only in cases where the legislator agreed in writing to support tort reform.[20]

After Senate passage of product liability reform, the public relations campaign went on hiatus. The radio, print, and TV ads were revived in 1996 when the bill moved on to the White House. President Clinton, under enormous pressure from ATLA, cited technical disagreements with the bill and promised to veto it. Business groups countered ATLA's executive branch lobbying with another grassroots campaign. Media consultants working for the business coalition bought air time in two important swing states, Kentucky and Michigan. The ads produced in 1995 were revived and aired in those states.[21] In order to demonstrate to the White House that vetoing the legislation could carry electoral consequences in 1996, the business coalition even commissioned a poll. The before-and-after poll conducted by private pollsters Public Opinion Strategies showed President Clinton's lead over Bob Dole evaporated among voters who saw the ads. The results were then transmitted to the White House. The business coalition's efforts were for naught, as the president vetoed the bill anyway, but their sophisticated media strategy, which incorporated polling and advertising, is emblematic of a change in the way interest groups attempt to influence elected officials.

Several of the legislative initiatives outlined briefly in the Contract were radical departures from the public policies of the past thirty years. The language used in the Contract may have seemed benign, but underlying calls for a return to personal responsibility and traditional American values was a pledge to dismantle many of the social programs produced during the Great Society. The welfare reform provision, for example, entailed a wholesale restructuring of federal programs for the poor. It would transfer welfare responsibility to the states, cap welfare spending, and limit recipients' eligibility in most cases to two years.[22] The plan was as ambitious as it was controversial. Other elements of the Contract broached supposedly untouchable social programs. The spending and tax cuts promised by the Republicans in the Contract forced them to adopt cuts in popular entitlement programs like Medicare. Attempts to reform Medicare, the supplemental insurance program for the elderly, are regarded warily by legislators because the program has a large constituent base that tends to vote in high numbers. In short, the policies championed by the House Republicans were bold and could prove perilous in the next election cycle. As a means of sustaining public support for their agenda, Republican leaders turned to the same consultants who marketed the Contract with America during the campaign.

In early 1995 Frank Luntz conducted several surveys at the behest of the House leadership to discern the proper vocabulary to describe welfare reform. In a memo addressed to House Republicans interpreting his results, Luntz unwittingly affirmed the negative description of political consultants offered by Larry Sabato and Dan Nimmo. His memo is littered with obvious advice, such as stressing the work elements of the Republican plan, and cynical assesments of the public's understanding of welfare. Luntz was manifestly unconcerned with the long-range consequences of the Republican plan and admonished his political clients to adopt the same attitude. Republicans, he argues, should leave the debate about the effects of the bill to "social scientists and moral philosophers."[23] It is sage advice if you are simply concerned with getting reelected; it is horribly myopic if you care about the ramifications of public policy.

Frank Luntz's exercise in semantics and his fascination with metaphorical equivalents and synonyms would be curious except for the fact that his advice was taken seriously by House Republicans, who incorporated his words into their description of the welfare reform plan. Partisan debates over public policy are necessarily biased affairs. They are not, as E. E. Schattschneider accurately points out, "intercollegiate debates in which the opponents agree in advance on the definition of the issues."[24] Each side presents a sanitized version of their position while simultaneously denigrating their opponents' point of view. However, by describing their plan in terms chosen expressly to maximize public support, politicians have advanced beyond the traditional parameters of political rhetoric. Parroting back market-tested themes does not enhance political discourse and, in some cases, could be construed as an exercise in purposeful disinformation. The Republican welfare plan was an innovative attempt to restructure a set of programs that many observers, liberal and conservative alike, considered to be failures. It was clearly a plan that deserved to be argued on its merits, but the short-term strategic advice offered by political consultants encouraged Republicans to avoid discussing the policy details in favor of pithy slogans and one-sentence sound bites.

Democrats were not merely bystanders in the message battle. In March 1995 the House Democrats scored their first significant public relations victory over the Republicans in the school lunch debate. As part of the Contract's commitment to return powers to the states, the Republicans had proposed replacing the existing school lunch program with direct cash payments to the states. The plan would save money as well by removing an unneeded layer of federal bureaucracy. Yet the debate rarely touched upon the efficacy of block grants in lieu of federal management. Instead, Democrats seized upon a 1.8 percent decrease in future spending and defined the Republican proposal as a cold hearted attempt to take hot lunches away from needy children. It was an emotional, evocative metaphor and one that Democratic consultants encouraged their clients to repeat at every opportunity. A Democratic media counter offensive paid for by liberal interest groups and produced by Democratic consultants portrayed the Republicans as mean spirited and harped on their alleged callous disregard for the poor. In an ad sponsored by the AFL-CIO, the Democrats exploited the dark side of Republican austerity. The ad warned "The new Congress is cutting jobs, wages, health, safety, housing for senior citizens, even school lunches so they can give tax breaks to big business and the rich."[25] Their argument was strengthened by polls that indicated public support for Republicans was slipping. According to Democratic pollster Geoff Garin, "People only know one thing about the Republican welfare reform plan, that it cuts school lunches."[26] As a rallying cry for demoralized Democratic lawmakers, the school lunch debate fulfilled its mission. However, it was a far cry from an honest portrayal of the Republican intentions and it did much to engender animosity between the two parties. Consultants did not create this animus, but by encouraging their political clients to use poll-tested words they may have amplified it.

The rhetorical gamesmanship was not confined to special-order speeches and orchestrated press events. The House Democrats used committee hearings as a venue for their public relations campaign against the Republican agenda. Instead of offering Democratic substitutes for Republican bills and engaging in constructive debate during committee markups, many members simply used the time to decry the "mean spirited" priorities embodied in Republican legislation. During the tax reform debate, for example, Democratic members of the House Ways and Means Committee confined their efforts to villifying the Republican bill as a "war on the poor" and did not attempt to draft amendments or even offer a Democratic substitute. The theatrics were evidence of a public strategy crafted expressly to embarass the Republicans.[27] The Democrats theme-driven assault on Republican plans could only work in the modern Congress, where gavel-to-gavel television coverage gives members an opportunity to spread a coherent message to a larger audience. C-SPAN, introduced in the House in 1981, has turned committee hearings into parade grounds for media showhorses.[28]

The preparations leading up to the Medicare debate reveal how pervasive the "permanent campaign" mentality is among elected officials. Months before the Republicans introduced legislation concerning Medicare, a select group of party officials and political consultants worked feverishly behind the scenes to devise a persuasive message strategy. Speaker Gingrich and the House Republican leadership viewed finding a compelling way to explain the Republican plan to the general public as important as crafting the policy details. Throughout the spring and summer of 1995, Republican pollsters Linda DiVall, Bill McInturff, and Frank Luntz conducted dozens of focus groups and polls to tease out the vocabulary used in the Medicare debate. They encouraged members to drop the revolutionary rhetoric and adopt a soothing tone that evoked stability. According to their research, words like "change, cut, cap and freeze" created anxiety among voters, but the words "improve, protect, and preserve" engendered positive responses.[29] This advice may seem silly and patently superficial, but these linguistic maneuverings have real consequences. Consider the objective facts of the Republican Medicare proposal. If it were adopted, it would lower the projected benefits of future Medicare recipients as a way of prolonging the life of the program. The size of the Medicare budget would continue to grow, just at a slower rate. In order to avoid electoral retribution for "cutting" Medicare, the Republicans needed to convince the voters that their plan would "preserve Medicare for future generations." Given the overwhelming popularity of Medicare and the constituency it serves, any policy that is viewed by the public as an attempt to change Medicare could result in a disaster at the ballot box.

Meanwhile Democratic consultants produced a powerful counterargument based on their own survey research. They urged congressional Democrats and the president to create a linkage between Medicare cuts and tax breaks for the rich. Focus group data revealed a strong negative reaction to any policy proposal that benefited the wealthy at the expense of the middle class. The Republicans inadvertently provided Democratic consultants with rhetorical ammunition. Speaker Gingrich, in a speech to the American Conservative Union, used the unfortunate phrase "wither on the vine" while articulating his hope for a future in which Medicare would be unnecessary. Democratic consultants captialized immediately on the gaffe. "Within hours," according to *Washington Post* reporter David Maraniss, "consultants at the DNC had drafted a response ad that began: The Republicans in Congress. They never believed in Medicare and now they want it to wither on the vine."[30] In the White House, erstwhile Republican consultant Dick Morris advised President Clinton to seize upon popular Republican initiatives like balancing the federal budget while simultaneously branding the GOP as the enemy of the middle class. As it played out over the media, the partisan battle over Medicare proved to be the high point of poll-tested phraseology.

Political Consultants and Democratic Accountability

Concerns about the accountability of political consultants generally come in two forms. First, scholars and public interest advocates believe that the new roles played by consultants come, according to James Thurber, "perilously close to that of a lobbyist, but without the disclosure requirements that apply to registered advocates."[31] The fear that some observers have is that corporations and trade associations that lobby Congress will use political consultants as a means of bypassing regulated contact with elected officials. Second and unrelated to the first, there is growing apprehension that the issue advocacy work produced by consultants and conducted on behalf of interest groups may be adulterating existing campaign finance laws. Direct-mail outreach and media advertising are subject to legal restrictions if they are part of a candidate's campaign, but the same activities are unregulated for issue advocacy. This sort of electronic lobbying troubles some scholars, who argue that it amplifies the influence of established interests at the expense of average citizens. Darrell West maintains, "[There] is the potential of high-tech campaigns to skew public policy making. Not all groups can afford the cost of electronic advocacy. Resource rich groups are in a much stronger position to use these new communication technologies."[32]

The Republican victory in the 1994 congressional elections proved to be a financial windfall for many Republican consultants. Those who were directly involved in selling the Contract with America basked in the reflected glow of the Republican leaders and soon attracted a number of high-profile corporate clients. In early 1995 Frank Luntz was hired by several groups with keen interests in legislation emanating from the Contract.[33] Luntz's relationships with private groups and his continued presence as a political strategist with close connections to House Republican leaders raise questions about his role. Is he a lobbyist or a political consultant? As a pollster and political consultant, Luntz is not covered by lobbying restrictions and disclosure requirements. Yet an objective observer could easily conclude Luntz's work closely resembles lobbying. Luntz consistently maintained that he never lobbied, nor was he asked to lobby on behalf of his corporate clients.[34] Subsequent interviews with his corporate clientele, however, show a more opaque distinction. According to John Tuck, the former executive director of the Competitive Long Distance Coalition, the coalition hired Frank Luntz in part because he represented a pipeline to the Speaker's office. "Frank Luntz," Tuck stated, "has a knowledge of the new leadership of the House of Representatives and the thinking of its component parts, and that is of value [to us]."[35] It would appear, leaving Luntz's protestations aside, that political consultants in similar circumstances would eventually encounter a conflict of interest between their political clients and their private-sector clients. One can easily envision private clients interests conflating with the political advice offered to elected officials. Under these circumstances, political consultants who advocate an interest group's position under the guise of strategic advice violate the spirit, if not the letter, of lobbying restrictions.

Frank Luntz was not the only consultant to enjoy the Speaker's confidence. Republican consultant Joe Gaylord functioned essentially as Newt Gingrich's shadow chief of staff. Although he did not hold an official position in the Speaker's office, he was a guiding force at policy meetings. According to a Republican leadership aide, "Joe is the closest to Newt. He is the overseer of Newt's life [and] helps select his staff and fix the payroll."[36] It was not unusual or improper for political advisors to be present during official staff meetings or to frequent the legislator's office. Yet the responsibilities handled by Joe Gaylord transcended the normal advisory function and appeared to violate House ethics rules that prohibit using private citizens in an official capacity. Gaylord's ambiguous presence in the Speaker's office eventually resulted in an ethics complaint filed by Democratic congressman George Miller. The House Committee on Standards of Official Conduct (the Ethics Committee) affirmed the allegations made by Representative Miller and concluded, "The routine presence of Mr. Gaylord in Representative Gingrich's congressional office created the appearance of improper commingling of political and official resources and was inappropriate."[37] Mr. Gaylord was not accused of using his relationship with the Speaker to benefit an outside party. However, as the House Ethics committee pointed out, his unfettered access to the Speaker coupled with his private business interests is a situation ripe for exploitation.

Issue advocacy campaigns are another element of consultant activity that is largely unregulated. Direct-mail outreach and media advertising that promote a particular issue but do not explicitly champion a legislator or political party are not covered by campaign finance regulation. The United States Supreme Court, building from a rationale laid out in *Buckley v. Valeo*, has consistently affirmed the right of individuals and groups to spend unlimited amounts of money on issue advocacy. Controlling these expenditures, says the Court, is tantamount to an abridgment of the 1st Amendment guarantee to free speech. The loophole created by *Buckley v. Valeo* has had some predictable effects. Campaign money, like water rolling downhill, seeks the path of least resistance. Spending by interest groups on issue advocacy has exploded in the last decade because, unlike donations to candidates and political parties, there are virtually no limits on spending and no reporting requirements. Since the FEC is not required to keep statistics on issue advocacy, a complete assessment is impossible. Nevertheless, according to study produced by the Annenberg Public Policy Center at the University of Pennsylvania, during the 1995 and 1996 election cycle interest groups spent close to $150 million on issue advocacy.[38] But critics, who include members of the FEC as well as self-styled public interest watchdogs, contend that issue advocacy is simply a form of mass media lobbying that should be regulated just like face-to-face contact with legislators. As part of their argument for regulation, these critics point to the deceptive tactics practiced by interest groups. Corporations, advocacy groups, and trade associations often form ad hoc coalitions with benign names like the American Property Rights Alliance and the Small Business Survival Committee to sponsor issue ads and coordinate media campaigns. The public and even some members of Congress are usually unaware of what groups are financing the public relations campaign. The anonymity covertly intertwines narrow, private interests with broader public concerns. An advertisement, for example, that decries excessive environmental regulation of private land may be directed at the small-property owner, but is in fact sponsored by industrial farming and mining interests.[39]

The tremendous growth of issue advocacy is a concern to scholars studying interest-group behavior, campaign finance, and political consulting. Consultants, it must be said, should not be held accountable for the proliferation of issue advocacy advertising. It would be more accurate to describe them as the beneficiaries. Their role, however, cannot be characterized as passive and deserves critical attention. From a power perspective, consultants collaborating with corporations revives the fears expressed by C. Wright Mills in his seminal work, *The Power Elite*, as echoed by various authors writing on the consulting industry. They warn that a small group of elites dominates the communications media at the expense of average citizens. They can make a credible argument that by virtue of consultants' mastery over technically sophisticated forms of communication, political consultants provide a megaphone for established interests and as a result widen the influence gap between the haves and have nots. Darrell West observes that "high-tech lobbying tools are expensive, and lobbying strategies based on these models are not equally available to all groups."[40] To paraphrase former Senate Majority Leader Bob Dole, there are no political consultants who work for the poor.

The Efficacy of Political Consulting

As political consultants take on more issue-related business and continue to work closely with their political clients in a post-electoral capacity, one question remains unasked by the participants: Are campaign methods suitable in governing? There are a number of instances related to the Contract with America that challenge the appropriateness of direct mail and polling as means of influencing public policy. The grassroots campaign organized on behalf of the Competitive Long Distance Coalition (CLDC) illustrates the pitfalls associated with these tactics. During the 104th Congress, the CLDC, a group of telecommunications companies lobbying for greater market freedom in telephone service, engaged a political consulting firm to raise public awareness of their position. The campaign was intended to produce constituent pressure on legislators through phone calls and telegrams. The popularity of this strategy was predicated on the logical assumption that congressmen are inherently risk averse and will avoid taking an unpopular stand if a significant number of their constituents make their opinions known. In the case of the CLDC, the firm they hired perpetrated a fraud by forwarding telegrams to members of Congress without the approval of the signatories. In essence, the firm took a list of names, forged their signatures, and passed them on to Congress in order to create the impression that there was a groundswell of public support for the CLDC's position.[41] Firms that specialize in grassroots advocacy steadfastly maintain that this type of fraud is rare, but there is no way to be sure. In fact, there is reason to believe the contrary is true. In a fast-growing, cutthroat industry like grassroots advocacy, the pressure to produce for clients could induce some companies to commit fraud. The temptation is fueled by a lack of legal controls covering correspondence to Congress. The firm that submitted forged telegrams on behalf of the CLDC went unpunished because no laws exist prohibiting sending false letters to Congress.

Misusing direct mail is simply one way political consultants can pressure legislators. A different example is provided by the American Association of Retired Persons. During the Balanced Budget Amendment (BBA) debate, the AARP, who vigorously opposed the amendment, sponsored a poll that showed public support for a balanced budget to be soft. The poll, which contradicted several other private polls and polls by respected institutions like Gallup and the Roper Center, indicated that support for the amendment, particularly among senior citizens, was contingent upon sustained levels of entitlement spending. In this instance, pollsters produced evidence to bolster their client's position in a policy debate. The completed poll was then used by the AARP to persuade several wavering Democratic senators to oppose the amendment. According to John Rother, the head of governmental relations for the AARP, the poll, and the possible electoral consequences it presaged, contributed to their decision to vote against the BBA.[42] The AARP's innovative use of a poll as an offensive weapon revives old questions about the place of public opinion in policy making and raises new ones about the validity of agenda-driven issue polls. Despite advances in methodology and technology, polls remain an inexact measure of public sentiment. Their accuracy can be further compromised by slanted questions that produce faulty data. A poll produced to support an agenda should be viewed with skepticism, but polls, with their patina of scientific credibility, are often assigned value they do not deserve. The AARP's poll, for instance, was touted as an accurate rendering of public opinion even though its results were disputed by other polls conducted by the Gallup organization.[43]

Elected officials are by far the largest consumers of polls and with the high level of consumption comes a greater susceptibility to flawed advice. During the 104th Congress, leaders in both parties regularly used polls to plot strategy. In some cases, polls produced a vivid snapshot of the public mood; a useful glimpse of the public's reaction to a new idea such as eliminating federal mandates. In other cases, however, polls served to thwart the prospects of negotiation and bolstered the recalcitrant positions taken by both sides. The tense budget battle between the Clinton administration and the House Republicans in 1995 is a fine illustration of the hazards presented by poll-driven advice. In this instance, polls may have served to prolong a government shutdown. The House Republican leadership was given poll data by their own party pollsters that showed the public supported their principled stand against the president. Conversely, the president's pollsters supplied him with numbers that unequivocally backed his position.[44] Both polls presented a sanitized version of public opinion skewed to reflect a particular viewpoint. Using polls in this fashion endangers political compromise. It instills a malign form of righteousness in debate, as each side claims to be speaking for the public.

To this point, the discussion has focused almost exclusively on actions pertaining to the House, but in order for the Contract to complete its transformation into new public policies it needed to pass the Senate and be signed into law by President Clinton. Gingrich's bouyant confidence aside, he and his lieutenants realized that passage of the entire Contract was a long shot. Nevertheless, as the Contract moved swiftly through the House the Republican leadership became more optimistic for its chances in the Senate. The Senate, however, was reluctant to rubber stamp the House agenda and, as Table 5.2 shows, only passed two Contract-related bills with minor amendments. The remainder were either defeated outright or were changed substantially. Even though the Senate was controlled by Republicans, the priorities outlined in the Contract were not universally embraced by their membership. Senate Republicans had, in fact, unveiled their own seven-plank platform in September that stood apart from the Contract

Table 5.2
Legislative Successes of the Contract with America

Contract Item	House Action	Senate Action	Enacted
Congressional Accountability Act	Passed January 5, 1995	Passed January 11, 1995	Yes
Balanced Budget Amendment	Passed January 26, 1995	Failed March 2, 1995	No
Line-Item Veto	Passed February 6, 1995	Passed March 23, 1995	Partial
Taking Back the Streets Act	Passed February 7, 1995	No action taken	No
Personal Responsibility Act	Passed March 24, 1995	Passed in amended fashion	Partial
Unfunded Mandate Reform Act	Passed February 1, 1995	Passed January 27, 1995	Yes
American Dream Restoration Act	Passed April 4, 1995	Passed in amended fashion	Partial
National Security Restoration Act	Passed February 16, 1995	No action taken	No
Senior Citizens Equity Act	Passed March 12, 1995	No action taken	Partial
Job Creation and Wage Enhancement Act	Passed February 22, 1995	Passed in amended fashion	Partial
Common Sense Legal Reform Act	Passed March 7, 1995	Passed in amended fashion	No

with America. The Senate plan, entitled "Seven More in '94," included a pledge on health care reform and did not mention unfunded mandates, a line-item veto, term limits, a capital gains tax cut, or an overhaul in product liability law.[45] The fact that the Senate was unwilling to meekly accept a junior role regarding the Contract is unsurprising, given its unique political and institutional characteristics.

From a political perspective, Senate Republicans are considered less ideological than their counterparts in the House. ACU ratings (a measure of conservatism based on selected roll-call votes) show that Senate Republicans draw a lower overall score than House Republicans.[46] This was especially true in the 104th Congress. In addition, moderate figures such as Sen. Mark Hatfield (R-OR), James Jeffords (R-VT), and John Chaffee (R-RI) held positions of influence within the Senate. Aside from their party affiliation, these senators had little in common with firebrands in the House and staked out positions that put them in direct conflict with House Republicans. Senator Hatfield, for example, cast the deciding vote against the Balanced Budget Amendment and was pilloried in the House for his opposition. Even Senate Majority Leader Bob Dole, whose pedigree as a conservative is impeccable, was taken aback by the revolutionary fervor and irreverent behavior seen in the House. Dole was perhaps influenced by his own ambition. Dole, as the prohibitive favorite for the 1996 Republican presidential nomination, faced a dilemma. He could ill afford to alienate party stalwarts by actively obstructing the House agenda. Yet he could not appear to the public as Gingrich's handmaiden, lest he isolate independent and moderate voters. The contrasting political atmosphere provides one explanation for the Senate's lack of enthusiasm for the Contract, but institutional factors also played a role. The Senate's cool reception to some Contract items is an affirmation of the chamber's design. The Senate was intended, according to notes taken during the Constitutional Convention and the *Federalist Papers*, to serve as a check against the volatile House. James Madison, writing under the psuedonym Publius, outlined the purpose of the Senate in *Federalist 62*, stating, "The necessity of a senate is not less indicated by the propensity of all single and numerous assemblies to yield to the impulse of sudden and violent passions and to be seduced by factious leaders into intemperate and pernicious revolutions."[47] Madison's words could be interpreted as an uncanny forecast of the 104th Congress. Thus, the Senate's decision to slow the legislative pace appears to be a natural reaction to the House's hyperactive 100 days.

The Senate's predilection for reflection and methodogical action is indulged by Senators' electoral circumstances. Unlike House members, who must stand for reelection every two years, senators serve six-year terms. The longer term and staggered elections protect them from the more pernicious effects of the permanent campaign. I am not suggesting that senators do not take electoral consequences into account when making policy decisions. I am, however, suggesting that the Senate is more shock resistant to short-term flucuations in public opinion and, thus, less likely to be concerned with issue polls and less vulnerable to pressure applied by mass media advertising. In this institutional environment, the public relations strategies developed by consultants are apt to be less effective.

CONCLUSION

Using pollsters and political consultants as a means of promoting or denigrating policies represents an evolutionary change in the way political actors communicate with the general public. Stumping for a particular piece of legislation is not a new phenomenon. Our history is replete with examples of presidents and, to a lesser extent, legislators campaigning for programs between elections. However, the use of professional campaign operatives who utilize social science and mass marketing techniques is qualitatively different from earlier instances of public outreach.

It is tempting to draw normative conclusions about this turn of events. For some observers, the permanent campaign and the presence of political consultants at the heart of policy debates is a perversion of political discourse. Policy filtered through consultants seems cynical and somehow phony. Other critics delve deeper than political aesthetics. Journalists and public-interest advocates, for example, are dismayed by the enormous sums being funneled through political consultants to devise issue advocacy campaigns and produce polls. They contend that it is another symptom of a diseased process poisoned by money. Well-heeled interests employing consultants drown out the voices of average citizens and the exorbitant fees political consultants charge virtually precludes their use by groups without vast financial resources.[48] Although political consultants do not possess a knowledge monopoly as medical doctors and attorneys do, their specialized expertise puts them in a similar category. Just as the average citizen is incapable of performing surgery, he or she also cannot conduct a poll or organize a direct-mail campaign.

Political scholars have also offered criticism of the consulting industry's new focus. Academics such as Kathleen Hall Jamieson and James Thurber question whether consultants violate the principles of democratic accountability by providing strategic advice to elected officials, while simultaneously selling their services to private interests. It is not difficult to imagine a scenario in which the consultant doctors advice to political clients in order to appease private-sector clients. These are all valid concerns and important criticisms.

In terms of the effect on political rhetoric, consultants are often accused of channeling debate to the lowest common denominator: emotion. The Contract presents several examples where policy became obscured by emotionally charged symbolism. Through the artful work of political consultants, tort reform became a crusade to save Little League, and federal block grants were transformed into a nefarious plot to take hot lunches away from poor kids. These are visceral, powerful images that can often stir the most apathetic citizen into action. But is the political process enhanced by this sort of electronic demogoguery? On the one hand, efforts to engage the public in the debate could be seen as an enhanced form of pluralism. On the other hand, the reduction of complex issues to bold, overwrought metaphors is an affront to honest political discourse.

I would, however, caution against a broad indictment of the consulting profession, for several reasons. First, it may be unfair to single out political consultants for criticism as unelected and unaccountable figures in the policy process without mentioning similar activity by other Washington insiders. The interplay between consultants and the Republican leadership is not a frivolous matter, but they were just one of several groups who aided the Republicans. Lobbyists, for example, enjoyed a more substantial role shaping legislation than political consultants, who were primarily used to develop message strategies and cultivate public support. During the first 100 days, Republican Conference Chairman John Boehner hosted weekly meetings with representatives from the Chamber of Commerce, NFIB, and the Christian Coalition to discuss legislative priorities and, in some isolated cases, invited the groups to submit drafts of their own bills. In subsequent interviews Boehner unabashedly defended the close relationship some lobbyists had with Republican lawmakers, claiming, "The lobbyists share common principles about what the appropriate role of the federal government is."[49] As the first session wore on there were numerous examples of lobbyists coordinating vote-counting operations, putting together talking points for members, and conducting briefings for aides. All of this activity occurred despite legal restrictions and regulations governing contact between legislators and lobbyists. Activists from conservative think tanks were also involved in the legislative process. Organizations like the Heritage Foundation and the Competitive Enterprise Institute hosted orientation seminars for new members and even loaned policy experts to congressional offices for special projects.[50] Bringing to light the actions of lobbyists and think tank activists does not absolve consultants or justify their involvement in the legislative process, but it provides a context to evaluate their role.

Some of the criticism leveled at political consultants undoubtedly stems from their reputation as mercenaries. Concerns that they may be misleading their political clients for private gain are rooted in the image of the political consultant as an amoral, gun for hire. But the fact is that most of the consultants, with Dick Morris being the major exception, worked for clients whose political ideology matched their own. Frank Luntz, Bill McInturff, and Linda DiVall worked for Republicans because they are Republicans and support the party's mission. Democratic consultants such as Geoff Garin and Stan Greenberg were likely as motivated by the desire to promote a partisan agenda as they were by their lucrative contracts. As for the use of direct mail, media advertising, and polling to influence legislation, critics are on firmer ground. The Contract presents several disturbing examples where these methods were misused. The fraudulent and deceptive direct-mail campaign sponsored by the Competitive Long Distance Coalition and the push poll conducted on behalf of the AARP are egregious examples of misuse. Even honest direct-mail contact and issue polling raise questions about the legitimacy of constituent pressure. However, some of the opprobrium is overdrawn. Criticizing political consultants for using campaign tactics is little like blaming the army for warfare. Consultants run campaigns, not public education seminars. They are not hired to perform a public service.

In 1980 the political journalist cum presidential advisor Sidney Blumenthal wrote, "The campaign method of governing implies a vision of the voters as passive yet moveable; supportive of bold action, yet possessing shallow allegiances; willing to endorse new possibilities, yet afflicted with a short attention span."[51] In many respects the Contract with America is an affirmation of Blumenthal's description of the permanent campaign, as well as a testament to the media-oriented, image-laden politics practiced by modern politicians. Legislators are keenly focused on harnessing public opinion and on selling policies to an ever fickle public. Cultivating popular support is not especially newsworthy, but the appearance of a battery of political operatives to accomplish the goal is something that merits critical attention. The metamorphosis of campaign specialists into strategic policy advisors speaks to the value assigned to public opinion and public perception by our elected officials. In this environment, elections no longer provide mandates for governing. In fact, the election is simply one battle in an endless war of attrition fought over public sentiment.[52] It is inevitable that politicians with an eye to minute fluctuations of public opinion would seek the advice and services of the people best equipped to manage their public images.

NOTES

1. Maureen Dowd, "Capital's Virtual Reality: Gingrich Rides a Third Wave," *New York Times*, 1 January 1995, A1.

2. Ever since the APSA report, "Toward a More Responsible Party Government," was published in 1959, it has been accepted as a truism of American politics that legislators are incapable of unifying behind a national campaign agenda. Scholars such as Richard Fenno, David Mayhew, Morris Fiorina, and Gary Jacobson describe legislators as attentive to the particularized needs of their districts over calls for national party unity. The Contract with America is incongruent with this logic. See Richard Fenno, *Home Style: House Members and Their Districts* (Boston: Little, Brown & Co., 1978); David Mayhew, *Congress: The Electoral Connection* (New Haven: Yale University Press, 1974); Morris Fiorina, *Congress: Keystone of the Washington Establishment* (New Haven: Yale University Press, 1977); and Gary Jacobson, *The Politics of Congressional Elections*, 3rd ed. (New York: HarperCollins, 1992).

3. Donna Cassata, "Swift Progress of the Contract Inspires Awe and Concern," *CQ Weekly Report*, 1 April 1995, p. 90. For background on the dynamic between Congress and the president in the twentieth century see James Thurber, *Divided Democracy: Cooperation and Conflict between the President and Congress* (Washington, D.C.: CQ Press, 1991); Louis Fisher, *Constitutional Conflict between Congress and the President* 3rd ed. (Lawrence: University of Kansas Press, 1992). For a classic work on the ephemeral nature of presidential power see Richard Neustadt, *Presidential Power and the Modern Presidents* (New York: Free Press, 1990).

4. According to journalist Eleanor Clift, the political advisors in the Clinton White House wasted little time creating a PR machine. In early 1993, "[Stan] Greenberg proposed a policy program that would surpass even Wirthlin's: a nationwide survey each month to assess Clinton's job performance; issue surveys every other month; statewide surveys at least two a month; and six focus groups a month to allow a continuing conversation with the American people." Eleanor Clift, *War without Bloodshed* (New York: Simon and Schuster, 1996), 35.

5. Douglas Koopman, *Hostile Takeover: The House Republican Party 1980–1995* (Boston: Rowman & Littlefield, 1996).

6. James Smith, *The Idea Brokers: Think Tanks and the Rise of the New Policy Elite* (New York: The Free Press, 1991), 186.

7. Elizabeth Drew, *Showdown: The Struggle between the Gingrich Congress and the Clinton White House* (New York: Simon & Schuster, 1996), 29.

8. John Bader, *Taking the Initiative: Leadership Agendas in Congress and "The Contract with America"* (Washington, D.C.: Georgetown University Press, 1996), 78.

9. Michael Weisskopf, "Playing on the Public Pique," *Washington Post*, 27 October 1994, p. A1.

10. Despite the clever, well-financed media campaign, the vast majority of voters still did not recognize the Contract. According to a Gallup poll conducted in December 1994, fewer than 4 in 10 American voters were aware of the Contract with America. However, the same poll indicated widespread support for the Contract's initiatives, giving credence to Republican claims that the Contract was popular among the public even if they couldn't identify it. See Lydia Saad, "Contract with America Still Little Known, But Goals Have Widespread Appeal," *The Gallup Poll Monthly*, December 1994, p. 7.

11. L. Brent Bozell, "Official Media versus, the GOP," *National Review*, 12 June 1995, 47. The Republican claims were verified in a study conducted by the non-partisan

Center for Media and Public Affairs. Their research estimated that more than 8 in 10 comments about the Contract with America and congressional Republicans were negative.

12. See Samuel Kernell, *Going Public: New Strategies of Presidential Leadership* 2 ed. (Washington, D.C.: CQ Press, 1993); George C. Edwards III, *The Public Presidency* (New York: St. Martin's Press, 1983); Theodore Lowi, *The Personal President: Power Invested Promise Unfulfilled* (Ithaca: Cornell University Press, 1985); Jeffrey Tulis, *The Rhetorical Presidency* (Princeton: Princeton University Press, 1987).

13. During the initial congressional debates, Democrats touted their own poll results that showed a majority of Americans did not recognize the components of the Contract with America and that, taken as a whole, it did not represent a legislative mandate. See James Gimpel, *Fulfilling the Contract: The First 100 Days* (Boston: Allyn and Bacon, 1996).

14. Eliza Newlin Carney, "Air Strikes," *National Journal*, 15 June 1996, 1316.

15. *1998 Almanac of American Politics*, (Washington, D.C.: National Journal, 1999).

16. Doug Bandow, "Buying Justics, Plantiffs' Lawyers Reap Huge Dividends," *Richmond Dispatch*, 28 December 1999.

17. Estimated by the Center for Responsive Politics.

18. Eric Shine, "From the Folks Who Brought You Harry and Louise," *Business Week*, 17 April 1995, p. 47.

19. James Barnes, "Privatizing Politics," *National Journal*, 3 June 1995, 1313.

20. Elizabeth Kolbert, "The Special Interests Special Weapon," *New York Times*, 26 March 1995, A1.

21. Carney, "Air Strikes," 1317.

22. David Cloud and Jackie Koszczuk, "GOP's All-or-Nothing Approach Hangs on a Balanced Budget," *CQ Weekly Report*, 9 December 1995, 3713.

23. Ann Devroy, "House Republicans Get Their Talking Points," *Washington Post*, 2 February 1995, A10.

24. E.E. Schattschneider, *The Semisovereign People: A Realist's View of Democracy in America* (New York: Holt, Reinhart and Winston, 1960), 68.

25. Howard Kurtz, "In Politics, the Spin Is In," *Washington Post*, 2 April 1995, A1.

26. John Harwood, "GOP, Given Power by Voters Angry over Welfare, Seeks a Compassionate Image in Reform Debate," *Wall Street Journal*, 22 March 1995, A18.

27. Gimpel, *Fulfilling the Contract*, 96.

28. Stephen Frantzich and John Sullivan, *The C-span Revolution*. (Norman : University of Oklahoma Press, 1996).

29. Michael Weisskopf and David Maraniss, "Republican Leaders Win Battle by Defining Terms of Combat," *Washington Post*, 29 October 1995, A1.

30. David Maraniss and Michael Weisskopf, *Tell Newt to Shut Up* (New York: Simon and Schuster, 1996), 143.

31. Peter Stone, "Man with a Message," *National Journal*, 19 April 1997, 750.

32. Darrell West and Richard Francis, "Electronic Advocacy: Interest Groups and Public Policy Making," *PS: Political Science & Politics* 29 (1996): 25–29.

33. Peter Stone, "A Contract That Paid Off," *National Journal*, 11 February 1995, 362.

34. Stone, "Man with a Message," 751.

35. Barnes, "Privatizing Politics," 1315.

36. Richard Cohen, "The Gingrich Team: Joe Gaylord," *National Journal*, 14 January 1995, 73.

37. Congress, House, Committee on Standards of Official Conduct, *Summary of Activities 104th Congress* (Washington, D.C.: GPO, 1997), 13.

38. Deborah Beck, et. al. "Issue Advocacy Advertising During 1996: A Catalog," Annenberg Public Policy Center, University of Pennsylvania available at (www.appcpenn.org).

39. The industry coalition that helped pass several Contract items was called Project Relief. As *Washington Post* reporter David Maraniss ruefully notes, "The name is more befitting a 3rd world humanitarian aid effort rather than a corporate alliance working to roll back government regulations."

40. West and Francis, "Electronic Advocacy," *PS*, 28.

41. Kirk Victor, "Astroturf Lobbying Takes a Hit," *National Journal*, 23 September 1995, 2359.

42. Barnes, "Privatizing Politics," and Michael Wines, "Feeling Down? How About a New Pollster," *New York Times*, 7 May 1995.

43. A Gallup poll published in *USA Today* on May 22, 1996, showed that 86 percent of those surveyed favored a Balanced Budget Amendment.

44. Thomas Edsall, "Polls Bolster Both Sides in Bitter Fight over Balanced Budget," *Washington Post*, 25 December 1995, A12.

45. Steve Langdon, "Contract Dwarfs Senate GOP 's Pledge," *CQ Weekly Report*, 25 February 1995, 578.

46. Michael Barone, ed. *1996 Almanac of American Politics* (Washington, D.C.: National Journal, 1997).

47. *Federalist 62*, *The Federalist Papers,* ed. Clinton Rossiter (New York: Penguin, 1961), 379.

48. Darrell West and Burdett Loomis, *The Sound of Money: How Political Interests Get What They Want* (New York: WW. Norton, 1998).

49. Peter Stone, "Follow the Leaders," *National Journal*, 24 June 1995, 1640 and Jill Abramson, "In GOP Controlled Congress Lobbyists Remain As Powerful As Ever - And Perhaps More Visible," *Wall Street Journal*, 20 April 1995, A14.

50. Louis Jacobson, "Think Tanks on a Roll," *National Journal*, 8 July 1995, 1767.

51. Sidney Blumenthal, *The Permanent Campaign* (Boston: Beacon Press, 1980), p. 298.

52. The military metaphor is especially appropriate when discussing political consultants. Their lexicon is studded with military terminology such as "rapid response", "battle team" and "message warfare", etc.

6

The Prescription Drug Debate: Flo Makes Her Debut

The anticlimactic failure of the 1994 health care reform effort was a bitter disappointment to President Clinton, his allies on Capitol Hill, and the varied public-interest groups that had lobbied on behalf of national health insurance. Faint hopes for action on a smaller scale in the 104th Congress were dashed a few months later with the ascendance of the new Republican majority. The House Republican's ideological blueprint for governing, the Contract with America, pointedly ignored health care and focused instead on traditional conservative issues such as tax relief, welfare reform, and strengthening national defense. At the beginning of 1995 it was easy to see why health care reform advocates would be disheartened to the point of defeatism. They had squandered a golden opportunity and the subsequent shift in political power seemed to doom their agenda to the margins for the foreseeable future. Initially, their pessimistic outlook was confirmed by congressional retreat. Even congressional Democrats that had lent support to the concepts outlined by President Clinton were wary of tackling health care again. Many in the party attributed the stunning electoral defeat to the botched health care reform effort. Meanwhile, the new majority in Congress saw its success as a vindication of its steadfast opposition to nationalized health care. Yet the assorted policy problems associated with the American health care system, a lack of coverage for millions of Americans, skyrocketing costs, and the unmet health needs of America's elderly did not disappear, and in fact, by some objective economic measures, they grew worse. Prescient Washington observers concluded that it was simply a matter of time before health care would return to the forefront of the political debate.

Five years after his crushing defeat, President Clinton unveiled a new health care initiative to provide prescription drug coverage to seniors as part of Medicare. Although his proposal was not on the order of magnitude of his earlier efforts, establishing a new drug entitlement for America's 40 million Medicare-eligible seniors would cost the federal government several hundred billion dollars over the next decade. More significant, a drug benefit represented a major augmentation of government influence in the nation's haphazard private health care delivery system.[1] President Clinton's renewed interest in health care legislation was generated by an acknowledgment of a serious policy problem and a fairly facile political calculation. Spending on prescription drugs exploded during the 1990s. According to some estimates the average price of a prescription was growing by 10 percent a year, triple the rate of inflation, and total retail spending on prescription drugs was rising at an alarming rate of 20 percent per year.[2] The elderly bore the heaviest burden brought on by the meteoric rise in drug costs. Not only did they purchase more medicines than any other identifiable demographic group, they were also more likely to be living on a fixed income. One did not need an advanced degree in economics to understand that double-digit increases in drug costs could not be sustained within a population whose incomes remained stagnant. The long-range forecast was even gloomier. In 1998 the Congressional Budget Office estimated that drug spending by Medicare enrollees on drugs would total $1.3 trillion over the next decade, and per capita spending for the Medicare population would climb from $1,756 in 2000 to $4,4818 in 2011.[3] Senior citizens' groups were keenly aware of the looming crisis and had made instituting a drug benefit their number one legislative priority. Public outcry, however, was not confined to the elderly. Independent polling data indicated that a majority of Americans supported a new federal benefit to cover drug costs for seniors.[4] According to a national survey conducted by Harvard opinion researcher Robert Blendon in 2000, 87 percent of the survey sample supported a federal prescription drug benefit.[5] From a purely political perspective, the party that delivered a solution to the prescription drug problem could reap the rewards at the ballot box.

For scholars working in the vanguard of interest-group theory, the legislative battle over prescription drug coverage presents an excellent opportunity to test the validity of some conventional assumptions, such as the inherent imbalance of power between "business" interests and "public" interests, as well as the purported connection between campaign donations and legislative activity.[6] The list of organized interests actively lobbying the issue included membership goliaths like the AARP, professional medical associations such as the American Medical Association, and of course the insurance industry. The loudest voice in the Washington pressure community, however, belonged to America's drug manufacturers. The pharmaceutical industry has an unparalleled presence in Washington, with 625 registered lobbyists, more than any other industry, and a combined annual lobbying and campaign contribution-budget of $197 million.[7] Drugmakers were petrified that a new federal entitlement would inevitably lead to federal price controls on prescription medicines as a way to reduce costs. Drug-company executives universally viewed price controls as a catastrophe that would flatten their profits and cripple their research budgets simultaneously. In light of this serious threat, the pharmaceutical industry pledged an enormous sum of money to defeating the president's plan.

The debate over prescription drugs during the 106th Congress matched the 1994 health care reform battle in terms of partisan intensity. It further accented the vast differences between the two parties visions for the future of American health care, with Democrats favoring an expansion of an existing government program and Republicans touting market-based proposals that would channel benefits through private insurance companies. The two conflicts share another salient feature the presence of political consultants and the manifest use of campaign-style tactics. Interest groups on both sides of the issue funded television commercials and direct-mail appeals. They promulgated grassroots campaigns and made determined efforts to sway opinions at the elite level as well as in the general populace. The vast amount of money spent on paid media again drew scornful criticism from the White House and resulted in an unprecedented "summit" with drug industry CEO's to negotiate an end to their public campaign against the president's proposal. Meanwhile, pollsters employed by party leaders in Congress were instrumental in developing policy messages and charting legislative strategy. House Republicans, for example, jettisoned several core conservative principles and embraced a moderate approach after polling data revealed a potential electoral disaster in November.

The prescription drug debate, like health care reform and the Contract with America, offers an excellent opportunity to explore the impact political consultants and campaign-oriented tactics have on the legislative process. As in the earlier case studies, the involvement of political consultants and the use of campaign-style pressure tactics to influence the outcome of a public policy debate raise some important questions. First, there is reason to speculate that the mass media campaigns and direct-mail outreach heightened partisan tensions and served as a corrosive agent with respect to executive-congressional relations. Although the abiding animosity that existed between the Clinton Administration and the Republican Congress had reached its apex during the impeachment ordeal, the ad campaigns that attacked the president's plan only fueled the atmosphere of mutual distrust. The incontrovertible evidence of past cooperation between drugmakers and Republicans in Congress coupled with their mutual support for a free-market solution led the Clinton administration to forge a link between drug-company opposition and Republican policies. Second, interest groups that market a particular policy vision to the general public under the guise of voter education are often guilty of misrepresenting the facts. Simplistic ads and poll-tested catchphrases inflame public passions rather than enlighten citizens. Individuals and interest groups have a constitutionally guaranteed right to say what they want regardless of the accuracy or provenance. Yet the waves of propaganda that often follow a policy proposal can erode public confidence in our political institutions without revealing the nature of the problem. It is a normative question, but one that merits examination without prejudice. Finally, the enormous imbalance in spending by interest groups opposed to the Clinton proposal raises questions about the efficacy of issue advertisements and elite bias in American politics. The deep pockets of the pharmaceutical industry were used to great advantage, as they bombarded targeted audiences with anti government messages crafted by political consultants. Other groups with a vested interest in the outcome, namely impoverished senior citizens, were incapable of mounting such a campaign. Were unprompted grassroots voices drowned out by the cacophony of fabricated direct mail and astroturf lobbying?

MEDICARE AND PRESCRIPTION DRUGS: FROM ITS ORIGINS TO TODAY

When Medicare was enacted in 1965 it was heralded as a pivotal expansion of the social safety net. At the time, nearly half the elderly had no health insurance and many others had inadequate coverage. As I chronicled in Chapter 3, the path that policy makers followed included several frustrating dead ends before a successful avenue presented itself. Medicare's triumph, however, was not total. Indeed, the clever decision by Ways and Means Chairman Wilbur Mills to combine hospital coverage and physician services under Medicare, albeit with separate financing arrangements, may have been a political masterstroke, but one that fostered unintended problems. The creation of Medicare part A (hospital care) and part B (physician services), with different forms, insurance provisions, and fiscal intermediaries sowed the seeds for future dysfunction and, according to health policy scholar Ted Marmor, was a prime factor in the exponential increase in Medicare costs.[8] Aside from the obvious structural flaw, critics also noted that the lack of coverage for outpatient prescription drugs was an acute oversight. The decision to leave out prescription drug coverage was not taken lightly, but budgetary concerns as well as political expediency necessitated the omission. Moreover, no one in 1965 could foresee the astounding advances in pharmacological science that would lead to the dramatic increase in drug therapies.

Prior to 1999, policy makers made two major attempts to establish a prescription drug plan as part of Medicare. Both efforts ended in failure, one spectacularly so, and both efforts informed the actions of policy makers addressing the issue in 1999. In 1988 the Congress, with the grudging acquiescence of the Reagan administration, passed the Medicare Catastrophic Coverage Act (MCCA). The law was intended to protect seniors in the event of an expensive medical emergency that left them hospitalized for a long period. In addition, it expanded Medicare coverage for a host of needs, including hospice care, home health services, and mammography services, and provided extra financial help to impoverished elderly by guaranteeing premium payments for physician services. The bill also provided for the first time a prescription drug benefit for all outpatient drugs, subject to a $600 deductible. The entire package was to be financed through a new supplemental premium imposed on higher-income seniors. In essence, a tax was levied on wealthy seniors to pay for a benefit for all seniors.[9] The new superpremium was controversial, but Democratic congressional leaders and the AARP believed that the benefits greatly outweighed the inconvenience to a small set of seniors.

In less than a year the MCCA was repealed, mainly due to a firestorm of protests orchestrated by seniors groups that balked at the higher premiums. Led by an upstart seniors organization called the National Committee to Preserve Social Security and Medicare (NCPSM), throngs of seniors picketed the offices of senior congressional Democrats. The NCPSM also prompted a massive write-in campaign to congressional offices. The group sent out shrill direct-mail appeals to seniors distorting the financing details of the legislation and succeeded in creating the impression that all of the elderly, not just the affluent, would be burdened by the extra premium. In one memorable scene, Dan Rostenkowski, the powerful Chairman of the Ways and Means Committee, was filmed by a Chicago television news crew fleeing his district office with dozens of angry elderly protesters in his wake.[10] The intense protests caught many members by surprise, but they reacted swiftly. In November 1999 the MCCA was repealed by a wide margin in the House by a vote of 352 to 63. The Senate quickly followed suit and concurred unanimously. The immediate lesson learned by legislators was as simple as it was instructive: Any tampering with Medicare, even constructive tampering, risked stirring the opposition of a powerful, organized grassroots constituency. Future efforts needed the unwavering support of America's organized senior citizens or they would be doomed to failure. It also revealed a serious disconnect between the Washington-based leaders of the AARP and the elderly citizens living outside the beltway. Policy makers could no longer rely on the support of Washington-based advocates as an accurate proxy for elderly citizens' opinion. Seniors groups were diversifying and splintering, with smaller, more aggressive organizations making their voice heard.

In 1994 prescription drug coverage was merged into President Clinton's health care reform plan. Clinton's health care advisors, mindful of the 1988 debacle, sought the political support of the elderly by adding a prescription drug benefit and long-term care for the severely disabled to the existing Medicare framework without a premium increase. The overture failed because the various interest groups representing seniors deemed the modest incentives an inadequate response to the long-term care problems faced by the elderly. Also, by targeting benefits to a small segment of the elderly (those below the poverty threshold or close to it), President Clinton threatened to undermine the pillar of universality that kept the program popular among seniors. Seniors groups were outspoken in their criticism of what they perceived as a high-handed attempt to transform Medicare from a universal program to a means-tested welfare benefit.[11] A prescription drug benefit for seniors was never more than a small detail in the grand vision of universal coverage. Five years later, however, when congressional attention narrowed to focus on updating the Medicare program, prescription drugs became a driving force.

On 29 June 1999 President Clinton unveiled a plan that he claimed would keep Medicare solvent for the next generation of beneficiaries and make it behave more like a private insurance company. In the late 1990s, solvency was the watchword used by politicians anxious to preserve America's cumbersome entitlement system. There was growing concern, particularly among the baby boom generation, that Social Security and Medicare would buckle under the strain of providing for them during their retirement years. The fear was magnified by pessimistic reports produced by program trustees that predicted Social Security and Medicare would begin to run massive deficits in less than two decades. President Clinton's bold proposal to stabilize Medicare also contained an important expansion of the program through the addition of a prescription drug benefit. The drug benefit was considered crucial in order to attract the political support of America's powerful seniors' lobby. In his press conference the President declared, "This is a drug benefit our seniors can afford, at a price America can afford."[12] Participation in the drug plan was not compulsory, but the Clinton administration's health experts predicted that most people would choose it because it presented such a good bargain. For a small premium of $24 a month, Medicare would cover half the beneficiaries' prescription drug costs up to an annual limit of $2,000. The premium would increase gradually to $44 by 2008, and so would the benefit: to an annual maximum of $2,500.

The House Republicans greeted the president's magnanimous proposal with wary skepticism. Fiscal conservatives wondered how the president could accomplish his overarching goal of Medicare solvency while attaching a new benefit that reasonable estimates assumed would cost the government an additional $40 billion a year. Nevertheless, the Republican leadership, recognizing an important election-year issue, signaled a willingness to work with the White House. America's drug manufacturers, however, were quick to attack the plan as a subversive attempt to establish federal price controls for prescription medication. In testimony before the House and the Senate, drug-company executives linked their apprehension over a drug benefit to the impact it would have on the development of new medicines. They argued that building into Medicare a new federal drug entitlement would be inordinately expensive and that the resulting budgetary pressure to control costs would eventually lead to federally mandated price controls. Price controls would ruin the pharmaceutical industry by erasing the financial incentive for innovation and thus harm the consumer by drastically reducing the number of new medicines brought to market. Although President Clinton and his supporters in Congress were dismissive of the drug-company logic, it was not a frivolous argument.[13] Independent studies supported the contention that price controls would adversely impact research and development of new drugs. The drug companies concern for their profits, however, was not echoed in the White House. The enmity that existed between the Clinton administration and the pharmaceutical industry dated back to 1994, when administration officials eagerly cast the industry as villains in the health care drama. In the heat of battle, Hillary Clinton went so far as to claim that the industry was a heartless profiteering cartel that made its money on the backs of the elderly. The drug manufacturers, for their part, made no apologies for being profitable, but pointed out that for every success like Zocor or Praxil, there were thousands of unknown failures. The companies maintained that their financial reward was an accurate reflection of the risk they took to develop new drugs.[14]

According to the Clinton administration, the industry's alarmist accusations of price controls were gross exaggerations. The president's proposal envisioned the widespread use of pharmacy benefit managers to organize the market for elderly drug buyers and thereby give them the necessary purchasing power to extract discount rates. The rationale was simple: The elderly pay higher drug costs because their economic weight is dispersed. Pooling them into regional purchasing units would give them leverage. Pharmacy benefit managers had already proven their ability to lower drug costs for private health plans by nearly 25 percent. The Clinton administration hoped that their involvement would result in similar savings for the Medicare program.[15] Unsurprisingly, the drug companies had a different opinion.

Three weeks after President Clinton's announcement, the drug companies, through their trade association, The Pharmaceutical Manufacturers Association (PhRMA), outlined their opposition to the Clinton plan and declared their intention to fight it with a $30-million advertising campaign. Drug-company spokespeople made it clear that they did not oppose the addition of a drug benefit for Medicare per se, but remained adamantly opposed to any proposal that even hinted at price controls. They claimed that under the president's clever use of purchasing alliances, the Federal Health Care Financing Administration would become the world's largest drug purchaser. The arrangement would lead to de facto price controls as the government inevitably sought to regulate costs. It was, a drug-company representative later admitted, a stretch to conclude the president's plan called for price controls. Nevertheless, with the industry's future profits at risk, they began an expensive, coordinated campaign to defeat the president's plan.[16]

In July PhRMA hired Republican political consultant Alex Castellanos to develop an advertising campaign that would capitalize on public unease with big government initiatives. His ads would be built on a foundation of survey data produced by Republican pollster Bill McInturff. PhRMA also sought to generate grassroots pressure on Congress and hired the well-established APCO & Associates to coordinate its outside lobbying activities. The industry continued to pursue its agenda with a stable of Washington D.C.-based contract lobbyists, but the bulk of the lobbying money was dedicated to campaign-style issue advocacy.[17] PhRMA's onerous task was complicated by its poor public image. Opinion polls indicated that the general public did not hold the pharmaceutical manufacturers in high esteem. More to the point, the public overwhelmingly favored the president over them when it came to prescription drug policy. Executives understood from the outset that an overt attack on a popular new entitlement could result in a backlash. To shield itself from public ire, PhRMA helped create the innocuously titled Citizens for Better Medicare (CBM), a coalition whose self-described objective was to educate the public and advocate for seniors health care needs. Organized under Chapter 527 of the IRS Code, Citizens for Better Medicare was a non-profit entity that could spend unlimited amounts of money to "educate" the public with issue ads and direct mail as long as they did not campaign for federal candidates. Until 2000, 527 groups were not required by law to disclose information about donors or the amounts raised and spent. Public watchdog groups like Common Cause dubbed 527 groups "stealth PAC's" because they were usually used as auxiliary, unregulated outlets for campaign spending.[18]

Later in the summer of 1999, Citizens for Better Medicare introduced television viewers in the Washington, D.C., area to Flo, a sprightly elderly woman with a message about Medicare reform. Flo wanted seniors to know that Congress would soon consider legislation that could interfere with their current health care arrangement. According to Flo, a new, one-size-fits-all government program could result in federal bureaucrats overriding doctors' decisions on which drugs to prescribe. In Flo's debut commercial, she finished her appeal with a memorable tag line, "I don't want big government in my medicine cabinet," that hearkened back to the Harry and Louise commercials from 1994.[19] The second ad starring Flo had a more ominous message. She claimed that some of the ideas circulating on Capitol Hill would "chill promising research" and "displace existing private coverage with a big-government run plan." Although the ads skirted an outright denouncement of the Clinton proposal, the criticism was hardly ambiguous. Indeed, Citizens for Better Medicare was relying on viewers to draw a connection between news coverage of the president's plan and Flo's invective.[20] Spokesman Tim Ryan said, "The group was trying to raise awareness of the Medicare issue and point out or critique plans that don't meet our principles...advertising is an important way to communicate with a majority of Americans, particularly seniors who don't know the debate is going on here."[21] Citizens for Better Medicare previewed the ads for the Washington policy community, but it was clear that they intended to selectively air the ads around the country. During the August congressional recess, television viewers from Maine to Montana became acquainted with Flo.

In late September the White House summoned executives from six of the largest pharmaceutical companies to scold them for the propaganda campaign sponsored by Citizens for Better Medicare. Administration spokesman Chris Jennings told the media that President Clinton believed the ads were "false, misleading, inaccurate, unfair and destructive." The president's objective for the closed-door session was to dissuade the executives from poisoning the public debate before legislative work even began. The White House wanted to avoid responding to the charges made in the commercials directly, a mistake President Clinton made in 1994 when he essentially bestowed greater visibility and credibility upon Harry and Louise by attacking them in the press. Drug industry CEO's, for their part, were anxious to steer clear of a destructive confrontation with a president who was adept at using the bully pulpit.[22] The summit, however, was a failure, in part because industry fears over price controls were stronger than their fear of the president's wrath. President Clinton's personal attempt to cajole the industry gave way to a harsher, more combative tone. In October the White House initiated a political offensive tailored to rebut Flo's criticisms and simultaneously portray the industry as an obstinate, greedy interest group that put selfish profits ahead of the public good. White House health policy advisor Joel Johnson said of the drug manufacturers, "The pharmaceutical industry has chosen the path of confrontation rather than cooperation. The president extended an olive branch to the Industry. They snapped it off. Their ad campaign is evidence of that." The president's belligerent posture came as Citizen's for Better Medicare was orchestrating a write-in campaign to Congress among senior citizens, urging members to reject the Clinton plan.[23]

By January the limitations of a paid media campaign became apparent, especially in light of the free media advantage owned by the president. Presidential scholars such as Richard Neustadt, Samuel Kernell, and Jeffrey Tulis have identified the president's ability to shape and lead public opinion as his preeminent informal power.[24] His ability to set an agenda and promote a policy vision with a singular voice cannot be matched by any other political actor. An interest group, no matter how well funded and unified, is at a distinct disadvantage in a public relations battle with the president. Facing the threat of a public rebuke by President Clinton during his State of the Union address, drug-industry executives decided to suspend their issue-advocacy work and call a truce with the White House.[25]

To the casual observer the partisan division of power, with Democrats occupying the White House and Republicans controlling both chambers of Congress, would lead one to assume that legislative gridlock is the norm. Moreover, the intense partisan tension that existed between President Clinton and his adversaries on Capitol Hill would seem to preclude any large-scale policy initiatives from moving forward. Conventional wisdom, however, can be misleading. In a study of divided government during the 1980s, conducted by David Mayhew of Yale University, he concluded that government was no less "productive" during periods of split party control as it was during unified periods.[26] Mayhew's study has yet to be replicated for President Clinton's tenure, but anecdotal evidence suggests that his argument is still valid. President Clinton's repeated clashes with congressional Republicans did not preclude passage of welfare reform, which is arguably the most sweeping social policy reform in two decades. Nor did it obstruct him from working with Republican leaders to pass a far-reaching modernization of banking law and a radical deregulation of the telecommunications industry. In each case, the president's determination was matched by willingness on the part of congressional Republicans to compromise. Partisanship notwithstanding, a prescription drug benefit was of interest to Republican congressional leaders as well as President Clinton.

Legislative work on the drug benefit began in earnest in early 2000. The House Republican leadership debuted their prescription drug plan in April. It provided a 100 percent government benefit for low-income elderly (defined as within 150% of the poverty threshold) and subsidized the voluntary purchase of insurance for drug coverage for other seniors. Like the president's plan, Republicans would utilize purchasing alliances to obtain an insurance discount for seniors. In addition, the government would pay 100 percent of drug costs over certain ceiling through private insurance subsidies. Interestingly, the GOP plan was criticized by seniors groups for being too generous to the poor and not generous enough to seniors in middle and upper income brackets.[27] The pharmaceutical companies did not endorse the Republican proposal, but it did meet their paramount concern: it did not contain language that could be construed as price controls. Savings would come from lower insurance premiums that would emerge from the creation of regional purchasing alliances. The urgent drive to pass a drug bill before the 106th Congress adjourned was propelled by polls that foretold of the potential for public retaliation in November if a plan did not emerge. In a memo to congressional Republicans, GOP pollster Glen Bolger stated, "It's very important that Republicans stick together and pass a bill. If they don't pass a bill they'll pay a price at the ballot box." Some Republican members admitted that it was more important to pass a bill than to argue over policy details.[28] On June 28, 2000 the House of Representatives passed Medicare Rx 2000 by a razor thin margin of 217 to 214. Whatever happened in the Senate, House Republicans could tell their constituents that they passed a drug bill.

In later negotiations with the Senate, House Republican leaders compromised on two critical parts. First, House Republicans agreed to make Medicare drug benefits an "entitlement," with all the attendant legal protections. Second, they agreed that drug companies must pay a return-on-investment fee to the Medicare program for government-funded research.[29] In anticipation of Senate action, Citizens for Better Medicare revived its mass media assault on the Clinton plan. Flo was retired shortly before the summer, but in her place were a new series of commercials crafted by Alex Castellanos as well a more aggressive cybernet strategy. In an unusual test of the burgeoning power of the Internet, CBM tried to entice young people to their Web site by offering free $10 phone cards and urging them to call their grandparents to talk about Medicare. It seems unlikely, however, that the quixotic bid for proxy lobbying had any impact on seniors' opinion. Another ad depicted a dispirited group of Canadian senior citizens taking a bus from Canada to the United States to escape their restrictive, highly regulated health care system. Citizens for Better Medicare continued to draw approbation from congressional Democrats. "Look at the name," grumbled Representative Rosa DeLauro (D-CT) "These are not citizens and they certainly aren't for better Medicare. Their interest is to distort the issue and frighten the elderly rather than have a debate on an affordable plan."[30]

POLITICAL CONSULTING, CAMPAIGN TACTICS, AND PRESCRIPTION DRUGS

For all the *sturm und drang* that accompanied the year-long prescription drug debate, it died a relatively quiet legislative death. Despite eleventh-hour negotiations by moderate members to craft an acceptable centrist bill, opposition in the Senate from ideologues in both parties prevented its consideration. In September 2000, Senator William Roth (R-DE), chairman of the Senate Finance Committee, offered a $31 billion temporary benefit for low-income seniors. GOP leadership pulled the bill from the Senate floor, however, out of concern that it would lose to a more generous Democratic alternative. The issue remained in the public spotlight throughout the fall due to the presidential campaign, but Governor Bush and Vice President Gore preferred to use the issue as a rhetorical foil. Passage of a prescription drug bill before the election would benefit neither candidate. Congressional leaders made a rational decision to wait until the next Congress, when a new man would occupy the White House.

Electronic issue advocacy has been connected to a number of failings in American politics, ranging from peddling falsehoods to depressing citizen confidence in our political institutions, but it is the conspicuous connection to well-funded interest groups that draws the most vociferous criticism.[31] Self-appointed public watchdog groups like Ralph Nader's PIRG organization and the government ethics group Common Cause were so dismayed by the proliferation of electronic issue advocacy that they made regulating the 527 political action groups that sponsor ads one of their legislative priorities. Clean-government groups, which tend to view the nexus of money and politics as the primary flaw in American democracy, are disturbed by wealthy interest groups brazen efforts to manipulate public sentiment through paid media. A number of political scientists share their concern and see electronic advocacy as a serious threat to pluralist democracy. Darrell West and Burdett Loomis, for example, see large, well-funded groups employing contrived grassroots movements, television ads, and direct mail to crowd out broad-based but poorly funded social movements.[32] Policy purists also argue that electronic advocacy and direct mail is often part of a larger misinformation campaign that plays on citizens' fears. Interest groups are not obligated to tell every side of the story, but the freedom to embellish and persuade should not be taken as a license to deceive the electorate.[33] All of the afore mentioned criticisms were on prominent display in the year-long political battle over a prescription drug benefit. Television, as all good political consultants know, is an excellent way to tell a story. Consultants have long recognized the persuasive power of arresting imagery and television allegories. Unfortunately, as a consequence of its brevity or perhaps the nature of the medium, a 30-second television ad has a strong inclination toward hyperbole and toward what critics often describe as fear mongering. The tendency is particularly evident in opposition ads. The Flo narratives contain several examples of half-truths and exaggerations that were intended to activate latent public fears. In one advertisement, for instance, Flo warns that President Clinton's proposal would "chill promising research with bureaucracy or price controls." The ad took an unlikely scenario, the advent of federal price controls, and presented it as an indisputable fact. With Flo's folksy delivery and non confrontational line of reasoning, the creators pursued the same strategy that worked well for the health insurance industry with Harry and Louise. In the first series of ads they refrained from attacking President Clinton or his plan explicitly. The objective during the early stages was to soften public support for a drug benefit by sowing the seeds of doubt. By raising concerns about the president's proposal, the drug industry could credibly claim that their campaign was an attempt to drive support to alternative plans.

The issue ads were part of a larger campaign to focus public attention on the lesser-known costs associated with a drug entitlement, rather than the more obvious benefits. Public support for a prescription drug benefit was high, but when survey participants were confronted with potential consequences, such as a reduction in the number of new medicines, support declined. Poll data emboldened consultants to accentuate the negative. It also provided them a reliable lexicon with which to build their arguments. The use of the pejorative phrase "big government," for example, was intended to prompt many Americans to put whatever conservative attitudes they harbored toward government to the forefront when thinking about prescription drug policy. Any proposal allied with big government automatically lacks credibility with a substantial number of citizens. It is no surprise, then, that the signature line uttered by Flo was "I don't want big government in my medicine cabinet." "Washington bureaucrat" is another phrase that elicits a visceral negative response. GOP pollster Frank Luntz encouraged Republican legislators to remind the public that Democratic proposals would put Washington bureaucrats in charge of their prescriptions. The irony is that the health care needs of most senior citizens are provided by a very popular, successful "big government" plan run by "Washington bureaucrats".[34]

Accusations of price controls infuriated the White House, but at least the first series of ads were presenting a defensible point of view. Other claims made by Citizens for Better Medicare in the Flo campaign were more dubious. In one ad Flo argues that the president's plan would "displace seniors existing private coverage with a big government run plan." The implication is that that government would force seniors to forfeit the insurance coverage they already enjoy. In reality, President Clinton's plan would supplement existing policies and provide a government safety net of last resort for poor seniors. Other opposition groups went further and crossed the line dividing fact and fiction by providing flagrantly misleading information. United Seniors Association, in a direct-mail broadside sent to its 500,000 dues-paying members, asserted that the new Medicare rules would prevent seniors from paying for private insurance outside the new government program. In essence, United Seniors accused the Clinton administration of criminalizing the purchase of supplemental health insurance. Under both prescription drug plans, Republican and Democrat, participation would be voluntary and would not, under any circumstance, interfere with seniors' freedom to purchase supplemental drug insurance. It is the general absence of specific information about the Clinton proposal that challenges the claim made by CBM that the ads were an attempt to educate the public.

Flo's creators as well as the authors of the inflammatory direct-mail outreach were operating from a simple premise based on a set of equally simple assumptions. It is as follows: the public, absent a national crisis, is generally risk averse and skeptical of large scale government initiatives; they are particularly sensitive to changes in well-established programs. Political consultants synthesize this anxiety and transform it into a commercial or a mailing. By using the right catchphrases they can dissuade or outright scare the public away from a proposal without ever specifying details or facts. The degradation of the public's confidence in government action is perhaps the most damaging consequence of the permanent campaign. Political consultants, acting on behalf of their clients, are naturally myopic when it comes to the institutional ramifications of their actions. They remain unburdened by such concerns because they have a simple, clear objective: promoting their client's interest. Political scholars, however, should be troubled by political consultants ability to diminish our collective willingness to take on challenges by tapping into suspicions and irrational fears.[35]

Flo never attained the near mythic status of Harry and Louise, in part because public support for a prescription drug benefit remained constant throughout 1999 and 2000. Despite the millions of dollars spent to create a negative impression of President Clinton's plan, public opinion did not shift. According to the Gallup organization, in a national survey conducted in September 2000 77 percent of the respondents supported greater government intervention to alleviate rising health care costs. In an explicit question about government expansion of the Medicare program to include a new prescription drug benefit, 57 percent of the respondents supported a new federal entitlement; only 26 percent supported a Republican alternative to provide tax subsidies to pay for private coverage.[36] A cursory evaluation of Citizens for Better Medicare's public relations campaign could rightly conclude that it was a colossal waste of money. After a full year, public opinion on the addition of a prescription drug benefit to Medicare remained virtually unchanged. Issue ads, however should not be judged in such limited terms. An issue ad campaign can be deemed a success if it provides essential political cover for policy makers who in turn support the position of the interest group sponsoring the ad. Legislators, for example, that are predisposed to a policy value independent ads that validate their stance. According to Kara Kennedy, a former communications aide to Speaker Newt Gingrich, "We had discussions with [outside] groups where we have told them that you need to do something for the member who has been out there on their issue. You need to show them why this is important."[37] Indeed, issue ads as part of a defensive strategy worked well. President Clinton's plan did not pass Congress and the argument against price controls prevailed, as evidenced by reluctance on the part of legislators to accept strict cost control measures. The ads also gave legislators packaged reasons why price controls would be harmful; reasons that could be recycled for constituents during the reelection campaign.

The issue ads draw most of the critical attention from the press, but an equally important element of the outside lobbying strategy is grassroots activity. Politicians and consultants alike recognize the power of grassroots advocacy. The quick congressional reaction to orchestrated protests following the passage of the MCCA is a prime example. Political consultants, for their part, understand that repeated citizen contact can trump all other forms of lobbying. Consultants specializing in citizen mobilization maintain that a major policy that does not possess an integrated grassroots advocacy component will not be taken seriously.[38] Grassroots contact, whether in the form of a mass mailing or whether it is a scheduled "drop by" of concerned citizens, will draw members' attention.

"Sure," says Todd Funk, legislative director for Congresswoman Nancy Johnson, "we keep a running count of mail, even if we know it is being generated by some interest group. Mail is mail."[39]

Grassroots advocacy is not limited to phone banks and postcard campaigns. The most sophisticated also utilize opinion primers, local community figures who can lead or organize greater numbers of citizens. The power of local opinion leaders was chronicled in Richard Fenno's seminal work, *Home Style*. Fenno described the various concentric circles of advisors that legislators' employ, and one of the most important are prominent local citizens who possess a particular expertise or insight.[40] Physicians, insurance agents, and religious leaders are just some of the local citizens that Fenno identifies as "primary constituents." Fenno's book was written in 1978, but his thesis is still valid, perhaps more so. Paid lobbyists cannot match the credibility of local citizens. The importance of citizen contact cannot be overstated, particularly in the current era of civic disengagement. With fewer and fewer Americans bothering to vote and a growing number refusing to identify with either political party, legislators understand that their political future is in the hands of a dwindling number of activists.

A number of interest groups used coordinated grassroots advocacy to influence policy makers during the prescription drug debate, all with varying degrees of success. Citizens for Better Medicare, accused by opponents of being a sham group, touted 100,000 members nationwide. The drive to recruit members was lead by APCO Associates, a well-established Washington, D.C.-based consultancy. The express goal was to get local opinion leaders to begin discussing the Clinton plan using the same terminology seen on the television ads starring Flo. The hoped-for result would be an echo chamber repeating the same message and reinforcing a negative impression of the plan. Ben Goddard, mastermind of the Harry and Louise campaign explained, "The target [of a media campaign] is really opinion leaders. We call these folks informed Americans and they are about 27% of the populace. And these are the folks who write letters to the editor, they write to politicians, they write checks, they volunteer in the community. They have a disproportionate impact. They are the folks who are actually going to talk to the member of Congress. They are the folks who are going to create the impression that there is a change of opinion going on."[41]

Smaller groups with less financial means relied heavily on grassroots action to counter the narratives promoted by the drug manufacturers. The National Council of Senior Citizens (NCSC), a liberal advocacy group sponsored by the AFL-CIO, boasted a 2.5-million person membership of citizen activists. At the height of the Flo ad campaign the group conducted a made-for-tv protest on Capitol Hill. The protesters, chanting, "Flo must go" and holding placards denouncing PhRMA, hoped to garner free media and amplify their message of support for President Clinton's drug coverage plan.[42] Attempts to capitalize on sympathetic news stories, however, are a poor substitute for a coordinated mass media campaign. Wealthy groups use their superior resources to frame the debate. The NCSC protest, in fact, highlights the impotence of poorer groups. They were forced to confront a fictional character rather than emphasize their policy goals. Herein lies the real value of political consultants within a policy-making context. By virtue of their experience and skill in developing and promoting campaign themes, they enable their clients to rise above the din of voices clamoring for the attention of policy-makers and citizens alike.

The failure to pass a prescription drug bill led to the usual exercise in partisan blame assignation. President Clinton accused Republicans of playing politics with the health needs of senior citizens, while Republicans derided the president's efforts as empty sloganeering. As mentioned earlier, the animus that existed between President Clinton and congressional Republicans, particularly the House leadership, transcended political styles. The ceaseless campaigning on both sides, however, exacerbated the tension. The permanent campaign ethic drove a wedge between the president and Congress regarding drug policy. The unfettered pursuit of public support encourages posturing and symbolic acts on the part of the president and his adversaries in Congress. The unrelenting drive to sell the policy to the people is not compatible with efforts to search for common ground. In essence, by adopting a campaign mentality with respect to public policy, it becomes less important to build toward a consensus and more important to score rhetorical points. The ultimate consequence of campaign-style gamesmanship is a breakdown of the tradition role of negotiation and compromise. President Clinton's prescription drug legislation and the version promoted by the congressional Republicans had a large number of similarities. Each party, however, chose to discount a centrist position and advocate their own divergent policy goals. The decision by the House Republican leadership to pass a prescription drug plan that had no chance of becoming law is an illustrative example of symbolism triumphing over substance.

Legislators loathe the implication that strategic decisions are poll driven. The suggestion that their reactions are solely attributable to the vacillating moods of the general public makes them appear weak and superficial. Yet, no one can dispute that polls play an integral part in developing and implementing a legislative strategy. The fact that the Republican party, supposedly the champion of the free market and the scourge of government growth, embraced the idea of adding an expensive new entitlement shows that polls can influence policy. Legislators are correct, however, to scoff at the simplistic notion that politicians use polls to select policies. The real value of polling for legislators is its capacity to discern effective message strategies. Polls are used to develop a good sales pitch.[43] During the prescription drug debate, Citizens for Better Medicare employed Republican pollster Bill McInturff to shape the language of the Flo campaign. Legislators and the President Clinton also used pollsters and survey research to bolster their position. President Clinton, for example, remained confident in his confrontation with the pharmaceutical industry because in-house polling and independent polls indicated that the public trusted him more than the companies or the Republicans on the issue. House Republicans used pollsters and word gurus like Frank Luntz to help them articulate an alternative to the Clinton proposal. Polls were not used to identify a popular position; they were used to provide symbolic and rhetorical ammunition to defend a position.

Although some commentators and journalists find the use of polls as a marketing tool to be subversive and inauthentic, using polls to map out a communication strategy is not inherently corrupting. In fact, one could argue that the unending string of polls is an affirmation of democratic responsiveness. A problem, however, emerges when message trumps substance, when jargon and poll-tested buzzwords obscure policy choices. Policy makers' reliance on survey research and focus groups to develop rhetoric is troublesome because it masks important policy considerations from public attention. Instituting a prescription drug entitlement has enormous consequences for the private health care market, medical research, and fiscal policy, to just name a few areas. Yet these considerations seem lost amid the euphemisms and linguistic gimmickry. Doctoring the discussion with these words and phrases degrades the quality of public debate. Polling also promotes symbolic action. Looking toward November, rank-and-file Republicans in the House of Representatives were more concerned with passing a prescription drug bill than they were with the policy details of the legislation. A floor vote was necessary to inoculate members from public criticism after a poll indicated that the voters would hold them responsible for inaction.

Political journalist Nicholas Lemann has called modern polling firms "word labs." According to Lemann, word labs "generate phrases and rhetorical strategies that are political effective, and then put them in the hands of candidates."[44] Modern pollsters, he claims, are working in a highly evolved field of word association called frame semantics. All of the pseudo-scientific wordsmithing was on display during the prescription drug debate. Pollsters working on behalf of both political parties used focus groups to develop their narratives. The practice is well-established and accepted by political leaders. As Lawrence Jacobs points out, politicians are under the thrall of consultants who tell them how to talk to the people and how to connect with their anxieties.[45] Unfortunately, burying hard policies choices and unpleasant details under a layer of euphemisms and buzzwords tested in focus groups, prevents citizens from exercising judgment and making informed decisions about what policies are best for them. CBM's effort to color public perception by using loaded terms like "big government" and "Washington bureaucrat" was a blatant attempt to create an aura of negativity around the president's plan. It was not a serious effort to "educate" the voters.

CONCLUSION

By 2000 politicians seemed to be accustomed to the television ads direct-mail appeals, endless polling, and assorted grassroots outreach activity that accompanies a public policy initiative. What was considered innovative in 1994 is merely another facet in a twenty-first century political contest. PhRMA's unflinching decision to spend up to $65 million on a mass media and grassroots lobbying campaign reveals how significant the events of the mid 1990s are in the minds of lobbying strategists. Indeed, the fact that the Flo advertisements are a carbon copy of the Harry and Louise venture is a testament to the impact it has had on outside lobbying. Imitation is the highest form of homage one political consultant can offer another. Today no one disputes that political consultants and pollsters play a role in the legislative process. They advise elected officials how to pitch their policies and they toil on behalf of interest groups to shape the language used in debate. Presence, however, is not synonymous with acceptance.

Familiarity, as the old adage goes, breeds contempt. Certainly in the case of prescription drugs political consultants' handiwork drew heaps of scorn from a number of quarters. Yet the outrage exhibited among the pundit class generated by the Flo campaign seems disproportionate to its impact on the outcome of the debate. Flo and her sponsors earned the ire of President Clinton for allegedly distorting and misrepresenting his plan to the public, but when faced with the unparalleled power of the presidential bully pulpit, the drug industry's resolve weakened and they quietly accepted some of the president's policy demands. The president clearly won the showdown, but his victory was tainted by the acknowledgment that the president of the United States was forced to the negotiating table with an interest group by a single television commercial. President Clinton's confrontation with the drug companies reveals how obsessed politicians are with public relations and how palpable is their fear of the "killer ad."

Electronic advocacy, Common Cause protestations to the contrary, is not the political equivalent of a weapon of mass destruction. The prescription drug debate also revealed an acute weakness of electronic advocacy. Political advertisements have a difficult time communicating subtlety. The drug makers, for instance, went to great lengths to declare their support for the "right" prescription drug plan. Their expression of support with important caveats, however, was lost on the average viewer. For some viewers, the ads only strengthened their negative perception of the pharmaceutical industry. The Harry and Louise campaign was successful, in part, because they did not have to negotiate this obstacle. Their message was concise and unambiguous: They opposed any attempt to federalize health care. Flo may have been opposed to big government in her medicine cabinet, but she was not against providing senior citizens with some form of government aid. Whereas Harry and Louise activated latent fears among some citizens of government mismanagement and bureaucratic sloth, Flo failed to fire the imagination of the viewing public. Although 23 percent of those surveyed in a Gallup poll admitted recognizing Flo, her message opposing a "big government" solution did not seem to penetrate the public mind. The exaggerated reactions elicited by Flo are less an indication of her power over public opinion, than it is a patent example of misplaced concern over political advertising.

The stereotype of political consultants as amoral guns for hire, bereft of any concern for public policy persists despite new research on profession.[46] The pollsters and political strategists who encouraged the House Republicans to pass a prescription drug bill, no matter what it included, were championing a cynical strategy. Ultimately, however, they were not responsible for the decision to cast a vote as a political shield. Political consultants have consistently been portrayed as mercenaries for hire whose principal guideline for taking a job is financial rather than ideological. James Thurber's study dispels this stereotype, but there are still many examples of consultants working for a candidate while pursuing a private client with contrary interests. One of Vice President Al Gore's well-compensated consultants, Carter Eskew, sought to handle the $30-million advertising campaign run by Citizens for Better Medicare. A short time later, he signed on as the vice president's chief media strategist and message developer. During his presidential campaign, the vice president has excoriated the industry, calling them price gougers, and claimed that Citizens for Better Medicare was a phony coalition.[47] At best, Eskew's about-face underscores his disinterest in consistent public policy; at worst it affirms Larry Sabato's biting characterization of political consultants as cynical purveyors of illusions.[48]

The nature of modern American politics virtually assures the continued presence of political consultants in policy debates. In the era of the permanent campaign, grassroots stimulation, public opinion polling, and political advertising are indispensable additions to the legislative process. Political consultants, by virtue of their training and expertise, are the obvious choice to lead the campaigns. What this means for the American political system will be addressed in greater depth in the next chapter.

NOTES

1. John Poisal et al, "Prescription Drug Coverage and Spending for Medicare Beneficiaries," *Health Care Financing Review*, 20, (1999), 15.

2. Peter Stone, "Drug Makers Have Developed a New Prescription for Easing Their Many Political, Legal and Regulatory Headaches," *National Journal*, 21 July 2001, 2315.

3. *Congressional Budget Office*, "Long Term Budgetary Pressures and Policy Options," Washington, D.C., May 1998, ch. 4.

4. Julie Rovner, "Voters Flip Flop on Healthcare Prescriptions, Survey Finds," *Congress Daily*, 26 January 2001.

5. Robert Blendon, "National Survey on Prescription Drugs", September 2000 , http://www.pbs.org/newshour/health/prescriptions/survey_summary.html (12 August 2002).

6. Kay Lehman Schlotzman and John Tierney, *Organized Interests and American Democracy*, (New York: Harper and Row, 1986); Mark Smith, *American Business and Political Power: Public Opinion, Elections, and Democracy* (Chicago: University of Chicago Press, 2001); Paul Herrnson, Ronald Shaiko, and Clyde Wilcox, eds. *The Interest Group Connection: Electioneering, Lobbying, and Policymaking*, (Boston: Chatham House, 1998).

7. Leslie Wayne and Melody Peterson, "A Muscular Lobby Rolls Up Its Sleeves," *New York Times*, 4 November 2001.

8. Theodore Marmor, *The Politics of Medicare*, 2nd ed., (Chicago: Aldine Publishing, 1998), 107.

9. Ibid, 110.

10. Richard Himelfarb, *Catastrophic Politics – The Rise and Fall of the MCCA of 1998*, (State College: Penn State University Press, 1995), 77.

11. Marmor, *The Politics of Medicare*, 134.

12. Robert Pear, "Clinton Lays Out Plan to Overhaul Medicare System," *New York Times*, 30 June 1999, A1.

13. Dan Morgan, "Health Care Lobby Targets GOP Senators on Air," *Washington Post*, 5 July 1999, A3.

14. David Broder and Haynes Johnson, *The System: America's Way of Politics at the Breaking Point*, (Boston: Little Brown & Co., 1996).

15. Robert Pear, "Tracking Just What the Doctor Ordered, *New York Times*, 13 July 1999, C1.

16. Robert Pear, "Drug Makers Fault the Details of the Clinton Medicare Proposal," *New York Times*, 16 July 1999, A14.

17. Peter Stone, "Kinder, Gentler Arm Twisting," *National Journal*, 17 July 1999, 2080.

18. In 2000, Congress passed a law that required 527s to register with the FEC and begin disclosing lists of donors and amounts expended. The move was inspired in part by press accounts of the estimated $30-million ad campaign coordinated by Citizen's for Better Medicare. Campaign finance reform advocates and supporters of a prescription drug benefit were furious that the drug industry was able to finance a negative issue advocacy campaign under the guise of public education.

19. Dan Morgan, "Drugmakers Launch Campaign on Medicare; Industry Wary of Prescription Cost Controls," *Washington Post*, 28 July 1999, A4. Even though the ads did not explicitly reference the Clinton plan, the commercials counted on viewers to draw a connection between the criticism and the ideas touted by the administration. The effect was subtler. It was an attempt to set the terms of the legislative debate before it began. By prompting people to accept certain terms,

20. According to the news archive at Vanderbilt University, President Clinton's announcement resulted in five network stories in June and sixteen more throughout the summer focusing on prescription drug and the plight of senior citizens. The presidential campaign boosted the profile of prescription drugs significantly. During 2000, fifty-four appeared on the network news, more than any other domestic issue relevant to senior citizens; calculated by author from data found at Vanderbilt Television News Archive http://tvnews.vanderbilt.edu (26 August 2002).

21. Ira Teinowitz, "As Lobbyist Flo Worth to Follow in Harry and Louise Footsteps," *Advertising Age*, 25 October 1999, 43.

22. Robert Pear, "Drug Makers Are Taken to Task for Criticism of Clinton Plan," *New York Times*, 23 September 1999, A16.

23. Robert Pear, "Clinton is Going on the Offensive to Offer the Elderly a Drug Plan, *New York Times*, 24 October 1999, A1.

24. See Richard Neustadt, *Presidential Power and the Modern Presidents* 3rd ed. (New York: The Free Press, 1990); Jeffrey Tulis, *The Rhetorical Presidency*, (Princeton: Princeton University Press, 1987); and Samuel Kernell, *Going Public: New Strategies of Presidential Leadership*, (Washington, D.C.: CQ Press, 1993).

25. Robert Pear, "Drug Makers Drop Their Opposition to Medicare Plan," *New York Times*, 13 January 2000, A1.

26. David Mayhew, *Divided We Govern*, (New Haven: Yale University Press, 1991).

27. Robert Pear, "GOP in House Offers Medicare Plan," *New York Times*, 13 April 2000, A1.

28. Robert Pear, "House GOP to Push Media Drug Plan," *New York Times*, 11 June 2000.

29. Robert Pear, "Bipartisan Effort on Drug Coverage Has Begun," *New York Times*, 27 May 2000, A10.

30. John Broder, "Clinton's Drug Plan Attacked by Industry," *New York Times*, 28 June 2000, A22.

31. Stephen Anslobehere and Shanto Iyengar, *Going Negative: How Political Advertisements Shrink and Polarize the Electorate* (New York: The Free Press, 1995).

32. Darrell West and Burdett Loomis. *The Sound of Money: How Political Interests Get What They Want*, (New York: WW. Norton, 1998). See also Ken Kollman *Outside Lobbying: Public Opinion & Interest Group Strategies*, (Princeton: Princeton University Press, 1998); Thomas Mann and Norman Ornstein, *The Permanent Campaign and Its Future*, (Washington, D.C: The Brookings Institution, 2000).

33. Tim Ryan, the executive director of Citizen's for Better Medicare, constantly referred to the Flo campaign as an educational outreach to America's seniors. In nearly every press report he steadfastly defended the accuracy of her statements and argued that the commercials were performing a public service by making senior citizens more aware of government activity.

34. Lawrence Jacobs and Robert Y. Shapiro, *Politicians Don't Pander: Political Manipulation and the Loss of Democratic Responsiveness* (Chicago: University of Chicago Press, 2000). Borrowing heavily from the successful strategy of Harry and Louise, survey data was also used to create the character of Flo. As a composite of the target audience, Flo was every bit the progeny of Harry and Louise. Like the fictitious middle class couple, Flo's character and appearance was the fruit of sophisticated opinion surveys conducted by Republican pollsters. Every detail, including the venue where Flo makes her pitch (a bowling alley), was carefully designed to maximize her appeal to elderly voters. Without question, Flo's demeanor and benign appearance strengthened her message.

35. Molly Ann Brodie, "Impact of Issue Ads and the Legacy of Harry and Louise," *Journal of Health Policy and the Law*, 26 (2001), 2035–2038.

36. "Health Care an Important Issue this Year," *Gallup Monthly*, 28 September 2000. The following questions were asked of 1,500 adults nationwide:

Question 1: Do you think the government should do more to regulate health care costs in this country, or not?

In January 2000, 77 percent answered affirmatively. Nine months later, 76 percent gave the same response.

Question 2: As you may know, Medicare the federal insurance program for senior citizens, does not provide coverage for prescription drugs. In order to deal with this do you think the federal government should expand Medicare to include prescription drug coverage as an entitlement for senior citizens or do you think the federal government should provide subsidies to encourage private insurance companies to offer seniors prescription drug coverage, but not make it an entitlement, or do you think no changes should be made to coverage at this time? In September 2000, 57 percent supported expansion, 26 percent supported federal tax subsidies, and 12 percent did not want changes made.

37. Kara Kennedy, Interview by author, 17 August 2000.

38. "Trends in Grassroots Lobbying," *Campaigns & Elections*, February 1999, 22.

39. Todd Funk, Interview by author, 21 August 2002.

40. Richard Fenno, *Home Style: House Members and Their Districts* (Boston: Little Brown, 1978)

41. Ben Goddard, Interview by author, 21 June 2000.

42. Marilyn Werber Serafini, "Say It Ain't So Flo," *National Journal*, 9 October 1999, 2910.

43. Jacobs and Shapiro, *Politicians Don't Pander*, 7. The thrust of Jacobs and Shapiro's argument is that the president and legislators carefully track public opinion in order to identify the words, argument, and symbols that are most likely to be effective in attracting favorable press coverage and ultimately "winning" public support for their desired policies. Politicians' attempts to change public sentiment toward their favored position convinces them that they can pursue their policy objective while minimizing the risks of electoral punishment.

44. Nicholas Lemann, "Word Labs," *The New Yorker*, 16 October 2000, 100–112.

45. Jacobs and Shapiro, *Politicians Don't Pander*, 10.

46. James Thurber and Candace Nelson, eds. *Campaign Warriors: Political Consultants in Elections* (Washington, D.C., The Brookings Institution, 2000).

47. Dan Balz and Dana Milbank, "Gore Aide Once Wooed Drug Group," *Washington Post*, 7 July 2000.

48. Larry Sabato, *The Rise of Political Consultants: New Ways of Winning Elections* (New York: Basic Books, 1981).

7

Expert Assessment of Post-Electoral Consulting

Over the past three decades, political consulting has undergone an evolutionary transformation. In the 1960s it was a small cottage industry dominated by a select group of general practitioners who considered themselves campaign junkies. By 2002 it had become a multi-billion dollar profession boasting experts in a wide range of subfields. The industry's maturity is exemplified by a robust professional association (the American Association of Political Consultants) with nearly 1,000 members and the existence of a glossy trade magazine (*Campaigns & Elections*) devoted to advancing the image of political consulting. Further evidence of the enhanced stature of the industry is readily found in our mainstream culture, where pollsters are well-known television pundits and political strategists earn six-figure fees to advise *Fortune 500* companies. As the industry matured and flourished, consultants penetrated all levels of political activity, including governing. The Contract with America, the Clinton health care reform effort, and the prescription drug debate illustrate clearly that political consulting is no longer relegated to the fairly limited confines of candidate-centered campaigns. In contemporary politics, media specialists, pollsters, and campaign strategists are routinely called upon to bring their expertise to bear in the governing realm. Post-electoral work has become so lucrative, and the demand for it is so widespread, that some political consultants are leaving electoral politics altogether to concentrate on issue advocacy.

At the outset of this study I posited four questions raised by the emergence of post-electoral consulting. First, by pursuing overt, campaign-oriented public strategies, do elected officials and interest groups make it more difficult to negotiate and seek compromise on policy matters behind closed doors? Political consultants did not create natural partisan and institutional tensions, but their influence can exacerbate an already tenuous situation. Second, does the presence of unelected, for-profit political operatives at the center of policy debates violate the principles of democratic accountability? There is reason to speculate that political consultants, as for-hire political advisors with multiple public and private sector clients, have become de facto lobbyists. Consultants, however, are not subject to the rules and laws that regulate contact between lobbyists and elected officials. Third, despite their technical proficiency and undeniable utility during a campaign, are the many specialized skills that consultants offer overestimated and ill suited for governing. Direct-mail appeals and television advertising use crass, emotion-laden rhetoric to inflame passions rather than inform citizens. Polls are an integral part of campaigns, but their inherent uncertainty coupled with normative concerns about the proper role of public opinion in a liberal democracy leave some critics wondering if they are an appropriate tool for making public policy. Fourth, does the use of high-priced campaign operatives to market public policies or influence debate raise concerns about elite bias in policy making? In addition to these questions, this chapter will explore other matters such as the extent to which consultants have moved beyond electoral politics and why have they done so, whether they are a permanent addition to the legislative process, and whether their methods actually work in a governing context.

The data presented in this chapter come from two sources. Primary material was obtained through in-depth interviews with a group of political consultants, lobbyists, and key congressional staff members (a complete list of the interviewees along with biographical information is found in the Appendix). All of those interviewed are relevant political actors with experience in legislative politics and are familiar with the events described in the case studies. The comments are based on a series of open-ended questions predicated on the main concerns set forth in this study. The primary material is supplemented with background information gathered from news reports, scholarly articles, and books. The interview sample is not large enough or diverse enough for a statistical analysis, but as explained in Chapter 1, the focus of this study is on qualitative issues that are not easily reducible for statistical analysis. It does not purport to present an empirically derived "theory" of post-electoral consulting. Nevertheless, the insight offered by the interview subjects is compelling evidence of the changes wrought on the legislative process by the advent of post-electoral consulting.

POLITICAL CONSULTANTS AND ISSUE-BASED CAMPAIGNS

In the early 1990s, Matt Reese, one of the pioneers in professional political consulting, declared that he had foresworn consulting on behalf of candidates and that he was concentrating on advising non political private sector clients exclusively. It was, he claimed, easier to do and the pay was much better.[1] Reese's decision to move beyond the candidate base is not uncommon and is in fact indicative of an industrywide shift away from traditional campaign work. According to a recent study conducted by James Thurber of American University, over 78 percent of the 200 consultants he surveyed stated that they engaged in non-candidate-related political consulting and a significant number claimed that private-sector work was the central focus of their firms.[2] The reasons they offered were manifold, ranging from better pay and greater job stability to a greater sense of personal accomplishment. Republican pollster Bill McInturff is typical of the new generation of political consultants who eschew political races for the opportunities presented by non-candidate consulting. He claimed that his firm's candidate campaign work dropped from roughly 80 percent of business in 1990 to 40 percent in 2000. The bulk of the work is now issues related.[3] In little over eight years McInturff's firm has cut its candidate work in half and replaced it with consulting on behalf of private-sector groups. McInturff and other members of his cohort are undoubtedly innovators, but they are also opportunists who have taken advantage of changes in the political environment. Post-electoral, issue-based consulting work has flourished because of a confluence of factors. Two important reasons often cited by academics and other experts are the weak controls on spending for issue advocacy as well as the modern politician's faith in the power of polls and advertising. Each trend will be discussed at greater length later in this chapter.

Those interviewed are unperturbed by the deemphasis of candidate consulting seeming to see it as an inevitable outgrowth of our political culture. Ben Goddard, principal partner with the consulting firm Goddard/Claussen, views the elevation of public policy issues over candidates as a natural realignment brought on by changes in American politics as well as by the lure of financial reward. Goddard explains:

In the nineties, consultants have become much more interested in public policy. Some of the interest is purely financial, but some of it is the result of things that are outside our control such as independent voters and weak political parties. I've actually not worked on a candidate campaign since 1988. By the end of the eighties we were completely out of candidate work. In the last five years we've begun to compete with candidate consultants who are moving into advocacy work.[4]

Goddard's comments underscore a commonly held assumption that political consultants gained their newfound notoriety at the expense of political parties. The theory of party decline has suffused political science so thoroughly that in some circles it is axiomatic to consider parties anemic, hollow, and increasingly irrelevant institutions.[5] In spite of a vigorous counterargument, the perception of the party as an ineffectual remnant of an earlier era persists. Among the scholars who study political consultants, party decline, and the consultants' role in advancing it, is a recurring theme.[6] However, the consultants I interviewed downplayed the supposed adversarial relationship with political parties. Instead, they viewed their presence in policy debates as an affirmation of their skill at energizing citizens, not as an assault on traditional party activities.

Interest groups have been quick to realize the post-electoral potential of political consulting and they have over the past decade created a vast market for consultant services. There are a number of reasons why interest groups hire political consultants. Some organizations seek out well-known consultants because they regard consultants as an access point to political decisionmakers. Frank

Luntz, for example, in the aftermath of the Contract with America, used his connections with the House Republican leadership to expand his private-sector client base.[7] Some of Luntz's contemporaries sneered at his brazen and occasionally clumsy efforts at self-promotion, but name-dropping is an accepted practice within the industry as a way of attracting new clients. For most interest groups, however, a consultant is not a totem or a conduit. Indeed, he is a valuable, cost-effective source of political intelligence and strategy. Political communications scholars Darrell West and Burdett Loomis insist that special interests have an overwhelming need to control the terms of debate and therefore are willing to spend enormous sums of money to develop narratives that resonate with opinion leaders, policy makers, and the general public (e.g., Harry and Louise).[8]

Democratic pollster Geoff Garin encourages groups with substantial financial resources to invest in a poll before mounting a full-scale lobbying effort. It makes sense, he says, for groups to inform their legislative campaigns through polls. He believes that clients can save in the long run by investing in a poll.[9] Garin's description of polling as a commonsense, affordable investment is accurate.[10] Over the past decade the number of competent private pollsters coupled with advances in technology depressed the cost of conducting a scientific poll. Thus, reliable polling is now widely available to nonprofit organizations and smaller interest groups. However, Garin's blithe endorsement of post-electoral consulting fails to take into account the prohibitive cost of the other components of a public relations campaign; namely media buys, direct mail, and advertising. What good is sound information if you are unable to capitalize on it? The concern over elite bias animates West and Loomis. In their book, *The Sound of Money*, the authors argue "Moneyed interests are able to construct stories more clearly and effectively than poorer organizations."[11]

The shift toward private-sector political advising is important because it signifies a systemic change in the way interest groups seek to influence policy. Traditional lobbying techniques such as face-to-face encounters are still applicable, but they are supplemented with regularity by mass media advertising and grassroots pressure. Charles Kahn, president of the Health Insurers' Association of America (HIAA), argues that interest groups that work on high-profile, controversial issues ignore public relations at their own peril:

In my area today, although there are some exceptions, because of the 1993 and 1994 period all health issues tend to be front page news and this affects your lobbying method. If someone wants to get a payment fix in Medicare it could be such a small detail that an inside strategy will suffice. Whereas patient protection or prescription drug issues become larger than life and thus the lobbying dynamic is affected by that. I would say that in the health care area those front page issues affect your strategy as to how you want to affect public policy and generally dictates some kind of full court press.[12]

Health care is an area that lends itself to emotional advertising appeals, sentimental public overtures, and demagogic mass mailings. All are areas of strength for political consultants. Thus, it is no surprise that, in the aftermath of the Clinton debacle, many major health care proposals including Medicare reform, prescription drug benefits, and cancer research, have been followed by a professionally administered public relations campaign complete with polls, focus groups, direct mail, and television commercials. During the 106th Congress, for example, public outcry over skyrocketing prescription drug costs and the corresponding legislative efforts to impose price controls spurred pharmaceutical companies to invest $65 million in a public relations campaign.[13] The tactics, however, are not exclusive to emotionally charged policies like health care. Political consultants are also applying their skills on more arcane, esoteric issues. Tom McCrocklin, former director of federal affairs for the Independent Insurance Agents of America (IIAA), believes that public relations can be just as useful for legislation that remains beneath public view:

All of the issues, even the ones the public doesn't know or care about, have a public relations component, a mass mailing, an advertising campaign, polls what have you. The reason being is even if you have a relatively small target audience you can use PR to motivate them, energize them and get them involved. A small-scale, but well conceived, strategy can be just as effective in certain circumstances as a big, blow out campaign.[14]

Not all lobbyists share this view. T. J. Petrizzo, head of the eponymous firm the Petrizzo Group and former chief of staff to Jennifer Dunn (R-WA), concedes that outside lobbying may be necessary for some issues, but he makes the point to differentiate issues that lend themselves to mass media outreach from small, lesser-known issues. "Technical matters," he asserts, "do not need outside lobbying. For instance, after a tax bill has passed you often have news stories of random items that were dropped in the Christmas tree. How those things got in the bill are much more personal. You don't need a commercial."[15]

Thus, special interests' innovative use of campaign techniques to supplement traditional lobbying has created a tremendous demand for the specialized skills political consultants possess. More important, it appears that the use of consultants is not limited to big-budget, high-profile issues. Small to medium-size organizations are also employing consultants to coordinate public relations campaigns to capture public attention. The continued growth of the trend alarms some observers who view it as another manifestation of elite bias in our political system.

Knowledgeable observers and practitioners generally cite two reasons for the recent explosion in post-electoral consulting. First, loopholes in campaign finance laws encourage groups to spend unlimited amounts of money on issue advocacy without regulation and, until very recently, without disclosure.[16] Second, there is a perception among elite decision makers, cultivated by political consultants, that public relations is an indispensable part of modern day lobbying. Politicians, inculcated with what Kathleen Hall Jamieson describes as an enduring fear of "the killer ad," have brought their sensitivity to the public policy realm. Interest groups and legislators are acutely aware that appearance and perception are valuable currency in American politics, and, in many cases, artifice can trump sober analysis.

In the mid-1970s Congress passed sweeping legislation designed to regulate money in politics. The fervor was ignited by public calls to clean up the system amidst the lingering disgust with the Watergate scandal.[17] Although the Supreme Court struck down some provisions of the early laws, many of the donation limitations and disclosure requirements withstood court challenges. The lawmakers who drafted the 1970s legislation deserve credit for being pioneers, but as critics and present-day reformers point out, the original laws and subsequent addenda are not comprehensive.

One of the omissions, augmented by the legal interpretations of the Supreme Court, enables interest groups and PACs to spend an unlimited amount of money advocating for a specific piece of legislation or public policy agenda. They are free to do so, provided that they do not promote a particular candidate exclusively and explicitly. Prior to 2000, ad hoc single-issue coalitions did not have to register with the FEC or disclose a list of contributors and expenditures.[18] The loophole has led to a mushrooming of small, fluid organizations with benign names like Citizens for Better Medicare, Citizens for State Power, and Clean Water for Our Future. These groups function as intermediaries for established interest groups to influence public opinion and shape the terms of the political debate.

The emergence of issue advocacy has been a financial windfall for political consultants, who manage virtually every aspect of the issue-based campaign. In Bill McInturff's estimation, the enormous amount of money spent on issue advocacy reflects decades of poor thinking with respect to campaign finance reform. Reformers, working to impose cost controls on inputs (donations and contributions) but ignoring outputs (the costs associated with running a campaign), have done nothing to diminish the demand for political money. The push for campaign finance reform, he states, "will mean that you will see more and more advocacy advertising. The money has to go somewhere and since that area is essentially unregulated it seems like a logical place."[19] The 106th Congress took limited action, but it remains to be seen if the disclosure requirements will dampen interest-group enthusiasm for issue advocacy.[20]

Irregularities in campaign finance law explain the opportunity for issue advocacy to appear, but the reason why it has flourished is due to a belief among the political elite, based on anecdotal evidence, that it works. Elected officials at all levels of government are sensitive to shifts in public opinion; yet legislators, in particular House members, owing to their short election cycle, possess an amplified acuity to fluctuations. Ted Van Der Meid, a chief aide to House Speaker Dennis Hastert, notes, "Members pay a lot of attention to their mail and their phone calls and any member worth his salt will try to find out where his constituents are on an issue. The public rarely becomes engaged in an issue so when they do, members take notice."[21] Successful issue advocacy work creates the impression that the public has strong views by showering legislators with feedback. The impressive power of issue advocacy was aptly demonstrated during the health care reform debate when several Ways and Means committee members expressed reservations about supporting the Clinton plan after experiencing a wave of grassroots pressure instigated by interest groups.[22] "It [the ads] almost destroyed the process," claims former Ways and Means Chairman Dan Rostenkowski, "Membership just became so conscious of those things that it looked as though we weren't going to have the possibility of having a bill."[23]

There is some debate whether the use of consultants to stimulate a negative public outcry can alter the trajectory of legislation on a consistent basis. However, it is an established fact that a vigorous public reaction will gain legislators' attention. The dynamic, states Dan Meyer, chief of staff to former Speaker Newt Gingrich, is easy to understand:

It [the ads] influence legislators to the extent that they feel their constituency is behind it. If they believe the public supports the ad campaign then the legislators pay careful attention. They count the letters, tally the phone calls, and keep track of the emails. Although it might only reinforce what they want to do. There are always a sizeable number of legislators who want to do nothing and advertisements can occasionally compel them to act.[24]

Darrell West and Burdett Loomis concur in their recent study of interest-group behavior: "The reason it works is simple," they argue, "Constituents have a high degree of credibility that no Washington lobbyist can match. They are not hired guns, they have not sold their soul for a special interest, and they reflect concerns of ordinary citizens."[25]

Barry Jackson, former communications director for the House Republican Conference, believes that members can distinguish contrived and genuine public pressure. He thinks that most members of Congress can tell the difference between real public outcry and Astroturf lobbying. Effective members, he asserts, go home and listen to the people they represent. Jackson, did not, however, dismiss the power of interest-group-sponsored activism. "Contrived grassroots can be effective," he mused, "I mean if the NRA can get people to send out thousands of postcards, the member is still going to pay attention. He knows it was prompted, but that doesn't mean the public won't remember come election day."[26] Dan Blankenburg, director of legislative affairs at the National Federation of Independent Businesses (NFIB), argued that it is crucial that grassroots campaigns have real people, not consultants, behind them: "If you really have a manufactured problem," he said, "that is one pushed from the top down rather than the bottom up, it eventually won't be successful because you don't have real people making the arguments. Members see right through that other stuff."[27] Nona Wegner, executive director of Citizens for Better Medicare concurred: "I honestly believe that people are smart enough to see through crafted messages. People live their lives, when something they are told doesn't gibe with their common sense, they discount it."[28] Wegner's comments are particularly interesting considering the furor that resulted from CBM's prescription drug campaign.

Political scientists have spent considerable energy analyzing the connection between public opinion and legislative behavior as well as arguing over the proper role public opinion should play in a liberal democracy.[29] The comments offered here are consistent with the macro theory presented by R. Douglas Arnold in *The Logic of Congressional Action*. Arnold suggests that "legislators choose among many policy proposals by estimating the likelihood that citizens might incorporate these policy preferences into their choices among candidates in subsequent elections."[30] Within the framework presented by Arnold, issue advocacy can serve as a cue for legislators. What consultants know and many politicians fail to realize is that the outcry created by a direct mailing or a TV commercial is an exaggeration of actual public sentiment. The Harry and Louise commercials, for example, elicited a reaction from legislators that was not commensurate with the scope of the ad campaign. When Rostenkowski lamented that the advertising "almost destroyed the process" he is giving too much credit to commercials that only appeared in select markets. An exasperated Stan Greenberg recalls "doing focus groups on Harry and Louise and people just hadn't seen it. Even in the markets where they were targeting members, people claimed they never saw it."[31] Indeed, subsequent analysis conducted by Kathleen Hall Jamieson argued that the widespread influence of Harry and Louise was an elaborate hoax, "as it evoked little short term recall among viewers."[32]

Post-electoral consulting at the legislative level did not emerge in a vacuum. Bill McInturff believes that the current fascination with issue advocacy in Congress is a result of the president's power to control the policy agenda through the mass media. The proliferation of PR campaigns on major public policy issues, he maintains, is partly in response to executive control of the bully pulpit. The president's natural advantage in communications has forced groups that disagree with his policies to spend money on professionals. I think the proliferation of PR campaigns on major public policy issues is partly in response to the executive control of the bully pulpit. The president's natural advantage in communications has forced groups that disagree with his policies to spend money on professionals. Interest groups, for example, that are working against a presidential proposal need consultants to counteract the inherent PR advantage owned by the White House.[33] The president's overwhelming media presence and his inherent ability to capture public attention is a source of frustration for congressional leaders, particularly in times of divided government. However, McInturff's assertion that clever public relations can equalize the advantage owned by the president does not resonate with some commentators. Ted Van Der Meid claims, "You can never beat the president at his own game. Gingrich tried and for a short while he succeeded, but it was fleeting. Look what happened to him in the end. He couldn't control his members, and he was nearly toppled."[34]

McInturff may have gotten carried away. Congress, for a host of reasons, will never challenge the executive branch for mass media supremacy. However, he is correct to suggest that Congress has taken lessons from the executive branch. Two recent presidents, Ronald Reagan and Bill Clinton, elevated the practice of campaign-style leadership to new heights. Reagan was a master at diffusing public opposition through symbolic gestures. However, the interview subjects claim that Clinton outdid Reagan and credit him with intensifying the governing-as-campaigning method. Charles Khan asserts, "The Clinton administration has set the campaign style approach to government at a new high. He may be aping Reagan in terms of posturing, but he went way beyond anything that Reagan did."[35] Dan Meyer came to the same conclusion: "Clinton's ability," he maintains, "combined with the campaign aspect of his administration has absolutely led Republicans to increase their communications efforts. It is still much more difficult for a legislature to compete with a president, but by using pros we can mitigate his natural advantage to some degree."[36] Haphazard regulation of issue advocacy coupled with a virtually unassailable faith in the power of advertising among political elites has created a vast market for post-electoral consulting. The desire among some members of Congress to use political consultants as policy strategists is also spurred by the president's ability to go public. Legislators and interest groups have witnessed presidents use the power of the bully pulpit to define policy problems and essentially win the debate before it even starts.

POST-ELECTORAL CONSULTING: A LASTING ADDITION TO THE LEGISLATIVE PROCESS?

Over the past twenty years, political consultants have branched out success-fully and established themselves as formidable actors in the legislative process. It is too early to conclude without equivocation that this is a permanent condition. Yet given the nature of modern political discourse and the entrenchment of mass media politics, it is reasonable to assume that experts in political communication will remain influential figures. The contemporary political era, to paraphrase Steven Medvic, relies heavily on speed and technology with respect to commu-nication. It also places heavy emphasis on the symbolic that, while present in earlier eras, has not been as pervasive as it is in the television age. Both characteristics shift the balance in favor of professional political consult-ants who are used to the fast pace of a campaign and are masters of sym-bolism and evocative imagery.[37]

It is pointless to belabor the extent to which technological advances in com-munications and the proliferation of the mass media have altered the behavior of elected officials. Suffice it to say that politicians at virtually every level have gained an appreciation for the value of public appearance and perception. In Congress, leadership strategy has changed as a result of a preoccupation with public relations and the mass media. It is, for instance, unlikely that the leader-ship will prod the members to support a high-profile piece of legislation without proffering a comprehensive sales strategy. Kara Kennedy, former communica-tions aide to Speaker Newt Gingrich, acknowledges the importance of develop-ing a coherent message. Kennedy claims, "Outside lobbying, media campaigns and grassroots activity, can help move legislation. While members need to nego-tiate and compromise, and make tough decisions I think outside lobbying can actually help at times because there is more information and feedback from the public."[38] Todd Funk, legislative director for Congresswoman Nancy Johnson, agrees with Kennedy to a certain degree: "I think it is absolutely necessary to have a message strategy but some times the reality is that individual members don't want it or for electoral purposes can't pitch the story sent down from lead-ership. However, we would use our own pollsters to help develop a message specifically tailored to the district. So in that respect it is not different."[39]

Cultivating a reliable message is a high priority for congressional leaders of both parties, but how closely do consultants work with congressional leadership offices to craft the message? During the Contract with America, some journalists attributed its success to the political consultants who helped develop the marketing strategy, even though the ideas espoused in the Contract were based on long standing conservative principles. [40] The undue credit paid to political consultants was a source of controversy. Dan Meyer bristled when asked about the media's characterization of the consultants' relationship with the Contract:

There is one consultant in particular [Frank Luntz] who has marketed his involvement in the Contract as if he were the sole author and the rest of us were just waiting around for him to give us our cue and I think that is outrageous. You have to remember that the conservatives on the Hill determined the substance of the Contract long ago. What Luntz was used for was determining the language with which to sell the ideas. [41]

Perhaps owing to the negative attention consultants drew during the 104th Congress, the House leadership in the 106th Congress tried to downplay the presence of consultants. Ted Van Der Meid claims that the Speaker's office does not use the services of political consultants:

We don't use them per se. The NRCC hires pollsters and media people to consult with our offices, but the Speaker never employs outside political operatives to test issues or what have you. The leadership has a press office that takes a long range and a short range strategy. They also have people who stage photo ops and write speeches. These activities are all coordinated under the direction of the House Republican Conference. [42]

Van Der Meid's insistence that consultants are involved only through surrogate agents such as the National Republican Congressional Committee (NRCC) or the Republican National Committee (RNC) does not alter the fact that the advice they provide shapes the way legislators behave. In the 106th Congress, during the contentious debate over prescription drug coverage for senior citizens, Republican pollster Glen Bolger contracted with the RNC to evaluate the issue. In a memo to House Republicans Bolger outlined the legislative strategy that they should follow. His memo included strategic advice, such as gathering support from conservative Democrats so that the plan would appear to be bipartisan, and tactical advice, like the language that Republicans should use when describing the plan. Bolger's memo prompted swift action from House Republicans. In staged media events and press conferences, Speaker Hastert and Majority Leader Armey used the phrases and descriptions touted by Bolger almost word for word, causing some reporters and House Democrats to suggest that the Republicans were following a "poll-tested script." [43]

One of the reasons legislators employ political consultants is to bypass or penetrate the mainstream mass media. As Timothy Cook explains in *Making Laws and Making News*, the way the press frames the issue is as important as whether or not it is covered at all. If the press characterizes a policy option one way early on in the decision-making process, it is often very difficult for officials to turn that image around to their preferred perspective.[44] Moreover, the way the press covers public policy issues is similar to the way they cover candidate campaigns. Congressional scholar Thomas Mann suggests that "reporters now increasingly cover policy battles in Congress and the White House as campaigns, with the focus on who is winning and losing and on the motives and machinations of the players, not on the stakes or the choices."[45] Media influence on public policy is so pronounced that some critics have taken to describing it as the fourth branch of government. The monolithic presence of the commercial media is a source of frustration and resentment for some legislators. The House Republicans during the 104th Congress sought alternatives to the traditional media outlets through outside consultants. Ted Van Der Meid explains the method, "What we try to do is bypass the Washington elite media and reach out to the public. We use talk radio and other outlets to work around traditional media. Consultants are a fixture in this process."[46] Political consultants enable politicians, in a limited fashion, to control the timing and content of their message.

The need to reach out to people beyond the beltway without having the message filtered or altered by the mainstream media is paramount, according to Republican strategist Ed Gillespie. Gillespie argues that the press can distort legislation and create inaccurate perceptions:

Take bankruptcy reform, here you have a very watered down, moderate measure that corrected a problem in the economy where the stigma of bankruptcy had diminished and people were filing chapter seven even though they could pay some of their debts. And this is a reasonable bill that protects responsible consumers from irresponsible ones. It has taken a lot of paid advocacy to get that message out because the media continues to erroneously report that this is going to hurt poor people. Paying back debts has been portrayed in the mass media and editorials as benefiting the credit card companies at the expense of the poor.[47]

Republican legislators justify the use of paid media because of their enduring suspicion of a liberal bias in the mainstream media. However, Democrats on the Hill also employ professional media strategists to promote their policies. The goal, explained Ben Goddard, is universal and non partisan: you want to create an echo chamber where you have paid media establishing the message and earned media (news reports, pundits, etc.) repeating it until it becomes a mantra. In this respect, the two major parties have proven less capable than interest groups. The Harry and Louise campaign is a textbook example. The ads were shown only in a limited market, but they generated such controversy that media reports began citing the ads, thus amplifying their visibility. The charges made by the fictitious couple and repeated in the press angered White House officials and provoked a stern response from the President. President Clinton's retort inadvertently gave the ads and the negative message greater notoriety. By the end of the health care debate, the ads had taken on a near mythic status. A similar ripple took place during the tort reform debate in the 104th Congress. Some of the ads sponsored by business groups became fodder for Sunday morning political talk shows. According to Ben Goddard, synergy is considered crucial to the overall success of the public relations campaign on high profile issues. Tom Edwards, president of the Washington, D.C. media firm Edwards & Associates concurs: "what you are doing here is sending your message to those who can retail it to others. This is a wholesale market. The audience you can reach, trade associations, news media, international press organizations, can get your message to the public and the world."[48]

The partisan efforts of political consultants in recent Congresses run counter to the mercenary stereotype promoted in early academic treatments of political consulting. Dan Nimmo, David Rosenbloom, and Larry Sabato all described consultants as independent contractors who thrived due to a confluence of weak political parties and independent candidacies. They were aloof to party politics and, although ideology played a role in client selection, many remained skeptical of party practices and avoided formal links to party leaders. Recent work by Temple University political scientist Robin Kolodny challenges these assumptions and establishes strong ties between consultants and political parties within government.

Today party leaders seek the assistance of highly specialized consultants to help them focus their message and issue stands with the hope of shoring up their strength at election time. Party leaders clearly indicated that the traditional feedback loop in the political party was no longer sufficient to meet their needs. Specialized pollsters and strategists are hired by the party in government directly to deal with their collective needs.[49]

The party connection described by Kolodny is an important aspect of post-electoral consulting because it signifies a reliance on outside strategists trusted by party leaders to supplement the work done by congressional staff. It also indicates a heretofore ignored degree of party loyalty on the part of political consultants. In short, it appears post-electoral consulting affects the legislative process in a variety of ways. Party leaders in Congress employ consultants to articulate poll-tested phraseology and to develop "thematic cover" for rank-and-file members. Consultants are also used to develop media strategy on controversial issues or to bypass traditional media outlets. In addition, as the earlier section discussed, post-electoral consulting offers another avenue for interest groups to influence legislation through direct mail and television advertising.

POST-ELECTORAL CONSULTING AND THE POLITICAL ENVIRONMENT

The comments made by the interview subjects coupled with events described in the case studies is strong evidence that post-electoral consulting is not a fleeting or random phenomenon. If this is true, then the question becomes what its effect is on the political system. Consultants and lobbyists, while eager to recount their success stories, are reluctant to assess their impact on a larger scale.

Although they admit their actions can affect the prospects for compromise, no one interviewed was willing to entertain the possibility that post-electoral consulting is a threat to the integrity of the legislative process. Moreover, the consultants suggested that the academics who have cast aspersions on their work are either misguided, naïve, or motivated by a hostile bias against political practitioners.

In *Going Public*, one of Samuel Kernell's central concerns with the president's predilection to use the bully pulpit was its impact on political bargaining. Kernell states, "To the extent that it [going public] fixes the president's bargaining position, posturing makes subsequent compromise with other practitioners more difficult. Because negotiators must be prepared to yield some of their client's preferences to make a deal, bargaining proceeds best behind closed doors."[50] Post-electoral consulting raises a similar concern for legislators. When the interview subjects were asked if they thought the incorporation of campaign techniques into governing made it harder to achieve compromise, the response was affirmative. Dan Meyer's comments are typical:

Yes it makes it harder. I mean sometimes the public is served by bringing issues out of the backrooms, but one of the downsides of that is if you take your case to the public there you have people who have invested in a particular solution and it makes compromise much more difficult. Public strategies also benefit junior members and it empowers them, making compromise with them even more tenuous.[51]

Nancy Libson, former Democratic staff member for the House Financial Services Committee agreed: "Absolutely, politics and political advantage (the campaign mode) have overtaken legislative deliberation and process which limits thoughtful discussion of issues. It clearly limits cooperation because everyone is looking to score political points."[52] Stan Greenberg, President Clinton's former pollster, concurs. He argues that going public has made it harder to achieve meaningful compromise. He uses the recent case of prescription drug benefits to make his point: "You have these hyperbolic ad campaigns paid for by Citizens for a Better Medicare, but really it is just a shell for the drug companies who are adamantly opposed to anything resembling price controls. And these ads scare old people and just plain create more hostility."[53]

Meyer and Greenberg agree, but for different reasons. Meyer claims that the inclination to use public relations hinders party leadership control over the agenda in Congress by creating "media" personalities. Ironically, Meyer's former boss, Newt Gingrich, was considered by many observers to be a legislator in that mold. Greenberg focuses his criticism on the inflammatory, often misleading, ads designed by consultants. He believes that the public debate is sullied by fear-mongering tactics. Kara Kennedy does not dispute the notion that political consulting has made closed-door negotiations more tenuous. However, she views the change as a blessing rather than a curse: "I think competition is part of the democratic process. Outside lobbying and campaigning is a right that all citizens enjoy and for some tht is the way they participate in the democratic process. If it makes it harder for lawmakers to negotiate, so be it."[54] Kennedy's assessment, however, fails to consider the normative implications of using visceral, emotion-laden rhetoric to trigger latent fears among the general public. There is a genuine difference between informing people and scaring them. Consider some of the gross exaggerations that passed for public education during the health care debate. Ads that claimed, for example, that senior citizens could be jailed for purchasing "extra" health care or that people would be forced to request permission from a government bureaucrat before changing doctors were outright fabrications.

Geoff Garin was an exception among the consultants interviewed. Public relations, he maintains, is a symptom of a much larger problem in governance. The root cause of legislative gridlock is not advertising or polling, but the increased level of partisanship that emerged in the 1980s and 1990s. Harsh, ideological battles between conservative Republicans and Democrats created an atmosphere of mistrust and animosity that is wholly unrelated to work done by political consultants.[55] Barry Jackson, Congressman John Boehner's chief of staff, shares some of Garin's doubts. He believes that issue campaigning can have an effect because behind-closed-door negotiations are only successful based on the level of trust in the room. Both parties know and accept that there will be some kind of rhetoric and spin used on the outside, but when trust is broken, then the public strategy can further alienate the negotiators.[56]

In response to the same question Ben Goddard offers an expanded interpretation of post-electoral consulting's impact:

There are times when it does make compromise more difficult; particularly when policy makers get backed into a public position that tends to limit their negotiating room. But by and large, I think that the legislative process hasn't changed that much. It's still a process of negotiation and accommodation. What really has changed is that an outside force is having a greater impact on legislative decisions. The policy campaign we run with grassroots, earned media, and paid media have changed the dynamic. There is a whole other leverage point to move Congress. I think what Harry and Louise have proved is that the most influential lobbyists don't live in Washington, D.C., they live out here where the people are.[57]

One of the common criticisms leveled at political consultants by both academics and politicians is that post-electoral consulting activity further exacerbates voter cynicism and saps public faith in our political institutions. Public-opinion scholars suggest that Americans possess a latent distrust of central authority and are naturally skeptical of grand schemes to solve complex problems.[58] During the health care reform battle, consultants working against the Clinton plan tapped into this sentiment by conjuring up negative images and using alarmist narratives. The result was a debilitating drain of popular support for the Clinton plan. The consultants' tactics disgusted some public officials, including Senator Jay Rockefeller, who railed against negative issue advocacy. Rockefeller claimed, "I think that the advertising is probably the most destructive effort that I can remember in 30 years political life, at trying to undermine public policy that this country desperately and definitely wants."[59] Even consultants who promote new policies cultivate cynicism. Communications scholar W. Lance Bennett suggests that politicians' dependence on political consultants feeds public cynicism by encouraging the spread of symbolic politics. Symbolic politics, in Bennett's estimation, fosters cynicism because it masks difficult public policy choices with pleasant sounding but ultimately illusory solutions. In other words, modern politics is awash in lofty rhetoric and engaging imagery, but short on concrete action.[60] Rockefeller and Bennett seem to suggest that consultants are an attenuating force in American politics because they tend to pander in the lowest common human factor: emotion. The general public is not served by boiling down complicated issues into easy-to-grasp metaphors and symbols.

Political consultants, not surprisingly, disagree with Senator Rockefeller and W. Lance Bennett. The consensus among the interview sample is that issue campaigning has a muffled, imprecise effect on voter attitudes and that in cases when it does bear fruit the consequences are positive. Dan Meyer believes that the American public is served by the growth and proliferation of issue campaigning. "I think it's good for the process," he further adds, "I think bringing these decisions out from behind closed doors is good for democracy. The move to employ grassroots to shape public opinion has helped draw people into politics."[61] Geoff Garin is also quick to defend issue advocacy and post-electoral consulting. Garin argues that the public is so disengaged from the policy process that any action that brings knowledge to them is good. Anything that penetrates the public conciousness is beneficial.[62] Garin and Meyer promote the polarizing effects of issue advocacy as a democratic good: getting more people involved and aware of the issues. However, they are indifferent to the method. It is qualitatively different to motivate a citizen with a positive message as opposed to prompting them into action with fear or anger. The danger, critics point out, is that the negativity will linger and leave the citizens with diminished faith in their elected representatives.

As political consultants strengthened their ties with successful clients in office and continued to branch out into lucrative issue advocacy work, critics began to suggest that the enhanced status of unelected political mercenaries posed a threat to democratic accountability. Charles Lewis, director of the Center for Public Integrity, a nonprofit watchdog group, claimed that political consultants who serve elected officials and private sector clients simultaneously present a serious conflict of interest.[63] Lewis's concern is echoed by some political scientists, who see an inherent elite bias in post-electoral consulting.[64] The actions of a select number of high-profile political consultants such as Frank Luntz and Dick Morris lend credibility to the afore mentioned criticisms. However, the appearance of impropriety is not proof of corruption. There is no evidence that consultants en masse have used their influence with political clients to advance the goals of other private-sector groups surreptitiously.

Stan Greenberg was often criticized by Republicans for his overt role in White House affairs while representing a number of private clients, but he claims his actions were no different or less ethical than those of ad hoc counselors from an earlier era.[65] Greenberg agrees that political consultants are playing a larger role in the policy process, whether they work for interest groups developing ads, advising the president, or testing ideas for legislators, but he doubts that the enhanced profile of consultants is cause for alarm. He points out correctly that there are a lot of unelected figures, including congressional staff, lobbyists, and civil servants who have more influence than consultants.[66]

Greenberg's description is self-serving and fails to acknowledge the most important difference between consultants and other unelected figures; namely, the presence of government oversight and regulation to which the others are subjected. Consultants, unlike lobbyists, for instance, do not have to register with the FEC, disclose client lists, or submit to periodic reviews. Nevertheless, Greenberg's basic point is valid. There are innumerable unelected figures who contribute to the policy-making process. Furthermore, strict lobbying regulations have not altered the public perception of ethical impropriety with regard to elected officials. In fact, it has been suggested that the proliferation of laws governing contact between lobbyists and government officials has created an environment ripe for scandal.[67] Under the new regime, innocuous acts can be interpreted as prima facie evidence of illegal activity. Thus, there is no reason to believe that imposing similar controls on consultants, as James Thurber and Darrell West argue, would have the desired effect.

The question of elite bias is harder to refute, especially in light of the expenses involved in conducting a full-scale public relations campaign. PhARMA's $65-million investment, for example, in a national advertising and educational campaign on a single issue is a sobering figure. Charles Kahn, however, believes the concern about elite bias is misplaced. In fact, Kahn submits that the effective use of campaign techniques can level the playing field between two mismatched foes:

Take us for example. The insurance industry is not a minor industry, but we don't have anywhere near the resources of the drug industry. On the issue of senior's drug coverage, the drug industry has staked out a firm position because they are very concerned about price controls. But we have also gotten a lot of attention on this issue because we have created a smart, strategically sound public relations campaign. The 900 pound gorilla is not always successful in getting attention in a campaign.[68]

Tom McCrocklin shares Kahn's view: "Smaller lobbies can vault themselves into a prime position of influence by virtue of a strong PR effort. If they pick their spots carefully, meaning they choose the right districts or members to concentrate on, then they can sometimes move the agenda in ways that belie their size. In the old days, big groups like AAIC would just roll you, now things are different."[69] TJ Petrizzo shrugs off concerns about elite biases and unfair advantage: "The idea that moneyed interests are not the people is just plain wrong. Businesses employ people, they provide for families, and they make communities. When you hear talk about special interests, you never hear about the people that make up those interests. Besides, unions and the AARP are very well funded and they claim to be representing the people. How are they different?"[70]

Kahn, McCrocklin and Petrizzo speak from experience, but their comments focus on the relative difference between large and medium-size lobbies and fail to address the underlying dilemma. Electronic advocacy and issue campaigning is a capital-intensive process that is not available to all political actors. Small groups and disorganized interests have traditionally lost policy battles to larger, better-organized adversaries. Critics fear, however, that the ascendance of post-electoral consulting will make the natural advantage owned by moneyed interests more pronounced since they will be able to disseminate their messages to a larger audience. Groups working against the Clinton health care plan, for example, outspent their opposition by a 4-to-1 margin.[71] "It's a variation of the same old story," claims Nancy Libson, "Groups with the cash come in and try to cajole or bully members. But now it's much worse because they can use their money to move public opinion or create false impressions of popular support."[72]

Consultants answer their academic critics with equal parts indignation and condescension. According to Bill McInturff, political scientists will never embrace consultants because consulting work does not fit into academic paradigms. Political scientists, he argues, are sensitive to consultants' effect on their work.[73] His comments reveal the disdain most practioners have for ivory-tower theorists. Democratic pollster Geoff Garin shares a similar viewpoint. Political scientists, he opines, either misunderstand or purposefully misconstrue what he does. Consultants don't fit neatly into the political science literature and therefore we are viewed with some suspicion. He further argues that academic preference for meritorious, logic-driven public policy leads them to take a dim view of populist efforts to energize the public.[74]

DOES IT REALLY WORK?

Consultants, as a group, exhibit a great deal of self-assurance. According to James Thurber's study of the profession, over half of the consultants he surveyed believed that they had a significant to fair amount of influence on the public policy agenda in the United States.[75] Legislators and interest groups also have a high degree of confidence in the powers of political consultants, and some of the praise is justified. In just the past few years, consultants have left their mark on a range of policy issues including, Medicare reform, trade with China, and electric utility deregulation. However, as Paul Herrnson points out, practitioners and clients tend to exaggerate the value of professional consulting: "Consultants have a built in incentive to inflate their role. After all, many consultants spend nearly as much time marketing their services as they do working on political campaigns."[76] Meanwhile, their clients put an inordinate amount of faith in a strategy that is difficult to evaluate (How do they know that a Senator changed his position because of a television commercial or a direct mailing?).

Once health care reform was officially removed from the congressional agenda in 1994, an embittered Hillary Clinton in an interview with the *New York Times* shared her conviction that health care was defeated by a coordinated assault of paid media and direct mail. She was utterly convinced that television commercials like Harry and Louise had turned the tide against health reform. However, in her book-length post-mortem of the Clinton plan, Theda Sckopol cautioned against placing blame (or credit, depending on your viewpoint) at the feet of political consultants. Explanations that point to advertising, she argues, are glib and unsatisfying because they diminish institutional factors and other dimensions of the public debate over national health care reform.[77] Without question, political consultants were influential figures during the health care debate, but even some consultants believe their actions have been taken out of context. "Harry and Louise," states Geoff Garin, "has taken on completely mythical power. I think the impact is overstated. The failure of health care reform, if you listed the reasons for failure, Harry and Louise would be far down the list."[78]

Hillary Clinton's condemnation of political consultants is an understandable, if disproportionate, reaction. Whether Harry and Louise defeated health care reform like she claims or whether they were merely window dressing misses the larger point. At a national level, political consultants have become indispensable advisors to decision makers on major policy matters. Furthermore, public relations, advertising, direct mail, and polling are widely accepted methods used by interest groups to effect public policy. In short, the focus on Harry and Louise is trivial by comparison to the change in interest group and legislative behavior.

A similar evaluation can be made with respect to the Contract with America. Consultant involvement with the Contract from its genesis as a campaign document to its metamorphosis into legislation was manifest. It would be a gross exaggeration to credit political consultants with the successes won by the House Republicans. Yet GOP consultants were instrumental in crafting the language used to sell Republican policies, and their Democratic counterparts were equally valuable in the pitched battle to stall the agenda. Consultants on both sides of the political spectrum helped the leadership of both parties in Congress develop strategy and provided crucial political intelligence. In spite of their undeniable presence, I believe that academic critics who single out consultants for approbation are selectively interpreting the historical record. Political consultants should not be elevated over unelected actors in the political drama. Conservative think tanks elucidated intellectual arguments that bolstered the Contract, and lobbyists provided technical and legal expertise needed to write many of the bills.

The permanent campaign has become so commonplace that the mere presence of political consultants elicits reflexsive criticism from some corners, criticism that is occasionally inflated or misplaced. During the prescription drug debate the pharmaceutical manufacturers spent nearly $100 million to defeat the Clinton proposal, with most of the money channeled through high-priced consultants, but the results were mixed. The companies were able to avoid a price control regime, yet failed to move public opinion to their preferred alternative or prevent congressional endorsement of new federal entitlement. Consultants may have contributed to the coarsening of public dialogue, or as one interview subject succinctly put it, "the dumbing down of political discourse," through commercials and direct mail. It is difficult, however, to disaggregate their influence from the host of other political actors.

There is no definitive way to gauge the impact post-electoral consulting has had on the legislative process.[79] It is a subjective exercise based mainly on the impressions of individuals intimately familiar with how laws are made. However, given the testimony of the interview subjects and the burgeoning source of secondary material, it seems that post-electoral consulting is not a curiosity or a faddish response to political fashion. Post-electoral consulting is a relatively new phenomenon, as demonstrated by comparing the Medicare case study with case studies taken from the 1990s. Public relations and opinion polling were present during the fight to pass Medicare, but the actions described in the Clinton health care reform and Contract with America case studies are so different in degree as to be different in kind. In both instances, the crucial difference was the presence of professional political consultants and the incorporation of campaign-style tactics into public policy making. It would be specious to suggest that slick packaging and poll-tested vocabulary supercede traditional, recognizable features of the legislative process, such as committee work, face-to-face lobbying, and interaction between the executive and legislative branches, but it would not be an exaggeration to claim that political leaders are just as concerned with selling a policy as they are with developing it. The final chapter will cover some of the normative implications concerning the ascendance of the permanent campaign and the position political consultants now occupy in the legislative process. In addition, it will offer speculation on the future of post-electoral consulting in such areas as initiatives and referenda and in new communications mediums such as the Internet.

NOTES

1. Michael Clark, "Selling the Issues," *Campaigns & Elections*, April/May 1993.

2. James Thurber and Candace Nelson eds. *Campaign Warriors: the Role of Political Consultants in Elections* (Washington, D.C.: The Brookings Institution, 2000).

3. Bill McInturff, interview by author, 25 April 2000.

4. Ben Goddard, interview by author, 13 June 2000.

5. Political scientists, particularly those that favor rational, coherent government, lament the weak party structure in the United States. The reasons why parties have never matured to the point seen in other Western democracies has been analyzed by a number of eminent scholars. See William Crotty ed. *The Party Symbol: Readings on Political Parties* (San Francisco: W.H. Freeman, 1980) and Ted Lowi and Joseph Romance, *A Republic of Parties? Debating the Two Party System* (New York: Rowman & Littlefield, 1998).

6. Larry Sabato, *The Rise of Political Consultants: New Ways of Winning Elections* (New York: Basic Books, 1981).

7. Peter Stone, "A Contract That Paid Off," *National Journal*, 11 February 1995, 362.

8. Darrell West and Burdett Loomis, *The Sound of Money: How Political Interests Get What They Want* (New York: W.W. Norton, 1998), 61.

9. Geoff Garin, interview by author, 12 May 2000.

10. Lawrence Grossman, *The Electronic Republic: Reshaping Democracy in the Information Age* (New York: Viking, 1995).

11. West and Loomis, *The Sound of Money*, 10.

12. Charles Kahn, interview by author, 25 April 2000.

13. John McCoy, "Citizens for Better Medicare,"*Public Citizen*, June 2000.

14. Tom McCrocklin, interview by author, 6 June 2000.

15. TJ Petrizzo, interview by author, 13 August 2002.

16. In June 2000 Congress passed legislation championed by Senator John McCain that closed the disclosure loophole. The reform law will force interest groups that sponsor *ad hoc* issue advocacy campaigns to provide lists of donors along with the amounts each group has contributed to the campaign. Although the bill does not limit or regulate the size of the donations, the public will at least know who is funding *ad hoc* alliances like Citizens for State Power and the Property Owners Coalition. See Eric Schmitt and Lizette Alvarez, "Senate Approves Step to Overhaul Campaign Finance," *New York Times*, 9 June 2000, A1.

17. Herbert Alexander ed.., *Financing Politics: Money, Elections, and Political Reform* 3rd ed. (Washington, D.C.: CQ Press, 1984).

18. When I use the term "interest group" in this context it is in the broadest sense of the word. The term covers the traditional professional associations, unions, and advocacy organizations. But it also includes corporations, consumer groups, universities, and religious organizations. Any interest group can create a tax exempt shell to engage in advocacy advertising.

19. Bill McInturff, interview by author, 25 April 2000.

20. As of this writing many groups are in the midst of changing their tax status to avoid disclosure requirements. By reconsituting themselves as non-profit organizations, issue advocacy groups will not have to divulge donor lists and will be able to defer spending reports to the FEC until after the election. Susan Schmidt, "Political Groups Change Status to Avoid Disclosure," *Washington Post*, 15 September 2000.

21. Ted Van Der Meid, interview by author, 12 May 2000.

22. David Broder and Haynes Johnson, *The System: The Way of American Politics at the Breaking Point* (Boston: Little, Brown & Co., 1996), 410–414.

23. Hedrick Smith, *The Unelected: the Media and the Lobbies* (PBS 1998, full transcript).

24. Dan Meyer, interview by author, 26 April 2000.

25. West and Loomis, *Sound of Money*, 61

26. Barry Jackson, interview by author, 31 May 2000.

27. Dan Blankenburg, interview by author, 17 August 2002.

28. Nona Wegner, interview by author, 10 August 2002.

29. Bruce Cain, John Ferejohn, and Morris Fiorina, *The Personal Vote: Constituency Service and Electoral Independence* (Cambridge, MA: Harvard University Press, 1987); Robert Bernstein, *Elections, Representation and Congressional Voting Behavior* (Washington, D.C.: CQ Press, 1989); and John Kingdon, *Congressmen's' Voting Decisions* (New York: Harper & Row, 1973).

30. R. Douglas Arnold, *The Logic of Congressional Action* (New Haven, CT: Yale University Press, 1990), 15.

31. Stan Greenberg, interview by author, 31 May 2000.

32. Kathleen Hall Jamieson, "When Harry Met Louise," *Washington Post*, 15 August 1994, A20.

33. Bill McInturff, interview by author, 25 April 2000.

34. Ted Van Der Meid, interview by author, 12 May 2000.

35. Charles Kahn, interview by author, 25 April 2000.

36. Dan Meyer, interview by author, 26 April 2000.

37. Stephen Medvic, "Is There a Spin Doctor in the House? The Impact of Political Consultants in Congressional Campaigns." Ph.D. diss., Purdue University, 1997

38. Kara Kennedy, interview by author, 13 August 2002.

39. Todd Funk, interview by author, 6 July 2000.

40. The laudatory and inflated assessment of political consultants is typified by articles such as Jerry Hagstrom, "Message Maestros," *National Journal*, 9 November 1996, 2458-2459; John Marks, "Meet the Puppetmasters," *US News and World Report*, 11 March 1996, 28-30; and Elizabeth Kolbert, "The Vocabulary of Votes," *New York Times Magazine*, 26 March 1995. It should be noted, however, that reporters are not solely responsible. Political consultants as a group are excellent self promoters who have made a habit out of exaggerating their prominence.

41. Dan Meyer, interview by author, 26 April 2000.

42. Ted Van Der Meid, interview by author, 12 May 2000.

43. "Prescription Politics" (ABC News, 20 June 2000).

44. Timothy Cook, *Making Laws and Making News: Media Strategies in the US House of Representatives* (Washington, D.C.: Brookings Institution, 1989), 123.

45. Thomas Mann and Norman Ornstein, *The Permanent Campaign and Its Future* (Washington, D.C.: The Brookings Institution, 2000), 221.

46. Ted Van Der Meid, interview by author, 12 May 2000.

47. Ed Gillespie, interview by author, 22 August 2002.

48. Dan Morgan, "Issues Give D.C. Stations Leading Edge," *Washington Post*, 2 May 2000.

49. Robin Kolodny, "Electoral Partnerships: Political Consultants and Political Parties," in *Campaign Warriors: Political Consultants in Elections*, James Thurber and Candace Nelson eds. (Washington, D.C.: the Brookings Institution, 2000), 114.

50. Samuel Kernell, *Going Public: New Strategies of Presidential Leadership* (Washington, D.C.: CQ Press, 1993), 4.

51. Dan Meyer, interview by author, 26 April 2000.

52. Nancy Libson, interview by author, 7 September 2002.

53. Stan Greenberg, interview by author, 31 May 2000.

54. Kara Kennedy, interview by author, 13 August 2002.

55. Geoff Garin, interview by author, 12 May 2000.

56. Barry Jackson, interview by author, 31 May 2000.

57. Ben Goddard, interview by author, 13 June 2000.

58. Michael Cobb and James Kuklinski, "Changing Minds: Political Arguments and Political Persuasion." *American Journal of Political Science* 1 (1997): 85-104.

59. Hedrick Smith, *The Unelected: the Media and Lobbies* (PBS, 1998 full transcript).

60. W. Lance Bennett, *The Governing Crisis: Media, Money and Marketing in American Elections* (New York: St. Martin's Press, 1992).

61. Dan Meyer, interview by author, 26 April 2000.

62. Geoff Garin, interview by author, 12 May 2000.

63. Peter Stone, "Man with a Message," *National Journal*, 19 April 1997, 750.

64. Darrell West and Richard Francis, "Electronic Advocacy: Interest Groups and Public Policy Making," *PS: Political Science & Politics* 29 (1996): 27.

65. Gwen Ifill, "Off the Books Advisors Giving Clinton a Big Lift," *New York Times*, 1 April 1993, A16.

66. Stan Greenberg, interview by author, 31 May 2000.

67. Peter Morgan and Glenn Reynolds, *The Appearance of Impropriety* (New York: The Free Press, 1997).

68. Charles Kahn, interview by author, 25 April 2000.

69. Tom McCrocklin, interview by author, 6 June 2000.

70. TJ Petrizzo, interview by author, 13 August 2002.

71. Robin Toner, "Making Sausage," *New York Times*, 4 September 1994.

72. Nancy Libson, interview by author, 7 September 2002.

73. Bill McInturff, interview by author, 25 April 2000.

74. Geoff Garin, interview by author, 12 May 2000.

75. Thurber and Nelson, *Campaign Warriors*, 198.

76. Paul Herrnson, "Hired Guns in House Races: Campaign Professionals in House Elections" in *Campaign Warriors: Political Consultants in Elections*, James Thurber and Candace Nelson eds. (Washington, D.C.: the Brookings Institution, 2000), 147.

77. Theda Skcopol, *Boomerang: Clinton's Health Security Effort and the Turn Against Government in US Politics*. New York: W.W. Norton & Co., 1996.

78. Geoff Garin, interview by author, 12 May 2000.

79. David Brady and Morris Fiorina, "Congress in the Era of the Permanent Campaign," in *The Permanent Campaign and Its Future*, Thomas Mann and Norman Ornstein eds., (Washington, D.C: The Brookings Institution, 2000).

8

Conclusions

"Consultants are the shamans in the political tribe – the ones who, through some combination of technical knowledge and good intuition, can supply verbiage that might make the difference between winning and losing."

Nicholas Lemann

During one of the interviews for this book I was pressed repeatedly by a political consultant for assurance that his comments would not appear, as he put it, in some hatchet-job magazine exposé. His concern, he said, was based on a prior experience where comments he had made in confidence to a researcher later surfaced in an unflattering article. He further stated that he was reluctant to do interviews because "we [political consultants] always get bad press."[1] It is ironic that these self-proclaimed public relations experts should suffer from such a poor public image. Consultants claim that their unsavory reputation is due, in part, to sensational press reports that alternately portray them as dirty tricksters or immoral manipulators. Two prime examples come to mind immediately: Ed Rollins and Dick Morris. Rollins was excoriated by reporters for his underhanded attempt to suppress the Black vote in a New Jersey campaign, and Morris was lampooned for his infamous telephone conversation with President Clinton while in bed with a prostitute. The negative image is reinforced by Hollywood, as the movie industry faithfully casts consultants as cynical, soulless villains in political films.[2] Consultants, it seems, are to political films what HMOs are to medical dramas. The academic literature on political consulting, unlike the popular press, offers a well-rounded portrait of the profession, with more detail than the caricature drawn by the mass media and the entertainment industry. However, scholars share some of the popular disdain for political consultants. Indeed, some authors blame them for the proliferation of a host of ills in the democratic process, such as the cost of conducting a campaign and the vicious tenor of political advertising.[3]

Perhaps one reason why the academic opinion of political consulting has been so disapproving is because few people have studied the subject. Although several scholars have written books exploring the nebulous world of "election men," the political science discipline, prior to the 1980s, largely overlooked the emergence of political consulting. By the latter part of the 1980s and early 1990s, political consulting had established itself as a force within American politics and political scientists began to pay closer attention to consultants' methods and their influence over candidates.[4] Now, scholars are rectifying the earlier oversight and are addressing pertinent questions, such as what the impact of political consultants on congressional campaigns, what their relationships with the political parties are, and what their role is in the growing trend of direct democracy (i.e., referendums and initiative campaigns).[5] Increased academic curiosity about political consulting has produced a robust body of literature in a relatively short time. Nevertheless, one notable blindspot has persisted. The vast majority of books and articles analyzing political consulting, whether impressionistic or empirical, remain focused on the consultants' natural milieu: campaigns. Over the past decade political consultants transcended the artificial boundary of candidate campaigns and have begun to explore opportunities in issue-advocacy work; essentially managing a campaign around an idea instead of a candidate. In addition to the new ventures, a significant number of consultants have reinvented themselves as policy advisors and continue to counsel their political clients once in office, providing tactical advice and plotting strategy. The purpose of this study has been to cast some light on the expanded role political consultants play in the policy-making process after the election.

The entry of political consulting into the policy-making process is more than a curiosity or a passing political fad. Post-electoral consulting represents a fundamental change in how legislators and interest groups attempt to move a policy agenda and engage the general public. As the campaign methods and tactics introduced by consultants gain favor with relevant political actors, lawmaking begins to take on the outward trappings of a modern campaign, complete with daily polls, mass media blitzes, and staged public relations events. The change is not incidental or merely aesthetic. The transformation has broad implications for governing, since many elements of campaigns such as the adversarial, winner-take-all ethic, the emphasis on appearance rather than substance, and the short-term strategic mindset, are antithetical to governing. Injecting campaign-style tactics into the legislative process can exacerbate partisan animosity and limit the prospects for legislative compromise. In addition, academic critics have expressed well-founded concerns that political consultants are another perfidious manifestation of elite bias in American politics. Profit-minded political consultants, they argue, further tip the balance in favor of privileged interests by using their communication expertise and mastery over political symbolism to manipulate public policy debates.[6]

From an historical standpoint, stumping for a new policy or an important piece of legislation is a commonplace occurrence in American politics. During the twentieth century, presidents used the bully pulpit to stir up public opinion with regularity. In 1919, for example, President Woodrow Wilson exhausted himself until he suffered a stroke while conducting a whistle-stop campaign for public support for the League of Nations. Advances in communications technology, most notably the invention of television, enabled future presidents to "campaign" without leaving the confines of the White House. Members of Congress, while not as ambitious as the president, have also toured locales and appeared on TV in an effort to create a groundswell behind a new idea. During the 1980s, former New Hampshire Senator Warren Rudman traveled the country trying to galvanize the public around the issue of deficit reduction. Yet the current situation is distinguished from past examples of public outreach by the presence of professional campaign operatives and pollsters. In the modern era, television commercials, direct-mail appeals, and other forms of political advertising coordinated by political consultants are used to exhort the public to support or oppose policy proposals. The ongoing prescription drug debate is a typical example. As legislation wound through the 106th Congress, the American public was bombarded with competing ads that delivered contrary narratives. Consumer groups and insurance companies that wanted to see some federal action with respect to drug prices produced ads that showed citizens fleeing to Canada in search of cheaper medicines. Meanwhile, their adversaries, the drug manufacturers, introduced us to "Flo," a spry elderly lady who was adamantly opposed to "big government" interference in health care.[7]

The difference between the past and the present is best understood by comparing lawmaking prior to the advent of the permanent campaign and the involvement of political consultants to contemporary examples. All four case studies exhibit features typically associated with lawmaking: fevered lobbying by interest groups, tedious committee work, back-channel negotiations between the president and members of Congress, and horse trading among legislators. Yet in the three modern examples – the Contract with America, the Clinton health care reform effort, and the battle over a prescription drug benefit – there was a great emphasis on marketing and selling the policies. The elevated status of political marketing (hence the need for political consultants) can be attributed to two basic changes in American politics. First, the ascendance of television and the corresponding explosion in mass media outlets has altered the way politicians engage in policy debates and communicate with the general public. Spreading information through television often necessitates the use of experts who are familiar in the subtleties and quirks of the medium. Second, and related to the first, today there is a more concerted effort on the part of policy makers and interest groups to draw the public into the policy battle. Interest groups and politicians spend a significant amount of time and money in an attempt to mobilize public opinion. Consultants, by virtue of their campaign pedigree, have the requisite experience and background to serve as interlocutors of policy messages. Thus, the triumph of mass media politics coupled with a desire on the part of politicians and interest groups to manipulate public opinion have made political consultants a coveted resource.

The absence of political consultants and the lack of campaign-style tactics create a clear distinction between the Medicare case study and the three later examples. In 1964 the principal actors responsible for Medicare were indifferent to public relations. Negotiations and legislative haggling were concentrated among a select group of lawmakers and the president. Neither the president nor congressional leaders expressed an interest in soliciting public support through public relations. President Lyndon Johnson's crushing victory over Senator Barry Goldwater and the corresponding tidal wave of new, liberal Democratic legislators was viewed as a mandate for a more activist government. Meanwhile, interest groups focused their energies on traditional "inside" lobbying. Political advertising, what little there was, had no discernible impact on the outcome. Contrast the Medicare experience with the Clinton health care reform effort, where legislators and White House officials seemed preoccupied with public perception and distracted by political ads. Interest groups complemented their usual lobbying approach with an expensive "outside" strategy, channeling millions of dollars through high-priced political consultants in the hopes of influencing the debate.

DIFFERENT CIRCUMSTANCES IN THE FOUR CASE STUDIES

Medicare presents an interesting case study of the legislative process before the advent of post-electoral consulting, but it begs the question: How are the events surrounding the Medicare debate distinct from later examples involving political consultants? I propose that there are three significant differences distinguishing Medicare from the Contract with America, the Clinton health care reform, and the prescription drug debate related to political consulting. First, in the thirty years that separated the Great Society from the Clinton administration, the political landscape underwent a great transformation, particularly in the field of communications. Technological advances, such as satellite communications and cable television, and the emergence of mass media forced politicians to adapt to a faster-paced, more fluid political environment. C-SPAN and 24-hour news channels have made the legislative process more transparent to the public eye and subsequently given politicians a greater appreciation for the importance of perception. The dawn of mass media politics has real consequences for how politicians behave and interact with each other. Contemporary presidents, for example, are disposed to "go public" rather than negotiate with public leaders behind the scenes. Legislators, for their part, seem just as intent on "making news" as they are on making laws.[8] This evolutionary change in the way politicians engage in policy debates and communicate with the general public has created a demand for the services of political consultants. Consultants, whose experience is in the heated, rhetorically charged atmosphere of campaigns, are ideally suited to provide policy advice to politicians in this context.

Second and related to the first, the venue where policy battles are fought has been expanded to include the virtual world of television and, more recently, cyberspace. In 1965 the combatants faced each other within the exclusive confines of Washington, D.C., power centers. Interest groups, for instance, focused extensively on "inside" strategies to affect policy change. The significant exception is the AMA's quixotic ad campaign against Medicare. The AMA's expensive but primitive political marketing effort was not successful and was barely noticed by legislators. Contrast this with the sophisticated advertising effort coordinated by the Heath Insurers Association of America to defeat the Clinton health care reform or the multi million dollar marketing effort behind Flo. Contemporary political actors have accepted the proposition, rightly or wrongly, that policy battles are won and lost around the "kitchen table." This is not to suggest public relations overshadows committee work and inter-governmental negotiations, but that grassroots activity by interest groups and government officials is a crucial part of an overall legislative strategy.[9] The similarity between grassroots activity and electoral campaigning is not superficial, creating yet another opportunity for political consultants to involve themselves in the policy process.

Finally, in a basic sense what public opinion means to lawmaking today is markedly different to what it meant during the Medicare debate. It would foolish, as well as incorrect, to claim that public opinion regarding Medicare was not important to Lyndon Johnson and his allies on Capitol Hill, but the historical record reveals policy makers were not obsessed with the public mood. Some political figures, such as Wilbur Mills, were disdainful of public opinion, and others, such as Wilbur Cohen, were wary of its role in shaping legislation. Johnson, for his part, understood that his opportunity to pass Medicare was predicated on the public's approval of his ambitious domestic agenda, but he did remarkably little to cultivate public support once the election was over. Instead, he preferred to concentrate on personal contact with members of Congress. Compare this with the furtive, incessant polling that followed the Contract and the Clinton health care reform efforts. In both cases, policy makers felt compelled to harness public opinion as a way of projecting an advantage. Their preoccupation with public sentiment created an insatiable appetite for polls. The elevated status of public opinion motivated politicians to employ political consultants, who are best equipped to interpret and manipulate it.

A host of scholars have addressed the changes wrought by the advancement of communications technology and the development of the mass media on American politics. I do not wish to do them a disservice by engaging in a slapdash, pasteurized summary of their work, so I will endeavor to keep my remarks focused on how the changes relate to the advent of post-electoral consulting. Essentially, politicians who chose to use the mass media, particularly television, to garner support for their policies routinely rely upon the figures who have the most experience manipulating the medium: political consultants. Moreover, the modern politicians nearly pathological fascination with public opinion leads them to employ pollsters as full time policy soothsayers. The decision to use political consultants is directly related to the challenges posed by communicating in a technically sophisticated mediated polity. Simply put, political consultants preeminence is an affirmation of the contemporary political condition, where selling a policy is just as crucial as developing it.

Lawmaking is much more transparent today than it was in the 1960s. During the Medicare debate politicians were shielded, to a degree, from scrutiny by the insularity of congressional politics. Affairs were not kept secret, print journalists and lobbyists paid keen attention, but the absence of television allowed legislators to conduct their business in relative anonymity. Now C-SPAN presents gavel-to-gavel coverage of the House and Senate, while other cable networks maintain a permanent presence on the Hill, ready to report a story at a moment's notice. Today's legislators live in what Paul Light refers to as "an environment of surveillance."[10] The increased attention and visibility has altered how legislators act, particularly with regard to high-profile issues.

As the mass media grew in stature, congressional scholars advanced a typology that divided legislators into two rough categories. Members of the first group, the "workhorses," were typically described as diligent, behind-the-scenes figures who shunned the glaring media spotlight. These members were usually old-guard politicians who generally supported the hierarchical arrangement and worked within the system to earn respect and power. The other group, the "showhorses," exploited media attention and sought it out with a variety of symbolic and controversial actions designed to gain publicity. These members tended to be younger and were less likely to accept the institutional confines established by more senior members. The difference between the two is more than stylistic or aesthetic and involves a conception of productive behavior that is fundamentally different. The new generation of media conscious legislators are willing to use mass media techniques to advance their policy goals. They prefer taking to the airwaves to solicit public support instead of toiling in the shadows to build a policy coalition.[11]

This crude dichotomy is simplistic and does not render a complete picture of congressional behavior, but it does serve as a departure point for a debate about how legislators make laws. In the case of Medicare, workhorse legislators dominated the process. Chairman Mills and his colleagues on the Ways and Means Committee were content to operate without provoking a maelstrom of media attention. Mills felt his primary obligation was to craft a viable bill that a majority of Democrats could support on the House floor. He was indifferent to public perception. His low regard for public opinion is exemplified by his decision not to hold public hearings on Medicare. In order to expedite the bill, Mills, with the support of the Democrats on the Ways and Means Committee, went straight to closed, executive session.[12] This is in sharp contrast to the spectacle that followed the latter two case studies. During the Contract with America, legislators in both parties held "theme team" meetings, often with affiliated political consultants, to develop daily messages tied to committee action. Legislators would then take to the House floor or use committee time to promote the message. The strategy is rooted in the understanding that hard work within the institutional setting can be for naught if the corresponding public perception is negative. Public relations is not a substitute for committee work, but the resources devoted to "spin control" indicate a commitment to capturing the terms of debate in addition to influencing the actual content of a bill.

The workhorse legislator is not extinct. In fact, there are many members who enjoy long, successful careers in Congress far away from the limelight. Yet even the most reticent, self-effacing member would acknowledge that media scrutiny has raised the profile and influence of self-promoting political entrepreneurs.

Consider the different political worlds inhabited by Wilbur Mills and Dan Rostenkowski. Rostenkowski, a protégé of Mills, was very comfortable in the cloistered world of lobbyists and committee markups. He was awkward in front of the camera and openly expressed derision for "blow dried politicians" who cultivated the media. In a recent Rostenkowski biography, Richard Cohen remarked that he was an old-style politician trapped in a media-oriented political world.[13] Unfortunately for Rostenkowski, he, unlike Mills, could not afford to ignore the media or treat members who took cues from the media with indifference. By the time Rostenkowski became chairman of the House Ways and Means Committee, the ability of a committee chairman to control its members had declined sharply. His impotence was demonstrated by his inability to fend off pressure generated by outside public relations campaigns. When it became clear that some Ways and Means Democrats were fearful of supporting the Clinton administrations bill due to bad publicity, Rostenkowski negotiated with the HIAA to have their attack ads taken off the air in return for some concessions in the bill. It is difficult to imagine Wilbur Mills succumbing to this type of pressure. In fact, the AMA's expensive public campaign to defeat Medicare went virtually unnoticed by Mills. Mills casual disregard for public relations and Rostenkowski's explicit acknowledgment of it illustrates the influence marketing and advertising have over the legislative process.

From the politician's perspective there is a dark side to the omnipresence of the media. Since the early 1970s, elected officials, liberals as well as conservatives, have criticized the media for what they perceive as undue, deliberate cynicism. It is now commonplace to hear politicians lament about snide comments, puerile coverage, and outright distortions that pervade the mainstream media. Their concern, while undoubtedly self-serving, has been echoed by scholars and knowledgeable observers of media behavior. According to media critics like James Fallows and Mark Rozell, empirical evidence supports the assertion that media coverage of Congress and the president has grown increasingly negative over the past thirty years. Indeed, James Fallows claims that today's journalists are inculcated with a condescending cynicism toward politicians. He states, "Reporters don't explicitly argue or analyze what they dislike in a political program but instead sound sneering and supercilious about the whole idea of politics."[14] In their jaundiced eyes policy motives are suspect and policy makers are all engaged in a great game. This persistent media bias has led some contemporary politicians to use consultants to manage their dealings with the press. During the first 100 days of the 104th Congress, the House Republicans used several consulting firms to peddle stories that put the Republican accomplishments in a positive light. Republicans claimed they had to resort to paid media and direct mail to penetrate the national media.[15]

The dawn of mass media politics has had pronounced consequences for the presidency as well. Over the past forty years it has become an accepted practice for the president to use the "electronic bully pulpit" to champion a new policy. Despite evidence of this phenomenon dating back to the 1930s, it is generally associated with the 1980s and 1990s. Samuel Kernell states, "The concept and legitimizing precedents of going public may have been established during FDR's time, but the emergence of presidents' who routinely do so to promote their policies in Washington awaited the development of modern systems of transportation and mass communication."[16] The strategy was perfected under Ronald Reagan, who effectively used television to exhort the public to support his economic plan during his first term. Bill Clinton was a president in Reagan's mold, comfortable in front of a camera and willing to use the media to leverage Congress. Throughout the health care debate, President Clinton used televised appeals, photo opportunities, and staged media events, all coordinated with the help of consultants from the DNC as well as those attached to the White House, to highlight the importance of health care reform. The philosophy was summed up by President Clinton's spokesman Mike McCurry: "Campaigns are about framing a choice for the American people. When you are responsible for governing you have to use the same tools of public persuasion to advance the program, to build public support for the direction you are attempting to lead."[17] McCurry's explanation highlights the irony of contemporary politics, in which the president must pander to the general public in order to "lead" it. Clinton's campaign-style issue management stands in sharp relief against the actions of Lyndon Johnson, who preferred a more personal strategy. Johnson's public pronouncements for Medicare were unambiguous, but they were isolated and not the centerpiece of his legislative strategy. Instead, he worked quietly with congressional leaders and other interested parties to build a stable coalition in support of Medicare.

After President Clinton introduced his health care plan, Bill Gradison, a former Republican Congressman and the president of the HIAA, told reporters that the lobbying battle on Capitol Hill would be intense, but that the war would be won or lost around America's kitchen tables.[18] Gradison's comments encapsulate the difference in interest group strategy from the 1960s to the 1990s. In the 1960s, lobbyists would roam the halls of Congress and meet with legislators and buttonhole them to make their arguments. In the 1990s, lobbyists are still fixtures on Capitol Hill, but their activities have been supplemented by grassroots pressure applied by average citizens. These grassroots efforts are often conducted and developed by political consultants and enhance the insider position by demonstrating public support for the issue. Some observers claim that during the health care debate nearly $50 million was spent on grassroots activity.[19] An equally impressive sum was spent by interest groups in connection with the Contract with America. With respect to the prescription drug battle, the figure quoted by pubic watchdog groups is close to $40 million, not including the millions spent on direct mail and television advertising. In all three modern cases, the bulk of the money was filtered through political consultants, who created the advertisements and conducted the direct-mail outreach. Although it is difficult to speculate about the impact that these contrived grassroots campaigns have on legislative decision making, consultants believe that they have changed the face of lobbying.[20] Grassroots lobbying was a novelty in the 1960s because the capability to contact millions of citizens did not exist. Groups with large, geographically dispersed memberships had difficulty generating enough constituent pressure to justify expensive grassroots efforts. Grassroots lobbying was so unreliable that Wilbur Cohen dissuaded the AFL-CIO from using it on behalf of Medicare. He believed it was clumsy and a waste of labor's limited resources.[21]

According to health policy analyst Lawrence Jacobs, "When the Medicare program was debated in 1964 under President Lyndon Johnson, 78 percent of Americans said that they trusted the federal government to do what is right; in 1994, when President Clinton was promoting his reform plan, only 22 percent expressed this level of trust."[22] Given this level of public skepticism, the president can hardly be blamed for resorting to an epic public relations campaign. What is significant about the difference, however, is not the radical drop in public faith in government; it is the idea that the government must constantly solicit public support. Politicians, particularly those in leadership positions, would undoubtedly disagree with the assertion that they chart public policy strategy always with a finger in the proverbial wind, but their behavior suggests they are in the thrall of public opinion polling. The proof is in their statements, in which they cite poll results as a justification for a policy, and in their actions, which respond to fluctuations in public opinion. Of course, there are individuals who have made a career by ignoring majority opinion, but they are considered mavericks whose fame is derived in large part because they are isolated voices.

During the Clinton health care reform and the Contract with America, pollsters occupied prominent positions as strategic advisors. Stan Greenberg, President Clinton's lead pollster in 1993 and 1994, played a crucial role in developing the marketing strategy behind the Clinton plan. He edited the president's speeches and suggested various ways to pitch the plan to the public. After the Republicans took control of Congress in 1995, Frank Luntz used his poll data to help the Republican majority implement the Contract. He and fellow GOP pollsters Bill McInturff and Linda DiVall were instrumental in crafting the vocabulary used by many Republican legislators to describe the party's goals. Both case studies provide ample instances in which focus groups and poll data were an integral part of the legislative strategy. There is nothing comparable regarding Medicare. The Johnson administration did employ pollsters, but they were not the masters of voter knowledge that they are today. Johnson's own appreciation for the power of public opinion was largely unformed and intuitive.[23] As for Congress, there is no evidence that any key member consulted a pollster in connection with Medicare. Mills had little use for a pollster and the members who did quote poll numbers invariably cited neutral polling organizations like Gallup or Roper.[24]

POLITICAL CONSULTING AND THE LEGISLATIVE PROCESS: WHAT HAS IT WROUGHT?

Political consultants did not create the conditions that have made them valuable assets in policy debates. It would be more accurate to describe them as beneficiaries of a new trend in politics. However, the fact that they are not responsible for how post-electoral consulting came to pass does not mean that they are absolved from the consequences their actions have on the legislative process. In Chapter 1 I suggested that the use of political consultants in an advisory capacity could adversely impact the chances for legislative compromise. The partisan attacks, the inflammatory advertising, and the public grandstanding urged on by political consultants can compromise bargaining opportunities. The events chronicled in the Contract with America, the Clinton health care reform, and prescription drugs case studies, supplemented with commentary from interview subjects, support this line of reasoning. President Clinton and the First Lady committed some extraordinary blunders in their attempt to pass health care reform, but even allowing for their tactical mistakes there is little doubt that the unrelenting advertising attacks on the health care plan helped dampen enthusiasm for reform and hardened the opposition. Ads criticizing the plan essentially scared some legislators away from a health care bill. During the 104th Congress, political consultants were instrumental in prolonging the government shutdown by presenting the House Republicans with polling data that indicated the public sympathized with their tough stance. Meanwhile, President Clinton received contrary intelligence from his pollsters.[25] Consultants were also used by congressional leaders in both parties to bolster their message-strategy and theme-development operations. Floor speeches and press events were occasions to trumpet poll-tested phrases and campaign-style bromides. During the early stages of the prescription drug debate, the issue was largely defined as a high-stakes contest between President Clinton and the pharmaceutical manufacturers. There were moments in all three cases when it seemed that staying on message and attacking the opposition took precedence over the substantive details of governing.[26] The principals involved in the prescription drug debate were keenly aware of their public image and spent enormous sums of money to sway public opinion. In a limited sense, the content of the legislation was overshadowed by the campaign. "Like it or not," claims Nona Wegner, "for an issue to have traction it has to have the capability to be reduced to a 30 second sound bite." Wegner further states that the need to sell a policy "politicizes the issue," sometimes to the point that meaningful dialogue is crowded out.[27]

It should come as no surprise that political consultants first instinct when confronted with an adversary is to attack. Political consultants' perception of politics is shaped by competitive elections, and their responses are honed under the duress of a campaign. A campaign is a high-stakes conflict in which there are clear winners and clear losers; it is not an intellectual exercise, like lawmaking, where the outcome is shaped by collaboration as well as combat. According to Thomas Mann, "Campaigning and campaigners use the language of war – opponents are enemies to be vanquished. Policy makers use the language of negotiation – today's adversaries may be tomorrow's allies."[28] Thus, a consultant's initial inclination is to simplify the policy-making process to a zero-sum game. That is, however, a distorting and potentially harmful reduction of the complex lawmaking ritual. An unrelenting attack may be appropriate in a campaign because your opponent has no influence on your future success. In governing, the person that you vilify and humiliate may be an important potential ally on another piece of legislation.[29]

Poll-tested slogans do not have to be aggressive or excessively hyperbolic to threaten the legislative process. First, platitudes can inspire a false level of expectation among the citizenry. Public disaffection with politics is partly the result of a loss of confidence in our political institutions. People hold elected officials in low regard because they rightly suspect that politicians often tell them what they want to hear. Using focus groups and polls to develop a sales pitch is a form of deception. Parroting back language derived from focus groups and polls should be viewed as a step backward in the evolution of political discourse. It is a purposeful exercise in citizen manipulation, not an improved means of sharing information with constituents. The fact that politicians spend a considerable amount of time and energy on measuring public opinion is not a cause for alarm, but there is something disconcerting about the use of social science to tap into voters' collective subconscious in order to find the most emotionally charged terminology with which to describe a policy proposal.

It would be foolish as well as grossly inaccurate to lay the blame for government gridlock at the feet of political consultants. No matter how much influence political consultants have over their clients, they are not the ones making the decisions. The collective responsibility for the actions or inaction of government lies ultimately with the people who hold elected office. Nevertheless, it would be equally foolish to shrug off the ubiquitous presence of political consultants as meaningless window dressing. Political consultants may not be the primary cause for the demise of a policy proposal, as Hillary Clinton suggested with respect to health care, but they have succeeded in making a tenuous situation more difficult by championing the winner-take-all campaign ethic.

Another serious concern raised by the introduction of consultants to the policy-making process stems from the suitability of their methods in a governing context. Is it proper to stimulate the general public with inflammatory ads and direct-mail appeals? It is questionable whether the public discourse is enhanced or whether people are made more aware of policies, as some consultants claim, by boiling complex social problems down to a thirty-second commercial or a two-page color mailing. Some of the consultants interviewed for this project suggested that ads perform a genuine public service by providing a heuristic shortcut for busy Americans who cannot spare a moment to focus on public policy. As for opinion polls and focus groups, the pseudo scientific authority vested in pollsters by other political actors is an exaggeration of their abilities. Given the obvious technical limitations of polls and, in particular, focus groups, there is good reason to fear their use in making policy.

When scholars criticize political advertising, and by proxy political consultants, the linkage they often seek to establish is between public cynicism and advertising.[30] Since the 1950s political scientists have watched public confidence in government plummet, along with levels of public participation.[31] Voting in national elections has dropped from 61.6 percent of the eligible populace in 1952 to 49 percent in 1996.[32] In addition, annual Gallup surveys show that public trust in the government's ability to solve national problems has declined steadily over the past twenty-five years.[33] According to knowledgeable observers, advertising, in particular negative ads, feed public cynicism by emphasizing public doubts and creating an atmosphere of distrust. The Harry and Louise commercials, for example, drove home the message of the government as an ineffectual, cumbersome, invasive entity that was bound to screw up American health care. Flo and her fellow bowlers made the same point about a prescription drug benefit. Even if this criticism is justified, the blanket condemnation of government lingers and fosters a well of permanent distrust in all government actions. According to a senior congressional staff member, "It is fair to say that most of the advocacy advertising out there is designed to put the fear of God in the average citizen. If you made them [the citizens] mad or scared, then you're half way home to creating a grassroots movement."[34] It should be noted that political consultants are not willfully trying to ruin our public faith in our political institutions. In fact, I surmise that most consultants would be appalled at such a suggestion.[35] Nonetheless, one of the long-range consequences of mass media and direct-mail assaults on policy proposals may be to accelerate the erosion of public confidence in the democratic process.

Politics has been called war without bloodshed. It is an evocative metaphor that reminds us that partisan battles over public policy are not genteel affairs. Harsh rhetoric and exaggeration will always be a part of the legislative process. The day-to-day activities of legislators, however, demand a modicum of decorum. It is no small detail that House and Senate rules prohibit members from engaging in personal attacks on the chamber floor and further require that members be referred to with the honorific "gentleman" or "gentlelady." The often stilted exchanges witnessed on C-SPAN disguise fierce partisanship. According to Eric Ulsaner, the precipitous decline in comity that followed the 1960s has had a deleterious effect on lawmaking. Ulsaner's theory is ably supported by research, but it does not take an elaborate political science analysis to understand that when people begin attacking one another it will harm the prospects for cooperation.[36] As Samuel Kernell points out, "going public" threatens to delegitimize your opponent's position and thus hardens resistance to a negotiated compromise.[37]

People who cling to the ideal of sober-minded, articulate, and rational public debates will always view political consultants with a jaundiced eye. Yet political consultants will be the first to admit that they are not responsible for civic education. They are hired experts who are expected to present their clients' positions in as strong and persuasive a manner as possible. If this means leaving out some pertinent facts or slanting the narrative to favor the client, so be it. According to James Thurber's survey of political consultants, an overwhelming number (97.5%) indicated that it was clearly unethical to make statements in political advertisements that were factually untrue. The sample was less decisive about other tactics, such as taking facts out of context (25.5% thought it was unethical) and using ads to frighten voters (14% thought it was unethical and 36.5% thought it was acceptable.)[38] Thurber's results are important and telling. In some cases, using facts out context or fabricating public alarm with scare tactics can be just as corrosive to the public debate as false propaganda. Informing the elderly, for example, that they could be put in jail for buying extra health care under President Clinton's plan does not enhance the public's understanding of the stake they have in health care reform.

Questionable advertising is subject to obvious criticism, but what about opinion polls and focus groups? American politicians' unshakeable addiction to polling has been dissected, analyzed, and critiqued ad nauseum by scholars. A substantial body of work explores the issue from a philosophical vantage point and addresses broad socio political questions about the role of public opinion in a representative democracy.[39] I would prefer to avoid recapping the rarified theoretical debate and instead concentrate on more pedestrian, but equally relevant, concerns: in particular, the utility of using polls to plot policy strategy. Relying too much on polls gives rise to a strain of political myopia where everything is viewed through a short-term lens. Large-scale problems with vast implications for future generations begin to be defined by the immediacy of public reaction. Reforming massive public benefit programs such as Social Security or Medicare, for example, will require long-range strategies. In fact, it is possible that protecting the continued viability of redistributive programs like Social Security will depend on unpopular short-term sacrifices. Using polls to chart a public policy course could prematurely limit options. During the 2002 congressional campaign, Democratic candidates, operating under the advice of Democratic pollsters, consistently raised the specter of "privatization" when criticizing Republican opponents. Whether one agrees with the conservative ideas for Social Security reform or not, fear mongering of this magnitude does nothing to advance the policy debate. As for focus groups, the potential danger is greater. Ever since famed sociologist Robert Merton introduced focus groups to American politics in the 1950s, they have been misused and inappropriately cited on a consistent basis. Supporters fancy them as an effective way to solicit in depth responses from "real people." Conventional wisdom has it that they are a good way for a politician to flavor his message with vocabulary that appeals to average citizens. It is, however, impossible to generalize the results of focus groups to the at-large populace.[40] Politicians who claim to have discovered the vox populi through focus groups are deceiving themselves.

The final issue related to post-electoral consulting centers on elite bias. When E. E. Schattschnieder wrote *The Semi-Sovereign People*, his trenchant critique of American-style pluralist politics, he claimed that one of the enduring failures of American politics was that interest group activity was dominated by elites. As he put it colorfully "the flaw in the pluralist heaven is that the heavenly chorus sings with an upper class accent."[41] The basis for Schattschneider's criticism has not changed over the years. In fact, the use of for-profit campaign professionals on behalf of parochial interests bolsters his contention of elite bias. Hiring a battery of political consultants to coordinate a public relations campaign is a capital-intensive process. Underfunded interest groups, which include almost all groups with the exception of big business and labor, are rarely able to afford consultants. It is a variation of the problem with candidate campaigns, where he who has the largest wallet will possess the loudest voice. Groups with deep financial reserves (i.e. the drug industry or the AFL-CIO) are able to drown out other voices by pounding out a message through paid media.[42] Aside from amplifying the message, political consultants advise their clients on how to frame their arguments so that they appeal to the general public. The ability of moneyed interests to tell a compelling story and spread it around to as many people as are willing to listen does not ensure that they will win the argument. If money always determined the outcome of a policy debate, then big tobacco would have nothing to fear from poorly funded anti-smoking crusaders. The pharmaceutical companies invested millions in issue advocacy only to be outmaneuvered by President Clinton. Yet the imbalance that Schattschneider identified forty years ago between rich and poor interests remains a valid criticism.[43] Given the events described in the case studies and the comments made by the interview subjects, it is reasonable to suggest that political consultants widen the disparity by putting their talents to work for wealthy groups.[44]

The marriage of interest groups and political consultants appears to have the hallmarks of a lasting partnership based on mutual need and benefit. Interest groups, generally speaking, have a narrow focus and a strong desire to see their issue(s) addressed favorably by the government. Groups used to accomplish their goals through backroom dealing and inside lobbying, but increasingly organized interests are turning to grassroots campaigns and public relations to pressure legislators. According to interest group scholar Ken Kollman, there are two basic reasons for the addition of an outside strategy:

"Outside lobbying accomplished two tasks simultaneously. First, at the elite level it communicates aspects of public opinion to policy makers. The many forms of outside lobbying – publicizing issue positions, mobilizing constituents to contact Congress, protesting or demonstrating – have the common purpose of trying to show policy makers that people really do care about some relevant policy issue...The second role for outside lobbying is to influence public opinion by changing how selected constituents consider and respond to policy issues."[45]

Some groups can sponsor grassroots action by relying on large, diffuse memberships. But for groups with a small number of ineffectual numbers, political consultants play a decisive role in crafting an effective outside strategy. Political consultants can create the impression that there is overwhelming public sentiment supporting their client's position.

THE FUTURE OF POST-ELECTORAL CONSULTING

In a relatively short time, political consultants have successfully migrated from candidate-centered campaigns to issue advocacy work and policy advising. In doing so, they have established a solid beachhead within the legislative process. But what does the future hold for post-electoral consulting? Several of the consultants interviewed for this project were intrigued by the possibilities offered by the Internet. Ben Goddard was particularly enthusiastic about connecting television and print ads to an interactive Web site where visitors could find out more information about an issue and dash off an e-mail to their congressman.[46] Indeed, in 2000 an ad campaign sponsored by Citizens for Better Medicare touted its Web address as a place where seniors can get the "facts" about prescription drugs and learn how to get involved.[47] Several political consultants also mentioned statewide initiatives and referendum campaigns as an area with tremendous growth potential. In the early 1930s in California, proto-political consultants Whitaker & Baxter sold their services to groups with ballot interests.[48] The inheritors of the Whitaker & Baxter tradition have turned ballot drives into a lucrative trade. In his latest book discussing the proliferation of lawmaking via plebiscite, David Broder writes,

[Government by initiative] is a big business in which lawyers and campaign consultants, signature gathering firms and other players sell their services to affluent interest groups or millionaire do-gooders with private policy and political agendas. These players, often not even from the state whose laws and constitutions they are rewriting, have learned that the initiative is a far more effective way of achieving their ends than the cumbersome process of supporting candidates for public office and then lobbying to pass or sign the measures they seek .[Initiatives and referendums] have spawned a huge industry devoted to the manipulation of public opinion. Campaign consultants, pollsters, media advisors, direct mail specialists, and others have made themselves in effect, the new bosses of American politics.[49]

Broder's disdain for political consultants and his alarm over their unfettered expansion is based in his belief that the integrity of representative democracy is under siege by political professionals. Broder certainly overstates the case, but his suspicions of the permanent campaign are not unfounded. Broder's concerns about false populism and manufactured public sentiment are not new. In fact, they are as old as the Republic. In the *Federalist Papers*, James Madison devotes a substantial portion of his writing wrestling with the dilemma of public opinion and the role that the public should play in governing. Madison was clearly concerned about the ascendancy of passion over reason, and in his defense of the republican concept he expressed ambivalence for popular control of public policy.[50] He was truly committed to the democratic process and believed in connecting the decisions of elected officials to the people through regularly scheduled elections. Yet his trust in public wisdom was far from complete. In his writings he cautions his fellow citizens not to trade one form of bad government (constitutional monarchy) for another (despotism masquerading as plebiscite). He believed, with good reason, that linking elected officials too closely to the fickle whims of the public would impair liberty and could lead to oligarchy.

The recent passage of a landmark campaign finance law raises another interesting question. Reform advocates succeeded in limiting "soft money" contributions to political parties, but the law leaves so-called issue-advocacy groups virtually untouched. Companies, labor unions, and trade associations are free to establish and financially support umbrella organizations to promote Social Security privatization, telecommunications reform, or any other issue. The advocacy organization can accept an unlimited amount of money from any source and spend an unlimited amount of money on advertising, phone banks, polls, or other forms of citizen outreach. The only curb on their activity lies in the conduct of federal campaigns for public office. They cannot endorse or even mention a candidate's name within a ninety-day window before an election. Ironically, the restriction on federal campaigning may encourage more spending on issue advocacy, since it is the last bastion of uncontrolled spending. One congressional aide deemed the new law to be a full-employment bill for election-law lawyers and political consultants.

Madison's concerns are just as relevant today, perhaps even more so considering modern politicians' access to political consultants and pollsters. Madison's admonitions also represent a veiled criticism of post-electoral consulting. Post-electoral consulting is a manifestation of two core premises. First, that public perception is more important than policy substance. Second, that public opinion must be harnessed before a policy proposal can proceed. Post-electoral consulting champions the introduction of campaign logic and strategy into the governing process. Earlier in the study it was stated that political practitioners view academic efforts to distinguish campaign activity governing as a contrivance that does not exist in the real world. To a limited degree they are correct. Elected officials rarely make important decisions without calculating the impact in the next election. However, it is folly to suggest that differences between campaigning and governing are the product of scholarly imagination or that campaigning and governing are fungible terms without meaningful distinction. As the Contract with America, the Clinton health reform, and the ongoing battle over a prescription drug benefit illustrate, the wholesale importation of campaign strategy and campaign experts has relevant consequences for lawmaking. To claim otherwise is to ignore the facts. Using political consultants to plot strategy, to craft the vocabulary and describe the policy, and to engage in paid media warfare over the support of the American public is a new way to influence legislation.

The real danger presented by the transformation of pollsters and consultants into policy advisors is that the other political actors, namely interest groups and elected officials, will abandon the necessary tools of compromise and accommodation that are most useful during periods of narrow partisan advantage. Campaigns are often about appearance and showmanship: policymaking should not be. The public does not benefit from empty sloganeering and focus-group-tested messages. Americans do not gain a valuable perspective when complex policy problems such as health care or tort reform are reduced to folksy narratives or emotional metaphors. For better or worse, political consultants are already established "kingmakers" in the electoral process. Although they may never occupy a similar station in the policy realm, the experience of the 1990s suggests that they will be a lasting addition to the legislative process.

Finally, it should be noted that the potential consequences of post-electoral consulting come with two important caveats. First, singling out political consultants carries with it a normative assessment of lawmaking. Implicit in the criticism of the permanent campaign is an endorsement of the proposition that lawmaking was more honest and forthright decades ago. It is not my intention to represent the politics of the past, and the legislative process in particular, as a glorified ideal that has been irrevocably corrupted by the appearance of political consultants. It is merely my assertion that the legislative process was different then and that some of the differences can be attributed to the advent of the permanent campaign. Second, while the focus of this book has been political consultants, it would misguided to identify them as the sole culprit behind the introduction of campaign tactics to policy making. As mentioned in an earlier chapter, consultants have had a hand in transforming the legislative process, but they are also the fortunate beneficiaries of technological advancements and cultural changes that they had no hand in creating.

NOTES

1. The interview subject requested anonymity when discussing the industry's relationship with the press.

2. Hollywood's swipe at political consulting began in 1972 with Robert Redford's movie *The Candidate*. The cynical, manipulative consultant played by Peter Boyle was inspired by David Garth, a pioneer in professional political consulting. *The Candidate* established a cinematic stereotype that has endured. Whether it is a light-hearted farce like *Dave* or a hardboiled political drama like *Power*, the consultant is always a villainous foil.

3. Steven Ansolabehere and Shanto Iyengar, *Going Negative: How Political Advertisements Shrink and Polarize the Electorate* (New York: The Free Press, 1995).

4. Larry Sabato, *The Rise of Political Consultants: New Ways of Winning Elections* (New York: Basic Books, 1981); Robert Friedenberg, *Communications Consultants in Political Campaigns* (Westport: Praeger, 1997); Nicholas O'shaughnessy, *The Phenomenon of Political Marketing* (New York: St. Martin's Press, 1990).

5. Stephen Medvic, "Is There a Spin Doctor in the House? The Impact of Political Consultants in Congressional Campaigns," (Ph.D. diss., Purdue University, 1997); Robin Kolodny, "Electoral Partnerships: Political Consultants and Political Parties," In *Campaign Warriors: Political Consultants in Elections,* James Thurber and Candace Nelson (Washington, D.C.: The Brookings Institution, 2000); David Broder, *Democracy Derailed: Initiative Campaigns and the Power of Money* (New York: Harcourt, 2000).

6. Darrell West and Burdett Loomis, *The Sound of Money: How Political Interests Get What They Want* (New York: W.W. Norton, 1998).

7. Dan Morgan, "On the Air and Rising," *Washington Post*, 2 May 2000.

8. See Samuel Kernell, Going Public: New Strategies of Presidential Leadership, (Washington, D.C.: CQ Press, 1993); Timothy Cook, Making Laws and Making News: Media Strategies in the US House of Representatives, (Washington, D.C.: The Brookings Institution, 1989).

9. Ken Kollman, *Outside Lobbying: Public Opinion & Interest Group Strategies* (Princeton: Princeton University Press, 1998).

10. Paul Light, *Domestic Policy Choice: From Eisenhower to Clinton* (Baltimore: Johns Hopkins University Press, 1999), 225.

11. David Brady and Morris Fiorina, "Congress in the Era of the Permanent Campaign," in *The Permanent Campaign and Its Future*, ed. Thomas Mann and Norman Ornstein, (Washington, D.C.: The Brookings Institution, 2000).

12. Joseph Loftus, "Medicare Action Begins Tomorrow," *New York Times*, 26 January 1965, A1.

13. Richard Cohen, *Rostenkowski: The Pursuit of Power and the End of Old Style Politics* (Chicago: Ivan R. Dee, 1998).

14. James Fallows, *Breaking the News: How the Media Undermine Our Democracy* (New York: Random House, 1996), 63.

15. According Peter Stone, Fred Sacher, a wealthy Republican, paid a Republican consulting firm "for a news media blitz to highlight and amplify support for the contract. Creative Response Concepts lined up talk show appearances by conservative advocacy and trade groups and inundated journalists with faxes, under the heading Contract Information Center, chronicling the contract's progress through the House." Sacher explained, "He felt the liberal media was very strongly representing the Democrats," and that in order for the public to understand the Contract the GOP needed to bypass the traditional media. Peter Stone, "Just the Right Spin," *National Journal*, 22 April 1995, 985.

16. Kernell, *Going Public*, 2.

17. Allison Mitchell, "Clinton Seems to Keep Running though the Race Is Run and Won," *New York Times*, 2 February 1997, A1.

18. David Broder and Haynes Johnson, *The System: The American Way of Politics at the Breaking Point* (Boston: Little, Brown, 1996), 67.

19. Robin Toner, "Making Sausage," *New York Times*, 4 September 1994.

20. Elizabeth Kolbert, "The Special Interests' Special Weapon," *New York Times*, 16 March 1995, A1.

21. Sheri David, *With Dignity: The Search for Medicare and Medicaid*, (Westport: Greenwood Press, 1985), 58.

22. Michael Zis, Lawrence Jacobs, and Robert Shapiro, "The Elusive Common Ground: The Politics of Public Opinion and Healthcare Reform," *Generations* (Summer 1996), 8.

23. Diane Heith, "White House Public Opinion Apparatus,"

24. Lawrence Jacobs, *Health of Nations: Public Opinion and the Making of British and American Health Policy*, (Ithaca: Cornell University Press, 1995), 145.

25. Elizabeth Drew, *Showdown: The Struggle between the Gingrich Congress and the Clinton White House* (New York: Simon and Schuster, 1996).

26. Kathleen Hall Jamieson, "Civility in the House of Representatives," *Annenberg Public Policy Center of the University of Pennsylvania*, March 1998 <http://www.

27. Nona Wegner, interview by author, 10 August 2002.

28. Thomas Mann and Norman Ornstein, eds., *The Permanent Campaign and Its Future* (Washington, D.C.: The Brookings Institution, 2000), 225.

29. Eric Ulsaner, *The Decline of Comity in the House* (Ann Arbor: University of Michigan Press, 1993).

30. See, for example, Lance Bennett, *The Governing Crisis: Media, Money and Marketing in American Elections* (New York: St. Martin's Press, 1992).

31. Seymour Martin Lipset and William Schneider, *The Confidence Gap: Business, Labor and Government in the Public Mind* (Baltimore: Johns Hopkins University Press, 1987).

32. US Bureau of the Census, *Statistical Abstract of the United States: 1999* (Washington, D.C., U.S. Bureau of the Census, 2000), 301.

33. The Gallup Poll, *Public Confidence in Institutions – Full Trend*, Gallup Organization, available: http://www.gallup.com (19 August 2003).

34. Tom McCrocklin, interview by author, 6 June 2000.

35. Thurber and Nelson, *Campaign Warriors*, 197.

36. Ulsaner, *The Decline of Comity*.

37. Kernell, *Going Public*, 154.

38. Thurber and Nelson, *Campaign Warriors*, 109.

39. V.O. Key and Susan Herbst.

40. Irving Crespi, *Public Opinion, Polling and Democracy* (Boulder: Westview Press, 1989).

41. E. E. Schattschneider, *The Semisovereign People: A Realist's View of Democracy in America* (New York: Holt, Reinhart, and Winston, 1960), 34.

42. James Gimpel, "Grassroots Equilibrium Cycles in Group Mobilization and Access," in *The Interest Group Connection*, Paul Herrnson ed. (Chatham: Chatham House, 1998).

43. Kathleen Hall Jamieson, *Everything You Think You Know About Politics...And Why You're Wrong* (New York: Basic Books, 2000), 137–140.

44. Schattschneider's animated concern for the disorganized and the impoverished is important. However, in recent years groups with meager financial resources have been able to draw attention to their issues with clever, occasionally ingenuous public relations spectacles. The panoply of environmentalists, human rights advocates, and trade unionists that disrupted the WTO meetings in Seattle in 1999 and the World Bank meetings in Washington in 2000 took advantage of the free media to present their case to the general public. They succeeded, in spite of the vast financial superiority enjoyed by corporate interests, in creating an awareness among the general public about the negative consequences of unfettered free trade.

45. Ken Kollman, *Outside Lobbying: Public Opinion & Interest Group Strategies* (Princeton: Princeton University Press, 1998), 8.

46. Ben Goddard, interview by author, 13 June 2000.

47. The Web site, http//www.bettermedicare.org, provides data and contact information targeted to senior citizens. The most innovative feature, however, allows seniors to simply type in their zip code and a letter with their name will be sent to Congress.

48. Greg Mitchell, *Campaign of the Century: Upton Sinclair's Race for Governor of California and the Birth of Media Politics* (New York: Random House, 1992).

49. Broder, *Democracy Derailed*, 5.

50. "Federalist 49," *The Federalist Papers*, ed. Clinton Rossiter, (New York: Mentor, 1961), 313–317.

Appendix

The Interview Subjects

Geoff Garin is a senior vice president of Peter D. Hart Research Associates, and he also serves as a partner in the firm's political division, the Garin, Hart, Yang Research Group. The firm represents fifteen members of the U.S. Senate, by far the most of any Democratic polling firm in the 1998 election cycle. Garin has polled for Senator Chuck Schumer, several Southern Democratic Senators, and Senator Russ Feingold. In addition to his candidate work Garin has polled for a wide range of interest groups and private sector organizations.

Bill McInturff is a partner and co founder of Public Opinion Strategies, a national political and public affairs survey research firm established in 1991. Public Opinion Strategies is one of the country's largest political polling firms and currently represents seven U.S. Senators, six governors, and more than forty Members of Congress. McInturff has completed research for some of the country's largest corporations and associations, including American Airlines, Bell Atlantic/NYNEX, NBC, the National Basketball Association, International Paper, Pfizer, and the aluminum, paper, and computer industries. Since 1991 the focus of much of his work has been health care reform, having completed more than seventy focus groups and more than twenty-five national studies. McInturff's health care clients include the Health Leadership Council, the American Hospital Association, the Association of American Medical Colleges, and the Federation of American Health Systems. His primary health care client is the Health Insurance Association of America, including conducting message and advertising testing for their series of Harry and Louise television commercials, called by *Advertising Age* "among the best conceived and executed public affairs advertising programs in history." His prior experience includes "hands-on" campaign-management experience at the local, congressional, and presidential levels, as well as holding senior positions with the Republican national party committees prior to entering the field of survey research. McInturff co writes a monthly column on trends and political strategy for *Campaigns & Elections* magazine, served as a consultant to CBS News for their coverage of the 1992 Republican convention and is a frequently quoted source on the topic of American politics, having appeared on *Nightline*, CNN's *Inside Politics*, and C-SPAN, and is frequently quoted by national news magazines and a variety of major newspapers.

Ben Goddard began his communications career over thirty years ago in television news. After establishing an advertising agency in Colorado, Goddard went on to build an impressive issue advocacy and political advertising practice, working for Jimmy Carter, Gary Hart, Bruce Babbitt, Dennis DeConcini, Mo Udall, and many others. He is widely regarded as one of the most capable and creative talents in the business, particularly in the area of issue advocacy, and has earned a number of awards for his winning media. Goddard continues to oversee all aspects of the firm's advertising, provides strategic counsel and planning services to clients, and directs the firm's message-development efforts.

Charles Kahn has focused principally on health care financing-one of the defining issues of the past two decades. As staff director of the Health Subcommittee of the House Ways and Means Committee (1995-1998), he played a critical role in the passage of the Health Insurance Portability and Accountability Act (HIPAA) and the Medicare provisions of the 1997 Balanced Budget Act. His earlier Capitol Hill experience included serving as minority health counsel to Ways and Means and as senior health policy advisor to Senator David Durenburger (R-MN) when the latter was chairman of the Senate Finance Committee's Health Subcommittee. Kahn also served as legislative assistant for health to Senator Dan Quayle (R-IN). Kahn is well acquainted with the issues critical to the health insurance industry. In 1993 and 1994 he was HIAA's executive vice president in charge of federal affairs, policy development, research, and communications. It was during his tenure that the association mounted the groundbreaking Harry and Louise advertising campaign that questioned the viability of the Clinton health plan.

T. J. Petrizzo is the president of the Petrizzo Group, a contract lobbying and public relations firm in Washington D.C. He is the former chief of staff to Congresswoman Jennifer Dunn. He was her principal staff member for the House Ways and Means Committee and her political advisor during her historic run for the Majority Leader position. He specializes in tax policy and health care issues.

Nona Wegner is the president of Citizens for Better Medicare, a grassroots organization founded with the help of the pharmaceutical manufacturers to advocate for Medicare reform. Citizens for Better Medicare was the principal sponsor of the Flo ad series and has been a major grassroots organizer on behalf of free-market reforms. Prior to her work with Citizens for Better Medicare, Ms. Wegner was the president of the Council for Affordable Health Insurance.

Ed Gillespe is a founder and principal of Quinn Gillespie & Associates, a bipartisan public affairs firm that provides strategic advice, public relations services, and government representation to corporations, trade associations and issue-based coalitions. Gillespie was senior communications advisor to the Bush-Cheney 2000 campaign, and served as a spokesman for the campaign during the Florida recount process. He is currently serving as general strategist to the Elizabeth Dole for Senate Campaign. In the spring of 2000 Gillespie was tapped by Governor George W. Bush to serve as his program chairman for the Republican National Convention in Philadelphia. Gillespie's work as "the convention's message guru" was roundly applauded, with the Philadelphia convention considered to be one of the most successful party conventions in modern history. *PR Week* magazine named him one of five public affairs professionals to watch in 2001. For more than a decade, Gillespie was a top aide to House Majority Leader Dick Armey. Gillespie served as the Republican National Committee's director of Communications and Congressional Affairs during the 1996 election. In 1994, as director of policy and communications of the House Republican Conference, Gillespie was a principal drafter of the Contract with America, the blueprint for the Republicans' sweep of Congress that year. Gillespie edited the paperback book Contract with America, which climbed to number two on the *New York Times* bestseller list.

Dan Blankenburg is a director of governmental affairs for the National Federation of Independent Businesses. NFIB is the largest association representing the interests of small business owners and entrepreneurs. He is the chairman of a coalition of interest groups aligned to repeal the estate tax. In this capacity he has guided grassroots lobbying, mass media advertising campaigns, and coordinated direct-mail activities. Prior to joining NFIB, Mr. Blankenburg was the legislative director for Congressman John Shimkus (R-IL).

Kara Kennedy is a principal with the Petrizzo Group. She is a former communications aide to Speaker Newt Gingrich and served in a similar capacity for Congresswoman Jennifer Dunn (R-WA). During her tenure on Capitol Hill she was involved in a Republican effort to develop a more "woman-friendly" message strategy for House Republicans.

Stan Greenberg is chairman and chief executive officer of Greenberg Research. Greenberg has served as polling advisor to President Bill Clinton, President Nelson Mandela, Prime Minister Tony Blair, German Chancellor Gerhard Schroeder, and Prime Minister Ehud Barak and their national campaigns. Greenberg also works for private-sector organizations, including major corporations, trade associations and public interest organizations. Greenberg founded the company in 1980 after a decade of teaching at Yale University, where he received a Guggenheim Fellowship. He was educated at Miami University and Harvard University, where he received his Ph.D. Greenberg specializes in managing change and reform, with an emphasis on globalization, international trade, corporate consolidation, technology, and the Internet. He has conducted surveys and focus groups for major corporations on both product and corporate identity and on corporate mission. He has conducted research for major corporations, both internally among employees and managers and externally with relevant stakeholders, opinion leaders and the general public. Greenberg has advised a broad range of political campaigns, including those of President Bill Clinton and Vice-President Al Gore; Senators Chris Dodd, Joe Lieberman, and Jeff Bingaman; former New Jersey Governor Jim Florio and gubernatorial candidate, Andy Young; former Vice-President Walter Mondale; and a number of candidates for the U.S. Congress. For many years he served as principal polling advisor to the Democratic National Committee. Greenberg has conducted extensive research in international settings, including Great Britain, France, Central Europe and the Balkans, Central and South America, and Africa. Greenberg continues to serve as polling advisor to the African National Congress in South Africa and the Labor Party in Great Britain.

Ted Van Der Meid is the chief counsel to Speaker of the House Dennis Hastert. As chief counsel Van Der Meid manages the floor operation for the Speaker and is a key policy advisor to the leadership team. Prior to joining the Speaker's office, Van Der Meid was chief counsel to the House Committee on Standards of Official Conduct (1995-1999). He also served in a similar capacity to former House Minority Leader Bob Michel (1989-1995).

Tom McCrocklin is senior staff counsel to the House Committee on Financial Services. He is formerly the director of federal affairs for the Independent Insurance Agents of America, the nation's largest insurance association and one of the most influential small-business groups in Washington, D.C. As a government affairs representative for IIAA, McCrocklin is responsible for tracking, analyzing, and researching a range of agent and insurance issues, including financial services reform, natural disaster policy, electronic commerce, and crop insurance concerns, and lobbying members of Congress on these important industry concerns. McCrocklin came to IIAA from the Capitol Hill office of Representative Bill Martini (R-N.J.). McCrocklin joined Representative Martini's office in March 1996 as a legislative assistant. In this capacity he was the congressman's principal legislative advisor on economic policy, judiciary, small business issues, and foreign affairs.

Dan Meyer is a principal with the Duberstein Group, a lobbying organization founded by Ronald Reagan's former chief of staff, Ken Duberstein. Before coming to the Duberstein Group, Meyer was the chief of staff to Speaker of the House Newt Gingrich (1995-1998). As a key advisor to the Speaker, Meyer was intimately involved with developing and coordinating the Republican message strategy during the first 100 days of the 104th Congress. As a registered lobbyist he continues to provide communications and political advice to corporations and private-interest groups.

Nancy Libson is the former Democratic staff director of the House Banking Committee (now the House Financial Services Committee. She spent nearly two decades on Capitol Hill, specializing in housing issues for former House Banking Chairman Henry B. Gonzalez (D-TX).

Barry Jackson is the former chief of staff to Congressman John Boehner (R-Ohio). Jackson was the communications director for Boehner when he was chairman of the House Republican Conference. In that capacity, Jackson was responsible for disseminating the Republican message to the rank-and-file membership as well as serving as liaison for outside groups working to promote GOP legislation.

Todd Funk is former legislative director for Congresswoman Nancy Johnson (R-CT). Funk worked for Rep. Johnson from1994 to 2003 and served as her chief liaison with the Ways and Means Committee as well as her top staff person on budgetary issues.

Bibliographic Essay

The academic community has largely ignored the growth of the political consulting industry. Until recently, scholarly works were outnumbered by a patchwork of journalistic exposés and insider chronicles. According to James Thurber part of the reason that the literature is so sparse and varied is due to the confusion over "what subfield houses the study of political consulting: elections and voting behavior; political parties; political communication; political advertising; or campaign management." To make matters worse, much of the work is atheoretical, consisting of "insider accounts and how to books."[1] The diversity can be viewed in a beneficial light, since a wide assortment of commentators should lead to a rich variety of insights. Journalism brings a dynamic perspective and enriches academic understanding by presenting accessible examples of political issues. Journalists are not bound by the conventions of social science and thus possess a greater interpretive range. A nimble writer can often tie disparate events together and make an extremely compelling and engaging argument. But journalistic reliance on narrative, anecdote, and vignette to support sweeping generalizations may cast doubt on the substance of their conclusions. Fortunately, the empirical void left by journalists can be filled by political science. What political science lacks in breadth and rhetorical flourish it makes up for in depth and prosaic exactness. Good political science moves beyond description and strives to explain the causes and the effects of a phenomenon through careful analysis and a theoretical foundation. Ideally, the two styles complement each other, providing a holistic picture of the subject. Regrettably, much of the journalistic and academic writing about political consulting is compromised by a normative bias toward the profession.

A review of the scholarly writings discloses more polemical indictments than sober evaluations. Some academics seem to approach political consulting with a disconcerting antipathy, resulting in value-laden conclusions exaggerating the negative aspects of the profession. Consultants are blamed for, among other things, hastening the collapse of the party system and fostering the banality of campaign rhetoric. Their proximity to a number of systemic problems has encouraged a guilt-by-association effect. Throughout the literature authors characterize consultants as a problem within the democratic system. Magazine and newspaper articles that strenuously condemn professional political consultants reinforce the negative image.[2] The most critical works also invest consultants with an enormous, some would say unwarranted, amount of power over campaigns and candidates. Consultants have not done themselves any favors with their penchant for self-aggrandizement and alarming disdain for political idealism.

The uniformly negative treatments have given way in recent years to more multidimensional works that resist casting consultants as the villains in every play. Contemporary books by Thomas Mann and Steven Medvic remain critical of the role political consultants have in our electoral system, but they rightly avoid indicting the profession for all the alleged problems in American politics that have arisen over the past two decades. Scholarship has been further enhanced by detailed survey research of political consultants conducted by James Thurber. His analysis challenges some of the conventional notions regarding political consultants, such as the stereotypical depiction of them as political mavericks operating completely outside the party structure.

The literature discussing political consulting can be divided roughly into four categories: academic writings prior to 1980, academic writings after 1980, journalistic exposes written by practitioners or reporters, and closely related writings stemming from work done in the field of political communication. This division is not based on methodology, but rather on stylistic similarities exhibited by the authors in each grouping. Scholars in political communication, for instance, share a common lexicon and employ standard terms to describe the behavior of political consultants and the effect they have on the democratic process. Academic writings prior to 1980 tend to be more descriptive than those appearing over the last two decades. Finally, journalistic accounts distinguish themselves with a here-and-now, insider perspective.

EARLY WORKS

The first significant work to address the development of political consulting is Stanley Kelley Jr.'s *Professional Public Relations and Political Power*. The book contains an in-depth analysis of five cases in which the author believes public relations played a critical role.[3] When Kelley wrote in 1956, the party system in the United States and the electoral process in general were in a transitional period. The bossism and autocratic party machines that typified the politics of the latter nineteenth and early twentieth century were in decline, yet "candidate-centered" campaigns were still two decades from becoming the dominant paradigm. Parties were still the most important unifying force in electoral politics, but the regional power brokers who dominated elections in the past were losing their influence. As the bosses faded into the background, a new generation of campaign operatives skilled in the ways of mass communication and marketing emerged as the driving force behind campaigns.

Kelley claims that the first truly professional political consulting firm was founded in California in 1935 by Clem Whitaker and Leona Baxter. Whitaker, a former political reporter, and Baxter, a corporate publicist, understood the nascent power of new communications technology and were pioneers in mass media campaigning. In their first major statewide race Whitaker and Baxter used movie shorts and mass mailings to defeat populist gubernatorial candidate Upton Sinclair. Their professionalism and staunch independence from political party hierarchy was a harbinger of things to come.[4]

The successful presidential campaign conducted by Dwight Eisenhower exemplifies a transformation of American electoral politics. His campaign was the first to incorporate Madison Avenue-style advertising effectively and devise a strategy based on the insights of business marketing.[5] According to Kelley, during the 1952 Eisenhower campaign public relations became an irreplaceable tool. A sharp ad campaign allows campaigners to present a vibrant, vigorous image even if the candidate is lackluster. Eisenhower was never considered an especially energetic or forceful campaigner, but his wooden demeanor was cosmetically suppressed by a team of public relations specialists. Their role was not limited to aesthetic presentation. Public relations men were instrumental in shaping Eisenhower campaign themes targeted to the undecided or disaffected voter. Kelley saw a natural affinity between modern campaigning and professional public relations. Beginning at the turn of the century, when industrialists created the demand for public relations in order to counter an increasingly negative public image, public relations always had a latent political dimension. Drawing upon earlier observations made by Edward Bernays, the acknowledged father of public relations, Kelley believed the marriage of politics and public relations was a logical and inevitable outcome. Cultivating and maintaining a positive public image is just as important, if not more so, for political leaders as it is for corporations.[6]

Despite its vintage, *Professional Public Relations and Political Power* remains a crucial work in the political consulting field. Kelley was the first academic to identify the public relations "man" (a forerunner to today's political consultant) as an autonomous actor in the political system. He described a person independent of the party hierarchy who, unlike a candidate's personal confidants, obtains his position through professional expertise. Kelley's contemporary relevance is reflected in the actions he describes in his case studies, which retain useful insights for current scholars. Strategies developed by 1950s public relations experts, mobilizing public sentiment, defining the terms of a political debate, and manipulating statistics, are familiar to today's political consultants and suggest a remarkable continuity within the profession.

Although his work lacks the transparent hostility toward political consulting that animates future scholarly writings, Kelley approaches the subject with wary skepticism. Due to the close connection most public relations men have with big business, Kelley expresses grave concern for the future in which electoral politics is shaped by corporate culture and dominated by their communications techniques. Kelley's trepidation is reinforced by the case studies he selected that reveal a strong conservative bent to public relations activities. Kelley contends public relations men in the service of elite interests can circumvent the will of the majority.[7] Despite Kelley's valid concerns, he is unwilling to demonize the profession. Unlike later writers, he does not characterize public relations men as the archenemies of political parties. Some readers may find his tepid speculations are a poor substitute for a clear argument, but Kelley's reticence to come to steadfast conclusions is understandable given the novelty of the phenomenon he was describing. His book is a superb descriptive account and he wisely left judgments to a future generation of scholars.

Fourteen years after Stanley Kelley Jr. published his groundbreaking analysis of professional campaign operatives, Dan Nimmo, a political communications scholar, revisited the topic in *The Political Persuaders*. He claims that in the intervening period, political consulting was transformed from an amateur pastime into a full-fledged cottage industry.[8] The expansion and maturity of the profession allowed Nimmo to write with more confidence. Whereas Kelley explored political consulting cautiously and demurred from bold statements, Nimmo exhibits none of Kelley's timidity and does not shy away from provocative statements. In Nimmo's estimation, political consultants wielding social science and unbridled technological power are a serious threat to the sanctity of participatory democracy. Under the auspices of professional campaigners, "Elections are approached neither as conflicts between parties nor as confrontations of principle. They are viewed instead as contests of personalities and, even more basically, they offer a choice between sophisticated engineers working on behalf of those personalities."[9] In other words, political consultants devalue the meaning of elections, a problem Nimmo associates with the palpable gimmickry practiced by candidates under the guidance of professional campaign figures. Nimmo's writing is insightful, but he takes a dim view of the tactics employed by political consultants and introduces a pessimistic tone that permeates the literature henceforth.

Nimmo is troubled by the declining influence of political parties as the principal organizing force behind campaign activity. In the 1970s personality-driven, candidate centered campaigns became the norm, to the dismay of many political observers.[10] Parties provided consistency and order to the electoral process. More important, they provided "honest" cues to voters in contrast to the cynically contrived images developed by consultants. Nimmo clearly prefers the old style of campaigning to the new style, which he characterizes throughout his book as impersonal, insubstantial and deceptive. Nimmo should not be chastised for lamenting the diminished stature of political parties, but the extent to which his romanticized vision of the past unfairly colors his perceptions of the current state of affairs must be noted. He is, for example, the first author to use the loaded term "mercenary" to describe political consultants. Although Nimmo does not blame consultants for political parties' diminished stature (for him the relationship between party decline and consultant rise is correlational), his arguments lay the foundation for future scholars to imply a causal connection.

Nimmo's apprehension is not solely based upon stylistic changes brought on by political consultants. The crux of his argument rests on the reasonable assumption that we live in a mediated political society, whereby information is transmitted and filtered to the mass electorate through a host of interlocutors rather than directly from the politician. Nimmo contends, "Instead of direct, spontaneous, personal contact between candidates and voters, we find professional management firms, pollsters and communications specialists mediating between political leaders and followers."[11] In the mediated world, those who possess sophisticated communication skills (i.e., political consultants) have disproportionate influence over the electoral process. Nimmo's concern is genuine and understandable. Entrepreneurial consultants who enjoy great influence over the electoral process can pose a threat. It does not take a pessimist to envision a scenario in which the voters are duped by a slick public relations campaign. However, Nimmo falls short in his argument because he fails to present evidence to support his assertions. None of the examples cited in his book reveal malevolent intent on the part of consultants or outright dishonesty during a campaign. Furthermore, Nimmo ignores the likely possibility that voters determine the issues and consultants generally react to their preferences.

Consultants bear the brunt of Nimmo's pointed criticism, but his broadsides are not exclusively aimed at the industry. In fact, consultants appear to be a symptom of the real danger to democracy: technology. Lodged within the subtext of *The Political Persuaders* is a critique of the rampant abuse of technology in campaigns. Nimmo is no Luddite, yet he is at great pains to illustrate the potential hazards created by television and other innovations. It seems incongruous that a communications scholar would express reservations about advancements in communications technology, but given Nimmo's suspicion of elite bias it is consistent with his earlier arguments. Like campaign specialists who peddle their expertise, the new technology will be employed by those who can afford the cost. Although Nimmo does not go so far as to claim technology will be used by the wealthy minority to oppress the majority, he assumes the obvious beneficiaries will be individuals with vast financial resources.[12]

In terms of content and analysis, *The Political Persuaders* is an improvement from Kelley's work. Nimmo presents a more theoretical argument pertaining to the effects that consultants have on the electoral process. Consultants, he argues, are one of several variables in a mediated polity. Nimmo identifies a number of mitigating factors, such as party affiliation, social preconceptions, and media saturation, as barriers to "professionally mediated campaigns." In order to motivate voters, consultants must suppress unfavorable factors and assimilate favorable factors. Although Nimmo grants consultants a broad range of powers, his argument confines their influence within a predetermined context. In other words, consultants cannot change the nature of the voting population, but they can stimulate voters and manipulate their natural tendencies. Nimmo also broadened the discussion of professional campaign operatives. Whereas Kelley limited his discussion to professional ad men, Nimmo included pollsters and other technical specialists.

David Rosenbloom, in his book *The Election Men*, was the first scholar to connect a change in the tempo of the electoral process with the professionalization of the campaign corps. Until the 1960s, Rosenbloom argues, campaigns had a predictable cyclical rhythm, typified by long periods of inactivity and short periods of frenetic action. But as campaigns became a business enterprise complete with their own professional class, the campaign cycle shortened and the lulls between elections disappeared.[13] The perpetual election wheel is a familiar phenomenon to congressional scholars and House members, where the two-year term lends an air of urgency to every member's efforts.[14] In the 1980s scholars noticed a similar trend in presidential politics. Rosenbloom is careful not to attribute the alteration solely to political consultants. Changes in fundraising laws and the advent of the open primary system are also responsible for the unceasing campaign, but he rightly suggests that consultants are the only people who have profited from the new system and have a clear financial stake in maintaining it.

Rosenbloom's 1973 book contributes to the study of political consultants and is an early survey of the practitioners. Kelley, and to a lesser extent Nimmo, conducted interviews with several full-time campaign operatives, yet neither author attempted to gain a sweeping view of the profession from them. Rosenbloom surveyed over fifty firms and received detailed responses from almost all of them. The survey results allowed Rosenbloom to look inside an evolving profession. Unfortunately, Rosenbloom's analysis is one-dimensional. Given the richness of his data, it is extremely disappointing that his portrayal of consultants flirts with caricature. He describes consultants as competitive political junkies who thrive on the energy of the campaign, committed to their profession but indifferent to post-electoral policy consequences. The campaign is analogous to a high-stakes sporting contest where victory is the singular goal. "The professional pollsters and campaign planners," he argues, "do not care about the substance of the issues or about what the people really think."[15] His characterization is not wrong; it is simply incomplete and does not account for other motivating factors, such as ideology. Stanley Kelley's case study of the California firm Campaigns Inc. revealed ideology to be a very important part of their decision to take on new clients. Profit may be a primary incentive, but it is erroneous to claim it is the only impulse. Ultimately, Rosenbloom, like Nimmo, affirms the notion of the consultant as a single-minded profiteer, a political mercenary in the service of the highest bidder. He maintains, "The people who run professional campaign management firms are professional politicians who have set up companies to enjoy the action of politics, get rich, gain political and organizational independence and to bask in the warm light of professional recognition and respect."[16]

In his concluding chapter, Rosenbloom offers his own interpretation of the negative impact professional campaign consultants will have on American democracy. Rosenbloom, echoing a refrain that guided the Founders, believes consultants violate the principles of democratic accountability. He points out, "Today many of the crucial decisions of elections, who shall run and what they say, are decided not by the people or even by their organizational leaders, but by small groups of professional managers and money men. Who is to check the professional campaign managers?"[17] His concern is laudable, but it is a weak argument since it speciously distinguishes political consultants from other "unaccountable" figures such as party bosses and nonprofessional fundraisers. His second worry is more compelling. He argues that the consultants overriding commitment to profit will inculcate a myopic view of public policy. Under the guidance of political consultants, unglamorous policy proposals will be abandoned in favor of pithy phrases and promises of instant gratification.

The dark view of political consulting reached its apogee in Larry Sabato's book, *The Rise of Political Consultants*. Since Kelley first wrote in 1956, the authors examining political consulting have grown progressively more negative. The basis for the animus is threefold. First, consultants cultivated a public image that inspired loathing among serious political scholars. Their cavalier approach to the linchpin of democracy and their tendency to mock the sanctity of elections offended many political scientists.[18] Second, consultants were rightly blamed for cultivating the commercialized campaign system. High priced, glitzy, yet vacuous campaigns were seen as the trademark of the political consultant. Last, by 1981 their virtual conquest of the electoral process seemed to be a foregone conclusion, and with their dominance came renewed calls for some sort of regulation. Consultants were no longer operating on the periphery and had become central figures in campaigns. Sabato expresses ambivalence in his book. He approaches consultants with a mixture of grudging admiration for the way they have exploited their environment and barely concealed contempt for their methods.

The Rise of Political Consultants is an important book for a number of reasons. Foremost, Sabato is the first author to offer an operational definition of political consulting. He presents a concise, yet expansive definition of a political consultant as "a campaign professional who is engaged primarily in the provision of advice and services (such as polling, media creation and production, direct mail fundraising) to candidates, their campaigns, and other political committees."[19] To this point, scholars had used terms like "professional campaign operatives" or "political public relations men." Unfortunately, these terms are not always synonymous and can lead to misunderstandings when they are used interchangeably. Is a pollster, for instance, considered a consultant? What about a person who provides strategic advice on a part-time basis or a person who volunteers his services? Sabato's definition introduces a reasonable standard and helps resolve some confusion when discussing consultants as a group. Sabato's other noteworthy contribution is a massive compilation of primary research, including interviews with high-profile consultants, a lengthy list of historical examples, and a thorough description of the craft. He is particularly effective at dissecting the profession, and explains every facet, from the solicitation of clients to the application of techniques, with great detail.[20] Sabato's description is a service to scholars and lay observers alike, since it dispels the aura of mystery surrounding political consultants. As Sabato points out, there is no magic formula for winning an election.

The video culture and the press must shoulder some blame for the debasement of electoral politics. Television, Sabato argues, is a font of deception and chicanery. His argument is filled with familiar indictments, such as television's role in the triumph of image politics and its culpability for the shortened attention span of the average citizen. Sabato's quixotic attack on television is understandable given his contempt for negative advertising and sound-bite politics, but he assigns too much blame to an inert medium. Despite Sabato's legitimate concerns, television is not an inherently malignant force in American politics. Sabato unfortunately conflates his argument against the misuse of television with television itself. Moreover, if his description of the video culture is accurate, it presents an unflattering reflection of the voting populace. Is he suggesting that we are all mindless zombies waiting to be duped by clever advertising? Sabato leaves his strongest criticism for journalists, whom he believes have abetted consultants in a variety of ways. He questions the cozy relationship some reporters develop with political consultants. In their zeal to obtain good copy, some reporters have inadvertently allowed themselves to become mouthpieces for the candidates they are covering. He also takes them to task for enabling political consultants to build up a mythology about their effectiveness. Reporters should be held accountable, Sabato maintains, for "not publicizing the shockingly unethical practices that are so pervasive" in the consulting profession.[21] Their inaction has made them complicit in the rise of political consulting.

Sabato's blunt, if one-sided, assessment of political consultants puts them at the center of a wrenching transformation of American politics. Clearly, he is impressed with their meteoric rise, but he is troubled by their utter lack of regard for the long-term consequences of their activities. Sabato's main proposition, briefly put, is as follows: Consultants, whatever else they do, insult the integrity of the democratic process. Although he is careful not to present a causal link between political consultants and the series of problems with the electoral system that he identifies in his book, his tone implies something else. His desire to cast political consultants as the villain in a political drama creates a confusing set of contradictions. In one breath he absolves political consultants of blame for the declining significance of parties in elections, but in the next sentence he claims, "They have helped grease the slippery poll down which the parties have slid."[22] Sabato's book is comprehensive, but it is compromised by the hostility that animates the author.

Not every author embraces the prevailing characterization of political consultants as soulless profiteers and political mercenaries. Frank Luntz, who would gain notoriety as the principal consultant behind the Contract with America, brings a new perspective to the subject in his book, *Candidates, Consultants, and Campaigns*. In a refreshing change, Luntz does not evince the same distaste for consultants that inspired some previous authors. Luntz may not present a superior analysis of the profession, since he sidesteps thorny issues such as the inflating costs of campaigns and the persistence of disingenuous advertising, but he distinguishes himself from the chorus by making several notable claims. First, he disputes the notion that technology is a threat to democracy. On the contrary, he believes that technological advancements ultimately benefit democracy by leading to a more informed electorate. Second, Luntz does not hold consultants responsible for new campaign styles. Instead he blames the campaign legislation of the 1970s for indenturing candidates to campaign professionals. Last, Luntz dispels a popular myth that consultants ignore ideology when considering clients. Earlier works portrayed consultants as single-minded entrepreneurs, indifferent to a candidate's views.

Most of the previous commentators would agree with Luntz's assertion that "modern campaign technology has changed, completely and forever, the traditional style of campaigning once common in American politics."[23] Where they diverge from Luntz is in their assessment of the change. Several authors were at pains to point out the hazards posed by new technology and how it could be appropriated by those with means to dominate the mass electorate. Luntz, on the other hand, prefers to look on the bright side of innovation. He maintains "modern campaign technology exposes candidates to the electorate and renders office holders accountable to their constituents."[24] The exponential expansion of news outlets, gavel-to-gavel coverage of House and Senate proceedings, and satellite communications enable people to learn a tremendous amount about their elected representatives. Perhaps the quality of the information is in question, but there can be no debate about the quantity. Luntz's cheery optimism may strike the reader as naïve, yet it serves as a valuable counterbalance to the anti technology positions staked out by earlier authors.

Political consultants have been censured by journalists and political scientists for corrupting the electoral process and for cultivating an environment where money and imagery trump substance and integrity. Luntz makes a subtle, persuasive argument that the real culprits are the well-intentioned reformers of the 1970s. Campaign laws that did away with big contributions did not eliminate the need for money nor control campaign costs. Thus, candidates were forced to spend more time raising money, especially after limitations on campaign expenditures were struck down by the Supreme Court.[25] Luntz argues, "Candidates, unless independently wealthy, had no choice but to turn to direct mail consultants and other fundraising specialists for the then primitive, but nevertheless proven, technology needed to raise the significant sums required to replace the now illegal large donations."[26] Political consultants certainly took advantage of the situation, but they had no hand in creating it.

In retrospect, some of what Luntz says can be viewed as self-serving. He went on to become an influential political consultant in his own right and his favorable analysis may be, in part, a manifestation of his desire to join their ranks. His fascination with demographic information and the specially tailored voter outreach practiced by direct-mail consultants is a case in point where his own analysis clearly influenced his professional behavior. In his book he describes the advantages of using survey research to determine which issues and phrases are most important to voters and which ones candidates should avoid. As a consultant, Luntz earned a reputation in Republican circles for his creative use of focus groups and polls to craft messages and phrases that resonate with voters.[27] Despite Luntz's benign, occasionally fawning, approach to political consulting, his book is an important work because it presents a different perspective and challenges the consensual assumption that consultants are a malevolent force in American politics.

RECENT WORKS

In the 1990s political consulting as a profession and political consultants as actors in the system began to draw more attention from political scientists. Congressional scholars such as Paul Herrnson and Stephen Medvic endeavored to test the empirical validity of the some of the claims made by earlier authors. For the first time, questions about the influence consultants have on campaigns were analyzed using quantitative methods. Political consultants also came under scrutiny from interest-group theorists who were chronicling the swift rise of "outside lobbying." Consultants are at the forefront of a new strategy to shape public policy debates.

To date the most empirically grounded study dealing with political consulting is Stephen Medvic's Ph.D. thesis, "Is There a Spin Doctor in the House?"[28] His contributions to the literature are twofold. First, he offers a novel explanation of consultant behavior and its relationship to voters and candidates that challenge the prevailing understanding of consultants as manipulators. Medvic also provides strong empirical evidence demonstrating the value of a consultant to a successful congressional campaign. Some critics suggest that his work simply reiterates commonly held assumptions, but Medvic establishes an empirical basis. Prior to his work, no one really knew whether consultants were instrumental or whether their reputation as king makers was the result of savvy self-promotion and candidate fear.

The cornerstone of Medvic's work is the theory of "deliberate priming." Deliberate priming posits that consultants, as experts in political communication, are singularly capable of stimulating voters. The stimulation occurs through the intentional use of symbols that trigger a reaction in the targeted set of voters. The difficulty, Medvic maintains, lies in determining the precise issues, since only a small number ever raise wide interest among the voting populace. At first glance this appears to be a conventional interpretation of political consultant activity; consultants manipulating voters through clever communication techniques. In actuality, Medvic refutes this representation, arguing that voters drive the campaign agendas and that consultants merely react to voters' wishes. Far from being manipulators, consultants are translators who take cues from the voters and use them to create sound campaign strategies for clients. Medvic's argument is important and persuasive because it elevates the public's role in elections. Moreover, it presents a reasonable description of political consulting that is not freighted with claims of fraud, voter manipulation, and the like.

Medvic's other major contribution is empirical. Using data from the 1992 House races, Medvic charts the number of candidates who hired consultants, the money they spent, and their success rate relative to candidates who did not employ consultants. After controlling for variables such as campaign spending, district partisanship, and presidential election year, Medvic discovered several statistically significant relationships. Although consultants did not appear to affect voter turnout, there is evidence of a positive relationship between consultant use and a candidate's chance of winning, ability to raise funds, and overall cost of the campaign. For the first time there is solid evidence that consultants can make a difference in a campaign. Medvic's research design is innovative and his observations are astute, but in his conclusion he makes it clear there is a lot more research to be done. Echoing a familiar cry, Medvic makes a plea for more investigation and claims his work should be viewed as "something of a springboard into further exploration."[29]

Medvic's plea for more substantial research by political scientists has been answered in recent years. In 1999 and 2000, two edited compilations were published that addressed political consulting and the maturation of the permanent campaign phenomenon. The first, *Campaign Warriors*, edited by James Thurber and Candace Nelson of American University, is a landmark survey of the consulting profession.[30] Thurber and his collaborators, with funding from the Pew Charitable Trust, were able to render an accurate portrait of the profession based on exhaustive primary research. In addition, the book contains a number of essays that challenge conventional stereotypes of political consulting. Robin Kolodny of Temple University, for example, debunks the myth of the political consultant as an anti-party mercenary. She argues impressively that many political consultants were trained by the national party organizations and retain strong ties to them. The second book, *The Permanent Campaign and Its Future*, is the first scholarly analysis of the permanent campaign.[31] Since Sidney Blumenthal coined the term in the early 1980s (roughly, the idea that everyday governing has taken on the trappings and tempo normally associated with a political campaign), journalists and political scientists have bandied it about without a clear understanding of its meaning or its implications for governing. Mann and Ornstein argue that "the line between campaigning and governing has all but disappeared, with campaigning increasingly dominant."[32] In the book, a number of eminent political scientists, such as Hugh Heclo, Morris Fiorina, and Charles O. Jones, address the permanent campaign and its impact on political institutions. Each book is an important step forward in the study of political consulting.

Darrell West and Burdett Loomis focus their attention on the burgeoning use of political consultants and campaign tactics by interest groups to affect the policy agenda. In their book, *The Sound of Money*, West and Loomis assert that, during the 1990s, "on issues from health care to tort reform to telecommunications and tobacco there has been extraordinary interest group spending in advertising, public relations, and grassroots."[33] Building from E. E. Schattschneider's well-known aphorism about interest groups singing with an upper-class accent, they maintain that the ability of "well-heeled" groups to purchase the services of talented consultants has further tipped the balance of power in favor of the wealthy and well organized. Interest groups willing to spend money on polls and advertising are able to craft narratives that become the centerpieces of policy debates. Although they reserve the bulk of their criticism for interest groups, their treatment of consultants evokes comparisons to earlier works.

In his book, *Outside Lobbying*, Ken Kollman delves deeper into the phenomenon. His analysis complements West and Loomis's work by presenting an operative definition of outside lobbying. Outside lobbying, he claims, can be divided into two categories: One form is directed at opinion leaders and policy makers at the elite level; the second is a genuine effort to change how ordinary citizens view and respond to certain policy issues.[34] Kollman's work is also interesting because, unlike West and Loomis, he eschews the injudicious assessment of outside lobbying as a contrived attempt on the part of wealthy elites to employ citizens as pawns. He blames the reaction on the entrenched cynicism of Washington pundits. According to Kollman, "The notion that the appearance of spontaneous uprising can be purchased is so widespread in Washington that commentators are attempted to relegate all of outside lobbying to same conceptual bill as campaign attack advertising: slick, one-sided, misleading propaganda."[35] Kollman does not deny that some grassroots efforts are manufactured; he is, however, unwilling to dismiss the importance of mobilized constituents. Even orchestrated events are a manifestation of public will.

POLITICAL COMMUNICATION

Earlier I mentioned that political consulting is an eclectic profession. Not only are the specialties diverse, ranging from public opinion polling to television advertising, but the backgrounds of the practitioners are equally varied, as advertising executives, journalists and political scientists are all represented in the upper echelons of the profession. For that reason, it seems appropriate that the academic field that has produced a major portion of the scholarly material devoted to political consulting is one that has been described by its adherents as "self-consciously cross disciplinary."[36] Scholars specializing in political communication draw upon sociology, psychology, and journalism, as well as communications and political science, in their quest to interpret political discourse. Traversing disciplinary boundaries is understandable considering the key areas of interest include rhetorical and propaganda analysis, vote studies, political learning, news media, communications technology, campaigns and elections, polling, marketing, and advertising.[37]

In terms of its contribution to the study of political consultants, political communication provides a basis for understanding how they have emerged to become powerful figures in our political system. Consultants, and most politicians, intuitively understand the importance of setting the terms of a debate. They know that the party that successfully defines an issue has a distinct advantage over its adversaries. This is best illustrated by rhetorical gamesmanship emanating from the Congress at the outset of a major policy initiative. Republicans, for example, want the public to know that they are trying to save Medicare for future generations, while the Democrats counter that the Republicans want to cut benefits to the elderly to allow a tax cut for the wealthy. In this respect, the technical details of the competing proposals are irrelevant. The crucial matter is owning the terms of debate and successfully casting yourself as the public's advocate, while simultaneously portraying your opponent as its enemy. Robert Denton and Gary Woodward summarize the nature of political communication as follows:

On most political questions (i.e. questions analyzing choices with competing advantages to different constituencies) the *Truth* [sic] is not easily located. This is because politics is not primarily about truth telling, but consensus seeking. Political conflict typically concerns itself with decisions implying values or preferences rather than determinations of fact, even though there may indeed, be relevant facts that should inform our political debate. The bulk of most practical discourse is centered on mobilization of public opinion: a process that involves fact finding but frequently denies a superior point of view.[38]

According to this logic, political reality is subjective and, like physical beauty, in the eye of the beholder. In this arena, those who possess the greatest persuasive skills and the most sophisticated means to express their message are dominant actors. Political consultants, whether they specialize in direct mail or television advertising, not only shape the context of debate; they provide the vocabulary. As the interpreters and amplifiers of the messages, they serve as a bridge between the politician and the general public. In a mediated political world, the person who creates the policy message is just as important as the person who crafts the policy.

Political communications scholars are intimately familiar with the value of symbolic interaction between public leaders and the general populace. Candidates on the stump and leaders in times of crisis often deliver speeches laden with symbolic imagery as a means of unifying and inspiring the audience, or to convey complex abstractions. Although politicians throughout American history have used evocative metaphors, some critics contend modern leaders exploit national symbols, delivering them to the public as palaver and a substitute for honest public policy. According to Murray Edelman, a pioneer in the political communication field, a new leadership strategy emerged in American politics after World War II that encouraged inauthenticity. The new strategy was embodied by leaders such as Ronald Reagan. Reagan was notorious for his excessive reliance on symbolism and was often criticized for cynically appropriating revered images such as the Statue of Liberty and the flag to advocate his conservative philosophy. Some authors linked the increased use of political symbolism to the campaign techniques practiced by political consultants.[39] These authors decried the artful use of imagery encouraged by consultants during campaigns because they tend to crowd out "real issues."[40] In essence, the antagonism toward political consultants stems from an idealistic vision of campaigns. Campaigns should present voters with reasonable and well-articulated programmatic policy choices, not vacuous, image-laden slogans.

The subtle migration of consumer-marketing techniques to the political campaign has given political communications scholars another opportunity to evaluate political consultants. While some authors are simply concerned with presenting "practical procedures for identifying effective strategies based upon marketing principles and techniques," others are concerned with the normative implications.[41] The arguments posed against marketing are familiar variations of those against symbolic politics; that marketing begets fakery and superficiality. The attitude is summed up by Nicholas O'shaughnessy, who states, "The art of politics becomes an exercise in the judicious manipulation of symbols to which task the pseudo-science of marketing lends its nefarious lore."[42] Most authors, however, do not believe marketing is inherently "nefarious." Gary Mauser argues that marketing suffers from an academic bias against *realpolitik,* stating, "Political marketing, like Machiavelli, is reviled, not because it is evil, but because it dares to analyze publicly what many political leaders prefer to discuss in private."[43] One scholar goes so far as to suggest that "it is possible that despite the self-serving nature of political advertising, it makes a positive contribution to the civic education" by providing heuristic shortcuts for voters.[44] In short, marketing only becomes harmful in the hands of amoral political consultants who use it without conscience.

References to political consulting within political communications literature disclose a reoccurring theme. According to this line of reasoning, the citizenry, by and large, are an undifferentiated mass who are easily duped by pleasing yet insubstantial narratives, and political consultants are corrupt, or at least morally indifferent, profiteers who dole out the propaganda. This section is not the proper forum to discuss if these assumptions are valid and constructive, but it is important to note that the assumptions inform subsequent observations about consultant behavior. In this sense, political consulting has been tarnished by criticisms that precede rather than follow sound analysis. I should be clear that I am not accusing political communications scholars of deliberately castigating political consulting, yet it seems many of them have opted for the easy way and linked consultants to a number of supposed problems in American politics (elite bias, voter apathy, etc.) with scant empirical evidence. Writers who parrot this theme without reflection are, to paraphrase Kenneth Burke, contributing more to our gratification than to our enlightenment.

JOURNALISTIC WORKS

A review of the political consulting literature would be incomplete without mentioning two important journalistic works, Sidney Blumenthal's *The Permanent Campaign* and David Chagall's *The New Kingmakers.*[45] Published in 1980 and 1981, respectively, both books use presidential campaigns as the backdrop for their analysis of political consulting. According to the authors, the Nixon, Carter, and Reagan campaigns are edifying snapshots of the evolutionary change in electoral politics. Like time-lapse photography of a growing flower, the campaigns show the incipient, middle, and mature stages of the consultant phenomenon. Blumenthal and Chagall distinguish themselves from the academics who preceded them by abandoning the stilted, detached vocabulary used by social scientists in favor of the brash, often vulgar language used by political consultants. They want to tell the story in the words of the people who created it. Neither work presents a "theory" of consultant activity or endeavors to go beyond vague, general observations about their effect on the political process.

Nevertheless, the books make a significant contribution due to the penetrating and colorful depictions of industry leaders. The vivid portraits found in each book reveal a complex culture shaped by elitism and cynicism, by capitalist impulses and ideological loyalty, and by technical acumen and sharp political instincts.

Although not written as a series, the books bear a striking resemblance and complement each other well. Aside from the obvious parallels drawn from the writing styles and interview subjects, a subtle yet palpable undercurrent guides both works. Each author is captivated by the success of Ronald Reagan and their reflections about the influence of political consultants is, in part, derived from the lessons of the Reagan revolution. Reagan, as a politician and public leader, represented a crowning achievement for political consulting. More than any other politician before him, Reagan embodied the triumph of image over substance. He was smooth and amiable and possessed an effortless charm in front of a camera. Most important, owing to his career as an actor he was eminently coachable and took direction well. However, his critics contended that behind this genial facade was a vacant mind. His fiercest opponents claimed his policies revealed a shallow, obtuse reactionary with a muted sense of compassion and a warped vision of reality. The Reagan ambivalence, the jovial grandfather figure who cuts social programs for the poor, is a source of frustration and fascination for both Blumenthal and Chagall.[46] Some of Reagan's uncanny ability to distance himself personally from unpopular political actions is attributed to his charisma and intuitive understanding of his audience. But Blumenthal and Chagall correctly point out the imperative role played by political consultants. The Reagan team was an efficient, effective PR machine that deflected blame for failures and ably took credit for successes. In Blumenthal's estimation, Reagan demonstrated "that success does not depend upon accomplishment, but on the projection of image and ideology."[47]

The image Chagall and Blumenthal paint of political consultants is harsh and uncompromising. The interviews they conducted show leading industry figures as self-confident, bordering on arrogant. Some consultants believe they have rightfully taken over for the party and function as unofficial gatekeepers, discouraging "unworthy" candidates and assisting talented ones. Pat Caddell, President Carter's former pollster and political advisor, is typical. Without a trace of guile, Caddell told Blumenthal, "Consultants really are serving as preselectors of the candidates, we decide who is best able to use the technology, who understands the technology."[48] Given their lucrative trade and impressive success rates, a degree of overconfidence can be excused. However, other interviews reveal a disturbing disdain for the sanctity of the democratic process. Consultant Hal Evry's comments to David Chagall have the bracing effect of a bucket of cold water and go a long way toward explaining the antipathy many academics feel toward the profession. Evry, who makes a comfortable living by electing candidates, stated "I've never voted in my life. And I never intend to vote. It doesn't make any difference to the system who gets elected. The society runs its own way, with or without politicians."[49] This level of cynicism is disturbing coming from an average citizen, but it is especially jarring coming from a professional political operative. Evry's indifference to political outcomes is hard to reconcile with his career choice unless one embraces the conception of the consultant as a mercenary. *The Permanent Campaign* and *The New Kingmakers* are not groundbreaking works. By that I mean they do not present an innovative argument about political consulting. However, the books succeed in a more significant fashion by bringing the topic to a broader audience. Their writing style is accessible and easy for the average citizen to comprehend, yet it is perceptive enough to interest a more sophisticated reader. Blumenthal, Chagall, and other journalists who write about consultants cast light on the profession and introduced the American public to a character type. Celebrity consultants, like James Carville, Ed Rollins, and Dick Morris, owe their exalted status, in part, to intrepid journalists who brought them out from behind the scenes.

In the 1990s political consultants become pop culture icons. James Carville and his wife Mary Matalin pitch cotton sheets and antacid tablets on television and Dick Morris is a regular guest on several cable television shows. In many campaigns consultants are more well known than their clients. But the greatest indication that political consultants have become part of the Zeitgeist is the development of a Hollywood stereotype. Beginning with *The Candidate* in 1972, political consultants have been represented in movies as amoral, cynical puppet masters who manipulate the political process.[50] In *Bob Roberts*, Tim Robbins's biting account of a fictional Pennsylvania senatorial race, consultants are depicted as either buffoons or nefarious crooks. In *Power*, the political consultant portrayed by Richard Gere is a ruthless, egomaniacal mercenary bereft of a moral compass. Even in more benign roles, such as Kathy Bates's character in *Primary Colors*, the political consultant is presented with a shifting sense of morality. Television shows such as the *West Wing* and *Mr. Sterling* also give the viewing public a glimpse of the exciting world inhabited by political operatives. All of these characters make for good drama, but they reflect a distorted image and unfortunately reinforce the negative characterizations that appear in the literature.

When Stanley Kelley wrote *Professional Public Relations and Political Power* in 1956, no one knew what a political consultant was; the term had yet to be invented. Today, it is hard to find a major campaign that does not employ one. Their ranks grow every year, as does their presence in campaigns. Given the rapid rise of the profession, it should not be a surprise to anyone that the literature evaluating political consulting would be spotty and eclectic. Early authors like Kelley, Nimmo, and Sabato should be commended for providing a common set of terms and definitions for the study of political consulting. They also put political consultants' actions in a larger context. In the time since they wrote about political consultants there has been a dramatic transformation of the profession. Political consultants are no longer operating on the periphery of American politics, and their entrance into the mainstream is reflected in the proliferation of books devoted to the profession. Although research gaps remain, most notably with respect to the relationship between political consultants and political parties, the study of political consulting is no longer a series of questions seeking answers.

NOTES

1. James Thurber, "The Study of Campaign Consultants," *PS: Political Science & Politics* 23 (1998): 144–145.

2. Jerry Hagstrom, "Message Maestros," *National Journal*, 9 November 1996, 2458–2459; John Marks, "Meet the Puppetmasters, *U.S. News and World Report*, 11 March 1996, 28–30.

3. The cases are as follows: A history of Whitaker and Baxter, the most prominent political consulting firm in California, a chronicle of the AMA's campaign to defeat President Truman's health care reform effort, the sophisticated public relations machinery behind the campaign to defeat Maryland Senator Millard Tydings, and a fascinating look at the public relations juggernaut put together by the Eisenhower campaign.

4. Stanley Kelley Jr. *Professional Public Relations and Political Power* (Baltimore, Johns Hopkins University Press, 1956), 23–40.

5. Executives at Batten, Barton, Durstine, and Osborn (BBD&O), a large New York advertising agency, took leaves of absence to help coordinate the Eisenhower campaign, see Ibid, chapter 4.

6. Ibid. 9–13.

7. Ibid. 37.

8. Dan Nimmo, *The Political Persuaders: The Techniques of Modern Elections* (Englewood Cliffs, Prentice-Hall, Inc., 1970). In 1969 a small group of full-time political consultants formed the American Association of Political Consultants. The formal organization indicated the practitioners considered themselves to be a profession no different from bankers, lawyers, or accountants. It also affirmed observers' fears that elections had become a big, profit-making enterprise.

9. Ibid. 197.

10. There are several significant works that autopsied political parties in the 1970s and 1980s. The reasons for the decline are manifold, ranging from social changes, such as the emergence of the "alienated voter," to legal reforms, such as the McGovern-Fraser commission and the triumph of the open primary system. See David Broder, *The Party's Over: The Failure of Politics in America* (New York: Harper and Row, 1971) and Nelson Polsby, *The Consequences of Party Reform* (New York: Oxford University Press, 1983).

11. Nimmo, *Political Persuaders*, 163.

12. Nimmo's assumption is based on the understanding of the free-market philosophy that pervades American politics. In the United States, political races are generally funded through private donations. Government funding of elections is negligible. Thus, the use of expensive political tools like consultants is confined to wealthy individuals or groups.

13. David Rosenbloom, *The Election Men: Professional Campaign Managers and American Democracy* (New York: Quadrangle Books, 1973).

14. The pressure on House members to be reelected is well documented and is a popular explanation for individual decision-making within the institution. Several classic works include, Richard Fenno, *Home Style: House Members and Their Districts* (Boston: Little Brown, 1973); David Mayhew, *Congress: The Electoral Connection* (New Haven: Yale University Press, 1975); and Gary Jacobson, *The Politics of Congressional Elections* 3rd ed. (Boston: Little, Brown, 1992).

15. Rosenbloom, *Election Men*, 35.

16. Ibid. 104.

17. Ibid. 157.

18. I am, of course, speaking broadly about the profession. There are assuredly a number of consultants who do not act in such an inflammatory fashion, but surveys conducted over the past two decades support a picture of consultants as a cynical group given to posturing. The latest results confirm this. See James Thurber, "Are Campaign Pros Destroying Democracy?" *Campaigns & Elections*, August 1998, 53–58.

19. Larry Sabato, *The Rise of Political Consultants: New Ways of Winning Elections*, (New York: Basic Books, 1981), 8.

20. Ironically, Sabato's laudable desire to produce a comprehensive portrait of the consulting profession also contributes to a serious flaw in his book. In his effort to illustrate his arguments he presents an endless stream of examples with a surfeit of detail. His explanation of the direct-mail system, for example, is tedious and pedantic.

21. Ibid. 311.

22. Ibid. 268.

23. Frank Luntz, *Candidates, Consultants and Campaigns: the Style and Substance of American Electioneering* (Oxford: Basil Blackwell., 1988), 2.

24. Ibid. 229.

25. In the landmark decision *Buckley v. Valeo*, the Supreme Court equated money with speech and stated limits on expenditures were an unconstitutional restriction of the First Amendment. Thereafter wealthy candidates could spend an unlimited amount of their personal fortune on their campaign. More importantly, it allowed PAC's to make unlimited "independent" expenditures (i.e. expenditures made without the knowledge or consent of a candidate) in congressional and presidential elections. As a result of the ruling, PAC's mushroomed and campaign spending exploded. See Larry Sabato, *PAC Power: Inside the World of Political Action Committees* (New York: W.W. Norton, 1985) and Paul Herrnson, *Congressional Elections: Campaigning at Home and in Washington*, (Washington, D.C., CQ Press, 1995).

26. Luntz, *Candidates*, 14.

27. For an engaging profile of Frank Luntz and a fascinating description of his infamous tactics see Elizabeth Kolbert, "The Vocabulary of Votes," *New York Times Magazine*, 15 March 1995, 46–49.

28. Stephen Medvic, "Is There a Spin Doctor in the House? The Impact of Political Consultants in Congressional Campaigns" (Ph.D. diss., Purdue University, 1997).

29. Ibid. 321.

30. James Thurber and Candace Nelson, eds., *Campaign Warriors: Political Consultants in Elections* (Washington, D.C.: The Brookings Institution, 2000).

31. Thomas Mann and Norman Ornstein, eds., *The Permanent Campaign and Its Future*, (Washington, D.C.: The Brookings Institution, 2001).

32. Ibid. iiv.

33. Darrell West and Burdett Loomis, *The Sound of Money: How Political Interests Get What They Want*, (New York: W.W. Norton, 1998), 4.

34. Ken Kollman, *Outside Lobbying: Public Opinion & Interest Group Strategies*, (Princeton: Princeton University Press, 1998), 8.

35. Ibid. 79

36. Dan Nimmo and Keith Sanders, "The Emergence of Political Communication as a Field," in *Handbook of Political Communication*, ed. Dan Nimmo and Keith Sanders, (Beverly Hills: Sage, 1981), 12.

37. Even though political communication is a relatively new academic field, it has an ancient pedigree. Political commentators throughout history, from Plato and Aristotle to Machiavelli, have explored issues that interest contemporary political communications scholars. Indeed, the staples of political communications research, mediated politics, agenda setting, and political learning, are rooted in antiquity.

38. Robert Denton and Gary Woodward, *Political Communication in America* 2nd ed., (New York: Praeger Publishers, 1990), 13.

39. Nicholas O'shaughnessy, *The Phenomenon of Political Marketing* (New York: St. Martin's Press, 1990) and W. Lance Bennett, *The Governing Crisis: Media, Money, and Marketing in American Elections*, (New York: St. Martin's Press, 1992).

40. Not every observer accepts this argument. Jean Elshtain, commenting on the 1988 presidential campaign which was cited by critics as a prime example of a vapid, hollow campaign, stated, "to claim then that candidates are trafficking in nonissues because they immerse themselves in weighty symbolism is to presume that which does not exist – a clear cut division between the symbolic and the real, between issues and emotional appeals." quoted in Denton and Woodward, 93.

41. Gary Mauser, *Political Marketing: An Approach to Campaign Strategy* (New York: Praeger, 1983), 1.

42. O'shaughnessy, *Phenomenon*, 83.

43. Mauser, *Political Marketing*, 5.

44. George Dionisopoulos, "Corporate Advocacy Advertising as Political communication." In *New Perspectives on Political Advertising*, ed. Lynda Kaid, Dan Nimmo, and Keith Sanders, (Carbondale, IL: Southern Illinois University Press, 1986), 95.

45. Blumenthal and Chagall are not the only journalists to recount the exploits of political consultants. In books exploring the 1994 health care reform, the 1995 budget showdown, and the Clinton White House, Elizabeth Drew, Bob Woodward, Hedrick Smith, and David Broder have presented compelling portraits of powerful consultants.

46. Chagall and Blumenthal are not alone. Many of President Reagan's foes and members of the press corps were consistently amazed at his relative immunity to criticism and his knack for avoiding blame. Steven Roberts, "Many Who See Failure in His Policies Don't Blame Their Affable President," *New York Times*, 2 March 1984, A14.

47. Sidney Blumenthal, *The Permanent Campaign* (New York: Simon and Schuster, 1982), 331. It is no small irony that after excoriating the Reagan administration for relying on polls, mass marketing, and other smoke-and-mirror techniques to sway the public, Blumenthal would attach himself to Reagan's grand successor, Bill Clinton. The Clinton administration's public relations apparatus was easily the equivalent of Reagan's and in many respects its superior.

48. Ibid. 74.

49. David Chagall, *The New Kingmakers* (New York: Harcourt, Brace and Jovanovich, 1981), 309.

50. In *The Permanent Campaign*, Sidney Blumenthal claims the role of the consultant in *The Candidate* was inspired by David Garth. Apparently Garth was even offered the part, but he refused because he felt it was an insult to his profession.

Bibliography

Abramson, Jill. "In GOP Controlled Congress Lobbyists Remain as Powerful as Ever, and Perhaps More Visible." *Wall Street Journal*, 20 April 1995, A20.

Alexander, Herbert, ed. *Financing Politics: Money, Elections, Political Reform* 3rd ed. Washington, D.C.: CQ Press, 1994.

Andrew, John A., III. *Lyndon Johnson and the Great Society*. Chicago: Ivan Dee, 1998.

Ansolabehere, Steven and Shanto Iyengar. *Going Negative: How Political Advertisements Shrink and Polarize the Electorate*. New York: The Free Press, 1995.

Armstrong, Richard. *The Next Hurrah: The Communications Revolution in American Politics*. New York: Beech Tree Books, 1988.

Arnold, R. Douglas. "Can Citizens Control Their Representatives?" In *Congress Reconsidered*, edited by Lawrence Dodd and Bruce Oppenheimer. Washington, D.C.: CQ Press, 1993.

————. *The Logic of Congressional Action*. New Haven: Yale University Press, 1990.

Asher, Herbert. *Polling and the Public: What Every Citizen Should Know*. Washington, D.C.: CQ Press, 1992.

Bader, John. *Taking the Initiative: Leadership Agendas in Congress and the Contract with America*. Washington, D.C.: Georgetown University Press, 1996.

Balz, Dan, and Dana Milbank. "Gore Aide Once Wooed Drug Group." *Washington Post*, 7 July 2000, A6.

Balz, Dan, and David Broder. "Players in Health Care Debate Mobilize Consultants and Lobbyists." *Washington Post*, 10 October 1993, A1.

Barnes, James. "Polls Apart." *National Journal*, 10 July 1993, 1753.

————. "Privatizing Politics." *National Journal*, 3 June 1995, 1311–1315.

Bennett, W. Lance. *The Governing Crisis: Media, Money, and Marketing in American Elections*. New York: St. Martin's Press, 1992.

Berke, Richard. "Clinton Aide Says Polls Had Role in Health Plan." *New York Times*, 9 December 1993, A1.

Bernstein, Robert. *Elections, Representation, and Congressional Voting Behavior*. Washington, D.C.: CQ Press, 1989.

Blankenburg, Dan. Interview by author, Washington, D.C., 17 August 2002.

Bloom, Melvyn. *Public Relations and Presidential Campaigns: A Crisis in Democracy.* New York: Thomas Crowell, 1973.

Blumenthal, Sidney. *The Permanent Campaign.* New York: Harcourt, Brace, and Jovanovich, 1981.

Bozell, L. Brent. "Official Media versus the GOP." *National Review,* 12 June 1995, 45–47.

Broder, David. *Democracy Derailed: Initiative Campaigns and the Power of Money.* New York: Harcourt, 2000.

———. "White House Takes on Harry and Louise." *Washington Post,* 8 July 1994, A1.

———. *The Party's Over: the Failure of Politics in America.* New York: Harper and Row Publishers, 1971.

Broder, David, and Haynes Johnson. *The System: The American Way of Politics at the Breaking Point.* Boston: Little Brown, 1996.

Broder, John. "Clinton's Drug Plan Attacked by Industry." *The New York Times,* 28 June 2000, A1.

Brown, Lawrence. "The Politics of Medicare and Health Reform, Then and Now." *Health Care Financing Review* 18 (1996): 160–167.

Carney, Eliza Newlin. "Air Strikes." *National Journal,* 15 June 1996, 1316.

———. "Cashing In." *National Journal,* 6 June 1996, 1295.

Carter, Bill. "Buying the Air Time, Foundation Fosters NBC Program on Health." *New York Times,* 4 May 1994, A1.

Cassata, Donna. "Swift Progress of the Contract Inspires Awe and Concern." *CQ Weekly Report,* 1 April 1995, 90.

Clark, Michael. "Selling the Issues." *Campaigns & Elections,* April/May 1993, 26–29.

Clift, Eleanor. *War without Bloodshed.* New York: Simon and Schuster, 1996.

Cloud, David, and Jackie Koszcuk. "GOP's All or Nothing Approach Hangs on a Balanced Budget." *CQ Weekly Report,* 9 December 1995, 3713.

Clymer, Adam. "Clinton Says Administration Was Misunderstood on Health Care." *New York Times,* 3 October 1994, A12.

Cobb, Michael and James Kuklinski. "Changing Minds: Political Arguments and Political Persuasion." *American Journal of Political Science* 1 (1997): 85–104.

Cohen, Richard. "The Gingrich Team: Joe Gaylord." *National Journal,* 14 January 1995, 73.

———. *Rostenkowski: The Pursuit of Power and the End of Old Style Politics.* Chicago: Ivan Dee, 1998.

Congress. House. Committee on Standards of Official Conduct. *Summary of Activities for the 104th Congress.* Washington, D.C.: GPO, 1997.

Cook, Timothy. *Making Laws and Making News: Media Strategies in the U.S. House of Representatives.* Washington, D.C.: The Brookings Institution, 1989.

Cooper, Joseph, and Gary Bombardier. "Presidential Leadership and Party Success." *Journal of Politics* 30 (1968): 1014–1031.

Corcoran, Paul. *Political Language and Rhetoric.* New York: Prentice-Hall, 1979.

Crespi, Irving. *Public Opinion Polling and Democracy.* Boulder: Westview Press, 1989.

Crotty, William, ed. *The Party Symbol: Readings on Political Parties.* San Francisco: W.H. Freeman, 1980.

Crotty, William, and Gary Jacobson. *American Parties in Decline.* Boston: Little, Brown, 1980.

David, Sheri. *With Dignity: The Search for Medicare and Medicaid.* Westport: Greenwood Press, 1985.

Davidson, Roger, and Walter Oleszek. *Congress and Its Members.* 4th ed. Washington, D.C.: CQ Press, 1994.

Denton, Robert, and Gary Woodward. *Political Communication in America.* 2nd ed. New York: Praeger, 1990.

Devroy, Ann. "House Republicans Get Their Talking Points." *Washington Post,* 2 February 1995, A10.

Diamond, Edwin, and Steven Bates. *The Spot.* Cambridge: MIT Press, 1984.

Dionisopoulos, George. "Corporate Advocacy Advertising as Political Communication." In *New Perspectives on Political Advertising,* edited by Lynda Kaid, Dan Nimmo, and Keith Sanders. Carbondale: Southern Illinois University Press, 1986.

Dowd, Maureen. "Capital's Virtual Reality: Gingrich Rides a Third Wave." *New York Times,* 1 January 1995, A1.

Drew, Elizabeth. *Showdown: The Struggle between the Gingrich Congress and the Clinton White House.* New York: Simon and Schuster, 1996.

Easterbrook, Greg. "Junk Mail Politics." *The New Republic,* 25 April 1988, 15–20.

Edsall, Thomas. "Polls Bolster Both Sides in Bitter Fight over Balanced Budget." *Washington Post,* 25 December 1995, A12.

Edwards, George C., III. *The Public Presidency.* New York: St. Martin's Press, 1983.

Eilperin, Juliet, and Thomas Edsall. "Ad Blitz Erodes Democrats Edge on Prescription Drugs." *Washington Post,* 27 October 2000, A14.

Engleberg, Steven. "A New Breed of Hired Hands Cultivates Grassroots Anger." *New York Times,* 17 March 1993, A1.

Ewan, Stuart. *PR! A Social History of Spin.* New York: Basic Books, 1996.

Fallows, James. *Breaking the News: How the Media Undermine American Democracy.* New York: Random House, 1996.

———. "A Triumph of Misinformation." *Atlantic Monthly,* January 1995, 26–30.

Feingold, Eugene. *Medicare Policy and Politics.* San Francisco: Chandler, 1966.

Feldman, Paul, and Richard Simon. "Zeroing In." *Los Angeles Times,* 31 October 1992, A21.

Fenno, Richard. *Home Style: House Members and Their Districts.* Boston: Little, Brown, 1973.

Fiorina, Morris. *Congress: Keystone of the Washington Establishment.* New Haven: Yale University Press, 1977.

———. *Divided Government.* New York: MacMillan, 1992.

Fisher, Louis. *The Politics of Shared Power: Congress and the Executive,* 4th ed. College Station: Texas A&M University Press, 1998.

Frantzich, Stephen, and John Sullivan. *The C-Span Revolution.* Norman: University of Oklahoma Press, 1996.

Friedenberg, Robert. *Communications Consultants in Political Campaigns.* Westport: Praeger Publishers, 1997.

Garin, Geoff. Interview by author. Washington, D.C., 12 May 2000.

Geer, John. *From Tea Leaves to Opinion Polls.* New York: Columbia University Press, 1996.

Gillespe, Ed. Interview by author. Washington, D.C., 22 August 2002.

Gimpel, James. *Fulfilling the Contract: The First 100 Days.* Boston: Allyn and Bacon, 1996.

Ginsberg, Benjamin, and Martin Shefter. *Politics by Other Means*. New York: Basic Books, 1990.

Goddard, Ben. Interview by author. Washington, D.C., 13 June 2000.

Goodwin, Doris Kearns. *Lyndon Johnson and the American Dream*. 2nd ed. New York: St. Martin's Press, 1991.

Graber, Doris. *Media Power and Politics*. Washington, D.C: CQ Press, 1984.

Greenberg, Stan. Interview by author. Washington, D.C., 31 May 2000.

Grossman, Lawrence. *The Electronic Republic: Reshaping Democracy in the Information Age*. New York: Viking, 1995.

Hagstrom, Jerry. "Message Maestros." *National Journal*, 9 November 1996, 2458–2459.

Harwood, John. "GOP, Given Power by Voters Angry over Welfare, Seeks a Compassionate Image in Reform Debate." *Wall Street Journal*, 22 March 1995, A18.

Headden, Susan. "The Little Lobby That Could." *U.S. News and World Report*, 12 September 1994, 45.

Herbst, Susan. *Numbered Voices: How Opinion Polling Has Shaped American Politics*. Chicago: University of Chicago Press, 1993.

Herrnson, Paul. *Congressional Elections: Campaigning at Home and in Washington*. Washington, D.C.: CQ Press, 1995.

Herrnson, Paul, et al. *The Interest Group Connection: Electioneering, Lobbying and Policy Making in Washington*. Chatham, NJ: Chatham House, 1998.

Himmelfarb, Richard. *Catastrophic Politics – The Rise and Fall of the MCCA of 1998*. State College: Penn State University Press, 1995.

Hosenball, Mark. "Flo's Big Dollar Backers." *Newsweek*, 25 September 2000, 26.

Jackson, Barry. Interview by author. Washington, D.C., 31 May 2000.

Jacobs, Lawrence. "Health Care Reform Impasse: The Politics of American Ambivalence toward Government." *Journal of Health Politics, Policy and Law* 18 (1993): 634–655.

———. *The Health of Nations: Public Opinion and the Making of the British and American Health Policy*. Ithaca: Cornell University Press, 1993.

Jacobs, Lawrence, Robert Y. Shapiro, and Eli Schulman. "The Polls and Poll Trends: Medical Care in the United States." *Public Opinion Quarterly* 57 (1993): 394–427.

Jacobs, Lawrence, and Robert Y. Shapiro. *Politicians Don't Pander: Political Manipulation and the Loss of Democratic Responsiveness*. Chicago: University of Chicago Press, 2000.

———. "Questioning Conventional Wisdom on Public Opinion Toward Health Reform." *PS: Political Science & Politics* 19 (1994): 208–211.

Jacobson, Gary. *The Politics of Congressional Elections*, 3rd ed. Boston: Little Brown, 1992.

Jacobson, Louis. "Think Tanks on a Roll." *National Journal*, 8 July 1995, 1767.

Jamieson, Kathleen Hall. *Everything You Think You Know about Politics, and Why You're Wrong*. New York: Basic Books, 2000.

———. "The Evolution of Political Advertising in America." In *New Perspectives on Political Advertising*, edited by Lynda Kaid, Dan Nimmo, and Keith Sanders. Carbondale: Southern Illinois University Press, 1986.

———. *Packaging the Presidency*. New York: Oxford University Press, 1988.

———. "When Harry Met Louise." *Washington Post*, 15 August 1994, A19.

Johnson, Dennis. *No Place for Amateurs: How Political Consultants Are Reshaping American Democracy*. New York: Routledge, 2001.

Kahn, Charles. Interview by author. Washington, D.C., 25 April 2000.

Kelley, Stanley, Jr. *Professional Public Relations and Political Power*. Baltimore, MD: Johns Hopkins University Press, 1956.

Kennedy, Kara. Interview by author. Washington, D.C., 13 August 2002.

Kernell, Samuel. *Going Public: New Strategies of Presidential Leadership*. 2nd ed. Washington, D.C.: CQ Press, 1993.

King, Anthony. *Running Scared: Why America's Politicians Campaign Too Much and Govern Too Little*. New York: The Free Press, 1997.

Kingdon, John. *Agendas, Alternatives, and Public Policies*. New York: HarperCollins, 1984.

———. *Congressmens' Voting Decisions*. 3rd ed. Ann Arbor: University of Michigan Press, 1989.

Klein, Joe. "Bloviational Fiesta." *Newsweek*, 22 August 1994, 21.

Kolbert, Elizabeth. "The Special Interests Special Weapon." *New York Times*, 26 March 1995, A1.

———. "The Vocabulary of Votes." *New York Times Magazine*, 26 March 1995, 46–51.

Kollman, Ken. *Outside Lobbying: Public Opinion & Interest Group Strategies*. Princeton: Princeton University Press, 1998.

Kolodny, Robin. "Electoral Partnerships: Political Consultants and Political Parties." In *Campaign Warriors: Political Consultants in Elections*, edited by James Thurber and Candace Nelson. Washington, D.C.: The Brookings Institution, 2000.

Koopman, Douglas. *Hostile Takeover: The House Republican Party 1980-1995*. Boston: Rowman and Littlefield, 1996.

Kurtz, Howard. "For Health Care Companies, a Major Ad Operation." *Washington Post*, 13 April 1993, A1.

———. "In Politics, the Spin Is In." *Washington Post*, 2 April 1995, A1.

Langdon, Steve. "Contract Dwarfs Senate GOP's Pledge." *CQ Weekly Report*, 25 February 1995, 578.

Lemann, Nicholas. "Word Labs." *The New Yorker*, 16 October 2000, 100–112.

Libson, Nancy. Interview by author, Annapolis, Md., 7 September 2002.

Lieberman, Trudy. "The Selling of Clinton Lite." *Columbia Journalism Review*, March/April 1994, 20–24.

Light, Paul. *Domestic Policy Choice: From Eisenhower to Clinton*. Baltimore: Johns Hopkins University Press, 1999.

———. "The Focusing Skill and Presidential Influence in Congress." In *Congressional Politics*, edited by Christopher Deering. Pacific Grove: Brooks/Cole, 1989.

Lipset, Seymour Martin, and William Schneider. *The Confidence Gap: Business, Labor and Government in the Public Mind*. Baltimore: Johns Hopkins University Press, 1987.

Loftus, Joseph. "Medicare Action Begins Tomorrow." *New York Times*, 26 January 1965, A1.

Lowi, Theodore. *The Personal President: Power Invested Promise Unfulfilled*. Ithaca: Cornell University Press, 1985.

Lowi, Theodore, and Joseph Romance. *A Republic of Parties? Debating the Two Party System*. New York: Rowman and Littlefield, 1998.

Luntz, Frank. *Candidates, Consultants, and Campaigns: The Style and Substance of American Electioneering*. Oxford: Basil Blackwell, 1988.

Mann, Thomas, and Norman Ornstein, eds. *The Permanent Campaign and Its Future*. Washington, D.C.: The Brookings Institution, 2000.

Marks, John. "Meet the Puppetmasters." *U.S. News and World Report*, 11 March 1996, 28–30.

Marmor, Theodore. *The Politics of Medicare*. Chicago: Aldine, 1970.

Mauser, Gary. *Political Marketing: An Approach to Campaign Strategy*. New York: Praeger, 1983.

Mayhew, David. *Congress: The Electoral Connection*. New Haven: Yale University Press, 1975.

————. *Divided We Govern*. New Haven: Yale University Press, 1991.

McCoy, John. "Citizens for a Better Medicare." *Public Citizen Watch*, June 2000.

McCrocklin, Tom. Interview by author, Arlington, Virginia, 6 June 2000.

McGinnis, Joe. *The Selling of the President: 1968*. New York: Trident Press, 1969.

McInturff, Bill. Interview by author. Alexandria, Va., 24 April 2000.

McVicar, Nancy. "Drug Lobby Accused of Airing Misleading Ads." *Ft. Lauderdale Sun Sentinel*, 29 June 2000.

Medvic, Stephen. "Is There a Spin Doctor in the House? The Impact of Political Consultants in Congressional Campaigns." Ph.D. diss., Purdue University, 1997.

Merida, Kevin. "The GOP's Town Criers." *Washington Post*, 10 July 1997, A1.

Meyer, Dan. Interview by author. Washington, D.C., 26 April 2000.

Mitchell, Allison. "Clinton Seems to Keep Running though the Race is Run and Won." *New York Times*, 2 February 1997, A1.

Mitchell, Greg. *Campaign of the Century: Upton Sinclair's Race for Governor of California and the Birth of Media Politics*. New York: Random House, 1992.

Moore, David. *The Superpollsters: How They Measure and Manipulate Public Opinion in America*. New York: Four Walls Eight Windows, 1992.

Morgan, Dan. "Drugmakers Launch Campaign on Medicare; Industry Wary of Prescription Cost Controls." *Washington Post*, 28 July 1999, A4.

————. "Heath Care Lobby Targets GOP Senators on Air." *Washington Post*, 5 July 1999, A3.

————. "Made for TV Windfall." *Washington Post*, 2 May 2000, A1.

————. "On the Air and Rising." *Washington Post*, 2 May 2000, A1.

Morris, Charles. "Health Care Economy Nothing to Fear." *Atlantic Monthly*, December 1999, 86–96.

Morris, John D. "Congress Begins, Johnson Reports State of the Nation." *New York Times*, 5 January 1965, A1.

————. "Senate Passes Medicare Bill." *New York Times*, 10 July 1965, A1.

Neustadt, Richard. *Presidential Power and the Modern Presidents*, 3rd ed. New York: The Free Press, 1990.

Nimmo, Dan. *The Political Persuaders: the Techniques of Modern Elections*. Englewood Cliffs: Prentice-Hall, 1970.

Nimmo, Dan, and Keith Sanders. "The Emergence of Political Communication as a Field." In *Handbook of Political Communication*, edited by Dan Nimmo and Keith Sanders. Beverly Hills: Sage, 1981.

O'Shaughnessy, Nicholas. *The Phenomenon of Political Marketing*. New York: St. Martin's Press, 1990.

Patterson, Thomas, and Robert McClure. *The Unseeing Eye: The Myth of Television Power in National Politics*. New York: G.P. Putnam, 1976.

Pear, Robert. "Bipartisan Effort on Drug Coverage Has Begun." *New York Times*, 27 May 2000, A10.

————. "Clinton Is Going on the Offensive to Offer the Elderly a Drug Plan." *New York Times*, 24 October 1999, A1.

————. "Clinton Lays Out Plan to Overhaul Medicare System." *New York Times*, 30 June 1999, A1.

————. "Drug Makers Are Taken to Task for Criticism of Clinton Plan." *New York Times*, 23 September 1999, A16.

————. "Drug Makers Drop Their Opposition to Medicare Plan." *New York Times*, 13 January 2000, A1.

————. "Drug Makers Fault the Details of the Clinton Medicare Proposal." *New York Times*, 16 July 1999, A14.

————. "GOP in House Offers Medicare Plan." *New York Times*, 13 April 2000, A1.

————. "House GOP to Push Medicare Drug Plan." *New York Times*, 11 June 2000, A1.

————. "Liars Attacking Health Plan to Scare Elderly, Groups Say." *New York Times*, 27 May 1994, A1.

————. "Tracking Just What the Doctor Ordered." *New York Times*, 13 July 1999, C1.

Petracca, Mark. "Political Consultants and Democratic Governance." *PS: Political Science & Politics* 14 (1989): 11–29.

Petrizzo, T. J. Interview by author. Washington, D.C., 13 August 2002.

Poisal, John et. al. "Prescription Drug Coverage and Spending for Medicare Beneficiaries." *Health Care Financing Review* 3 (1999): 15.

Polsby, Nelson. *The Consequences of Party Reform*. New York: Oxford University Press, 1983.

Priest, Dana. "Anonymity Is the Buzzword for Health Worker Bees." *Washington Post*, 17 February 1993, A13.

Pusateri, Eva. "Shock Mailers That Jolt Your Audience." *Campaigns & Elections*, May 1995, 42.

Risen, James. "Health Reform Sprouts Intense Grassroots Lobbying Outside the Beltway." *Los Angeles Times*, 1 August 1994, A5.

Roberts, Steven. "Many Who See Failure in His Policies Don't Blame Their Affable President." *New York Times*, 2 March 1984, A14.

Rosenbaum, David. "The Pill Box: The Gathering Storm over Prescription Drugs." *New York Times*, 14 November 1999, Sec. 4, p. 1.

Rosenbloom, David. *The Election Men: Professional Campaign Managers and American Democracy*. New York: Quadrangle Books, 1973.

Rovner, Julie. "Voters Flip Flop on Healthcare Prescriptions, Survey Finds." *Congress Daily*, 26 January 2001, 3.

Rubin, Alissa. "Two Ideological Polls Frame Debate over Reform." *CQ Weekly Report*, 8 January 1994, 23–26.

Saad, Lydia. "Contract with America Still Little Known, but Goals Have Widespread Appeal." *Gallup Poll Monthly*, December 1994, 7.

————. "Public Has Cold Feet on Health Care Reform." *Gallup Poll Monthly*, August 1994, 2–6.

Sabato, Larry. *PAC Power: Inside the World of Political Action Committees*. New York: WW. Norton, 1985.

————. *The Rise of Political Consultants: New Ways of Winning Elections*. New York: Basic Books, 1981.

Schattschneider, E. E. *The Semisovereign People: A Realist's View of Democracy in America*. New York: Holt, Reinhart & Winston, 1960.

Schlackman, Richard, and Jamie Douglas. "Attack Mail: The Silent Killer." *Campaigns & Elections*, July 1995, 25–27.

Schlesinger, Arthur. *The Imperial Presidency.* Boston: Houghton Mifflin, 1989.

Schlotzmann, Kay Lehman, and John Tierney. *Organized Interests and American Democracy.* New York: Harper and Row, 1986.

Schmitt, Eric, and Lizette Alvarez. "Senate Approves Step to Overhaul Campaign Finance." *New York Times,* 9 June 2000, A1.

Seigel, Barry. "Spin Doctors to the World." *Los Angeles Times Magazine,* 24 November 1991, 19–26.

Shelley, Mack, II. *The Permanent Majority: The Conservative Coalition in the United States Congress.* Tuscaloosa: University of Alabama Press, 1983.

Shine, Eric. "From the Folks Who Brought You Harry and Louise." *Business Week,* 17 April 1995, 47.

Skocpol, Theda. *Boomerang: Clinton's Health Security Effort and the Turn against Government in U.S. Politics.* New York: W. W. Norton, 1996.

Smith, James. *The Idea Brokers: Think Tanks and the Rise of the New Policy Elite.* New York: The Free Press, 1991.

Smith, Mark. *American Business and Political Power: Public Opinion, Elections, and Democracy.* Chicago: University of Chicago Press, 2001.

Span, Paula. "Ad Ventures in Health Care." *Washington Post,* 18 March 1994, A14.

Stone, Peter. "Drug Makers Have Developed a New Prescription for Easing Their Many Political, Legal and Regulatory Headaches." *National Journal,* 21 July 2001, 2315.

————. "Follow the Leaders." *National Journal,* 24 June 1995, 1640.

————. "Just the Right Spin." *National Journal,* 22 April 1995, 985.

————. "Kinder, Gentler Arm Twisting." *National Journal,* 17 July 1999, 2080.

————. "Man with a Message." *National Journal,* 19 April 1997, 750–753.

Stone, Roger. "Using the Internet to Build Citizen Armies." *Campaigns & Elections,* April 2001, 46.

Sundquist, James L. *Politics and Policy: The Eisenhower, Kennedy, and Johnson Years.* Washington, D.C.: The Brookings Institution, 1968.

Sweitzer, Don, and David Heller. "Radio Tips: 10 Ways to Give Your Campaign Ads More Punch." *Campaigns & Elections,* May 1996, 40.

Thurber, James. "Are Campaign Pros Destroying Democracy?" *Campaigns & Elections,* August 1998, 55–61.

————. *Divided Democracy: Cooperation and Conflict between the President and Congress.* Washington, D.C.: CQ Press, 1991.

————. "The Study of Campaign Consultants." *PS: Political Science & Politics* 23 (1998): 144–145.

Thurber, James, and Candace Nelson, eds. *Campaign Warriors: Political Consultants in Elections.* Washington, D.C.: The Brookings Institution, 2000.

Tienowitz, Ira. "As Lobbyist Flo Worthy to Follow in Harry and Louise Footsteps." *Advertising Age,* 25 October 1999, 46.

Toner, Robin. "Following the Crowd on Health Care, and Getting Lost." *New York Times,* 20 March 1994, Sec., 4, p. 1.

————. "Harry and Louise and a Guy Named Ben." *New York Times,* 30 September 1994, A22.

Tulis, Jeffrey. "The Interpretable Presidency." In *The Presidency and the Political System,* 3rd ed., edited by Marshall Nelson. Washington, D.C.: CQ Press, 1990.

————. *The Rhetorical Presidency.* Princeton: Princeton University Press, 1987.

Tye, Larry. *The Father of Spin: Edward Bernays and the Birth of Public Relations.* New York: Random House, 1998.

Ulsaner, Eric. *The Decline of Comity in the House.* Ann Arbor: University of Michigan Press, 1993.

Van Der Meid, Ted. Interview by author. Washington, D.C., 12 May 2000.

Victor, Kirk. "Astroturf Lobbying Takes a Hit." *National Journal*, 23 September 1995, 2359.

Wallace, Amy. "Buying Time for Candidates." *Los Angeles Times*, 25 April 1994, A1.

Wartzman, Rick. "Small Companies Misunderstand Clinton Health Plan." *Wall Street Journal*, 24 September 1993.

————. "Truth Lands in Intensive Care as New Ads Seek to Demonize Clinton's Health Reform Plan." *Wall Street Journal*, 29 April 1994, A21.

Wattenberg, Martin. *The Rise of Candidate Centered Politics: Presidential Elections of the 1980s.* Cambridge: Harvard University Press, 1991.

Wattenberg, Martin, and Craig Leonard Watkins. "Negative Campaign Advertising: Demobilizer or Mobilizer?" *American Political Science Review* 93 (1999): 891–899.

Wayne, Leslie, and Melody Peterson. "A Muscular Lobby Rolls Up Its Sleeves." *New York Times*, 4 November 2001, Sec. 3, p. 1.

Weber, Tracy. "The Darth Vaders of Direct Mail." *Los Angeles Times*, 3 March 1996, A1.

Wegner, Nona. Interview by author. Arlington, Va., 10 August 2002.

Weisskopf, Michael. "Harry and Louise to Vacation during Hearings." *Washington Post*, 24 May 1994, A1.

————. "Playing on the Public Pique." *Washington Post*, 27 October 1994, A1.

————. "The Professional's Touch." *Washington Post*, 8 November 1994, A1.

Weisskopf, Michael, and David Maraniss. *Tell Newt to Shut Up.* New York: Simon and Schuster, 1996.

West, Darrell, and Richard Francis. "Electronic Advocacy: Interest Groups and Public Policy Making." *PS: Political Science & Politics* 29 (1996): 25–29.

West, Darrell, Diane Heith, and Chris Goodwin. "Harry and Louise Go to Washington: Political Advertising and Health Reform." *Journal of Health Politics, Policy and Law* 21 (1996): 35–66.

West, Darrell, and Burdett Loomis. *The Sound of Money: How Political Interests Get What They Want.* New York: WW. Norton, 1998.

Wicker, Tom. "Medicare's Progress." *New York Times*, 25 March 1965, A1.

Wood, Robert. *Whatever Possessed the President? Academic Experts and Presidential Policy 1960–1988.* Amherst: University of Massachusetts Press, 1993.

Zeller, Shawn. "Say It Ain't So Flo," *National Journal*, 9 October 1999, 2910.

Zis, Michael, Lawrence Jacobs, and Robert Shapiro. "The Elusive Common Ground: The Politics of Public Opinion and Health Care Reform." *Generations*, Summer 1996, 7–13.

Index

ABOUT THE AUTHOR

Douglas A. Lathrop is a senior legislative aide to Congresswoman Jennifer Dunn (R-WA). Dr. Lathrop is her principal adviser for tax policy, the budget, Social Security, and retirement issues.